942·8 PEE

Please renew/return this item by the last date shown.

So that your telephone call is charged at local rate, please call the numbers as set out below:

	From Area codes 01923 or 020:	From the rest of Herts:
Renewals:	01923 471373	01438 737373
Enquiries:	01923 471333	01438 737333
Textphone:	01923 471599	01438 737599

L32   www.hertsdirect.org/librarycatalogue

D1491583

ALONG THE PENNINE WAY

ALONG THE PENNINE WAY

J. H. B. PEEL

DAVID & CHARLES
Newton Abbot · London · North Pomfret (Vt)

British Library Cataloguing in Publication Data

Peel, John Hugh Brignal
    Along the Pennine Way.—2nd ed.
    1. Pennine Way, Eng.
    I. Title
    914.28'04'857   DA670.P4

ISBN 0-7153-7833-3

© J. H. B. Peel 1972

All photographs by the author
First published by Cassell & Company Ltd 1972
This edition first published by David & Charles Ltd 1979

Printed in Great Britain
by Redwood Burn Ltd Trowbridge & Esher
for David & Charles (Publishers) Limited
Brunel House Newton Abbot Devon

Published in the United States of America
by David & Charles Inc
North Pomfret   Vermont 05053   USA

To

PAULINE and RODNEY MEAKIN

True Wayfarers

. . . when thou haply see'st
Some rare note-worthy object in thy travels,
Wish me partaker in thy happiness.

Shakespeare

CONTENTS

PREFACE TO THE SECOND EDITION

Dr Johnson said that the biographies of famous men ought to be rewritten every hundred years. Such a revision would certainly incorporate changing attitudes and newly discovered facts. When describing the British countryside, however, a writer is nowadays in danger of being outdated before his book has been published. Villages that were peaceful when he last saw them may within six months be deafened by a motorway, or defaced by a housing estate. Likewise the churches may become concert halls, warehouses, holiday homes; the coasts may be marred by caravan sites; the towns may be dwarfed by skyscraping offices; the quiet places may be publicised, and so lose their quietude. Nothing, it seems, is safe. Human greed has become a synonym for human need. But the process is not new; it began during the early years of the Industrial Revolution. When Gerard Manley Hopkins saw it in spate during the 1870s the sight harrowed him:

> . . . all is soiled with trade; bleared, smeared with toil;
> And wears man's smudge and shares man's smell . . .

These things being so, one may reasonably ask why this book has been reissued ten years after it was first published. That question is answered by the book itself, for the Pennine Way crosses such deep country that many parts of it look much the same as they did two centuries ago and as they may look two centuries hence. After all, it seems unlikely that anyone will build a bingo hall at Bleaklow Head, or a factory among the solitudes of Ogre Hill.

It would, of course, be absurd to claim that the route has remained exactly the same as when I explored it twelve years ago. For one thing, the rocks have been imperceptibly eroded; for another, some of the people whom I met by the Way have died, and others are a decade older. In addition, the familiar names of some of the old counties were changed in the 1974 local government reorganisation. But those changes will not concern a reader who wishes to know what the Way is like today. Admittedly, I did not make a second journey along the entire course, but I did make several recent journeys along sections of it, and I can therefore report that in 1979 they appeared very much as they did in 1967. Most of the changes will be found less among places than among people. Fewer men, for example, can now plough behind a horse, or build a drystone wall, or thatch a roof, or mow a meadow. Fewer women can make their own bread, their own butter, their own honey and cheese and wine. A generation is arising that probably could not, and certainly will not, work as hard as their grandfathers worked. Some people applaud those facts; others regret them.

If a reader has already explored the Pennine Way, or knows something of the country which it traverses, he will readily understand that the past decade cannot have wrought much alteration there. How well I remember the first few miles of the Way as it climbs northward through a bleak and unpeopled terrain: little risk of *that* being 'developed'. How well I remember the wild expanse between Hawes and Tan Hill Inn, England's highest tavern; and there, too, the risk of change is slight. As for Cross Fell, the summit of the Way, who would tamper with a mountain that can be climbed only on foot? Further yet, along the Scottish border, the solitude becomes even deeper, the farmsteads even fewer, the silence even louder.

'What we have loved,' said Wordsworth, 'others will love.' In an era which changes as rapidly and as radically as ours, Wordsworth's prediction may sound too hopeful. Nevertheless, the Pennine Way remains a refuge from noise and speed and fumes. If now and again we do escape from those banes, we reinforce our ability to withstand the stress of modern urban life. We find time to stand and to stare and to take stock of ourselves. We perceive that Nature, unlike mankind, never hurries, yet always arrives punctually; and in the presence of Nature we share Walter de la Mare's gratitude:

> Thine are the woods whereto my soul,
> Out of the noontide beam,
> Flees for a refuge green and cool
> And tranquil as a dream.

J. H. B. Peel 1979

ILLUSTRATIONS

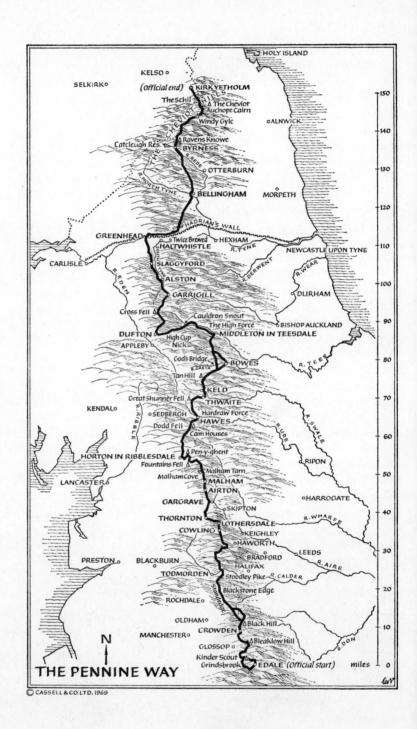

THE PENNINE WAY

© CASSELL & CO. LTD. 1969

1 *To Start With*

THIS is not the story of a walk; it is the pageant of a Way. The Way itself has evoked many handbooks for hikers, but this book is not among them.

I began exploring the Way long ago, chiefly its northern half, and usually in winter. I ended by making a detailed survey of the whole; that is, of those many features which, although they may lie off the Way, are conspicuously by the Way. Anything less than that kind of wholeness would seem dull indeed, even as the Way can seem dull, for it walks alone, far from the outward and visible signs of man's inward and spiritual life. To savour that solitude, and to distil it for others, is one of the tasks of this book. As you will discover, there were moments when to me it seemed the chief task. But—to make the point once again—I did not explore the Pennine Way in order to compose a soliloquy on solitude. I explored it because it crosses a country steeped in good stories, in memorable achievements, in stately buildings, in meetable people, both past and present. If you like, you may say that I travelled with a net, and cast it wide enough to catch a haunted castle or a dreaming poet, even although the net stretched a dozen miles to reach them.

The Way begins at Edale in Derbyshire and ends at Kirk Yetholm in Roxburghshire, having covered some two hundred and fifty miles of blistering and blustery solitude. Like a pre-Hadrianic Wall, it follows the northern backbone of England, through a skyscape which was first called Pennine by Charles Bertram in the eighteenth century. This devious route symbolizes an ambition that was fulfilled gradually, over several years and by courtesy of many landowners. To create it, new rights of way were devised; old footpaths, drove roads and bridleways were resurrected from their grassy graves; and together, like beads, they composed a necklace. That necklace was not designed to suit the

I

inconvenience caused by commercial travellers who demand to see as little as possible as swiftly as maybe. It was so designed that the Way—though it often grows narrow—seldom goes straight. Like a tentacle, it swerves in search of what is most worth finding.

Some of the going is good; much of it is hard; and none is consistently signposted. Without map and compass (and the ability to use them aright) a stranger will lose himself and very likely alarm himself, especially when rain or a mist blots out everything except the tip of his nose. Moreover, most of the Way is 1000 feet above the sea; much of it is more than 2000 feet above; some is nearly 3000 feet above. Wordsworth was climbing Helvellyn in his seventieth year, and a hale person can take the Pennine Way in his stride so long as he adjusts that stride to the weather and his own constitution. But if any man proposes to saunter from Dufton to Cross Fell and back again in time for tea, he is making one of the most arduous mistakes of his life. Like Meredith's Westermain, the Pennine Way utters a challenge:

> Enter these enchanted woods,
> You who dare . . .

It was said of old Wyoming that nowhere else in America could you gaze so far and see so little. Of the Pennine Way it may be said that nowhere else in Britain can you gaze so far and see so much. Granted, the sights are usually in the middle distance, and sometimes as faint as the horizon. Granted, too, that on several tracts you may walk for hours without noticing more than a faraway farm. Yet the sights are there—the castles, the priories, the peel towers, the mills and manors and viaducts—and invisible among them are the ghosts of poets, painters, engineers, warriors, statesmen, saints, sinners . . . all springing from the ultimate seedbed of human achievement, the families who live and die without leaving any trace except their name in a register or on a tombstone.

Because I knew much of the Way, I foresaw many of those ghosts as I stood at the start of my journey, sun-swept and wind-winced at Edale. I saw a priest, sitting alone in a remote house,

writing words that would sear the conscience of a nation. I saw
the cobbled street of a village, and on it a granite monolith in
memory of a local lad who became famous. I saw children crawling
through coalmines, and navvies hacking a railway through mountains. I saw a boy stealing apples from an orchard, not knowing
that he would one day wear a martyr's crown above the bishop's
mitre. I saw an angler so compleat that he became immortal. I
saw a plain-faced spinster, no longer young, whose beauty, a
century after her death, was praised by a great poet:

> Thou had'st all Passion's splendour,
> Thou had'st abounding store
> Of heaven's eternal jewels,
> Beloved; what would'st thou more?

Before I closed the eye of anticipation, I saw England's highest
inn, marooned among the bones of sheep and the ghosts of miners.
I saw Hadrian's Wall, looped like an indelible shadow across
unconquerable hills. I saw the smoke that was a by-product of the
brass which built Rochdale, Wigan, Oldham. And above them
all, and about them and beneath, I saw what William Langland
saw when he too gazed down upon England from a great height:

> A fair field full of folk . . .
> Of all manner of men, the rich and the poor,
> Working and wandering as the world asketh.

2 *Derbyshire*

MANY departures have been postponed by farewells, but few are marooned among greetings. Yet that is what happens at Edale. Having arrived, you are reluctant to leave. All around, the hills stand as it were on tiptoe, as though striving to become mountains; but the dale itself is so wide, and the grass so green, that the summits seem rather to uplift than to oppress.

The village of Edale lies five miles deep, along a winding lane from Hope, which is on the main road twenty miles south-west of Sheffield. Edale has attracted patrons ever since walking became a Peakland pastime, but it was only when the Pennine Way appeared that, like Lord Byron, the village could exclaim: 'I awoke one morning and found myself famous.' Edale, in short, has had thrust upon itself the greatness of being both an alpha and an omega of Britain's longest footpath; a place therefore pressed down and in summer overflowing with visitors.

Despite its fame, Edale remains pleasantly unaffected. It has an inn, a shop-cum-post office, an uninteresting church, and several comely cottages beside the tumbling river. A railway station serves the village, but no bus plies to and from the outer world. Some of the older people still walk the five miles into Hope, and do not despise their journey as a denial of social justice.

Edale must be set among those secluded villages which Thomas Hardy described as a 'little one-eyed, blinking sort o' place'. So far as I can discover, nothing has ever happened at Edale; no battle, no ducal elopement, not even a local lad who manufactured a knighthood. Instead, generations of farmfolk lived here and died here, and probably assumed that the Sahara (if they had ever heard of it) was very much like Edale itself, though rather warmer during August. But it is not the village alone that invites you to linger. In whatever direction you look, you are greeted by

Edale, Derbyshire: the start of the Way

The Way to Kinder Scout, Derbyshire

Malham, West Riding

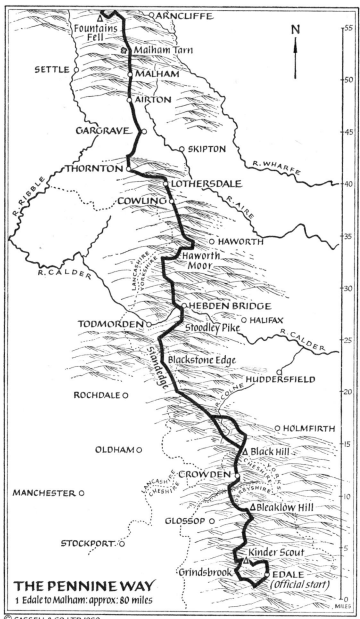

THE PENNINE WAY
1 Edale to Malham: approx: 80 miles

© CASSELL & CO. LTD. 1969

greatness. The greatness may lie within pleasant walking distance
—even, perhaps, within a few minutes by car—but whether on
foot or off, the greetings reach you and must be acknowledged:
Hathersage, for instance, away to the east.

Charlotte Brontë came to Hathersage as the guest of her
friend, Ellen Nussey, whose brother, the vicar, proposed to
Charlotte and was declined with thanks. Several members of
the ancient family of Eyre lived in the district, and one of them—
St John Eyre Rivers of Moorseats—supplied *Jane Eyre* with 'a
local habitation and a name'. In that story, Moorseats became
Moor House; the heroine became Miss Eyre; the missionary
became St John; and Hathersage was Morton. Charlotte Brontë
compared these Derbyshire hills with those around Lowood
School near the Westmorland border: 'not so lofty as those round
Lowood, nor so craggy . . . yet quiet and lonely hills. . . .'

Charlotte's writing-desk and some other Brontë relics are
preserved at Hathersage vicarage; and in the churchyard (they
say) lies Little John, the gigantic henchman of Robin Hood.
They say, too, that Little John's bow once hung in Hathersage
church; and among the sayers was Ashmole himself, a prince of
antiquists, who saw the bow three centuries ago. Thereafter it
hung awhile at Common Hall near Barnsley. Every year the
Ancient Order of Foresters' Friendly Society lays a wreath on
Little John's grave, woven of laurel or of grass taken from Hathersage moor. Scholars will frown at this, and cynics smile, but
Little John defies them all, for he is a national legend, and may
have been a specific man, writ several feet larger than life.

Meanwhile another sort of tallness is at hand, and the Way
must climb over it. My own departure from Edale was not
cordial. Rain hid the world, wind lashed it, thunder deafened. I
therefore eschewed the formal starting-point, and followed a foul-
weather route, which is said to be safer. Safer it may be, but it
could scarcely have been sloppier. The Way, in fact, was a waterfall, cluttered with boulders, railway sleepers, fag-ends, and twelve
tin cans cast overboard from a caravan site. Everyone had
assured me that the mist would lift. They were right. The mist
did lift, at a speed of two miles an hour, which, since it happened

to be my own speed, ensured that the mist became and remained a fellow-traveller. Andrew Young had received the same cold comfort:

> At first the River Noe
> Like a snake's belly gleamed below,
> And then in mist was lost;
> The hill too vanished like a ghost
> And all the day was gone
> Except the damp grey light that round me shone.

It was an unkindly light. Instead of leading me through the encircling gloom, it led me to encircle the gloom. I therefore gave up, and returned to Edale before that too became unattainable.

The next ascent took place in sunshine and along the fair-weather Way. A few yards beyond the Nag's Head Inn the path looks down on the roof of a cottage and then up at the lodge to a farm. After that it burrows into a wooded dell, through which the river carves a melodious course. Over the river it goes, via a rickety foot-bridge, and so up a steep bank to a gate; and after the gate to a tree whose roots have been exposed by uncountable boot-prints. Ahead lie the wild solitude of Grindsbrook Clough, a second bridge, another gulley, a long plateau . . . but, as I said to start with, this is a pageant, not a perambulation. So, after less than an hour, I stopped beside a pack-horse bridge at the foot of Jacob's Ladder, which is a rocky hill. What halted me was the sound of a stream, recalling the fairest and most gently-named of all Derbyshire rivers, the Dove, which Izaak Walton made famous and thereby himself became immortal. Edmund Blunden wrote a poem on the theme:

> Approach we then this classic ground,
> More gentle name was never found . . .

Alas, the truths of fantasy do not always tally with the facts of philology. The name Dove is a corruption of the British word *dubo*, meaning black or dark . . . a reference, perhaps, to trout pools.

As for Izaak Walton, he was born at Stafford, in 1593, and spent most of the first half of his life in London as a freeman of the Ironmongers' Company. Among his friends were Jonson, Donne, and Sir Henry Wotton. His first wife had been a descendant of Archbishop Cranmer; for his second (she left him twenty years a widower) he chose Anne, half-sister to Bishop Ken. Walton died when he was ninety, in the house of his son-in-law, a Winchester prebendary.

The last forty years of Walton's life were filled with leisure, literature, friendship, fishing; all of which were gathered together in his fishing-friendship with a Derbyshire landowner, Charles Cotton, who seems to have divided his time between getting into and out of debt. In 1674 Cotton built a one-room fishing lodge near the Dove; no doubt it made a change from the caves—he called them 'safe retreats'—in which he hid himself whenever his creditors and their lawful occasions demanded. At that lodge Walton and Cotton led the good life, talking about the one that got away.

Although Cotton lived chiefly by his pen in Grub Street, he returned to the Pennines whenever he could. Charles Lamb said of him that he 'smacked of the rough magnanimity of the old English vein'. One thing is certain; both Cotton and Walton knew this land and the streams thereof with an intimacy which few men have equalled. Their expertise was remembered in Cotton's poem for his 'dear and most worthy friend, Mr Isaac Walton':

> A day without too bright a Beam,
> A warm, but not a scorching Sun,
> A southern gale to curl the Stream,
> And (master) half our work is done.

Izaak Walton himself wrote several discerning biographies— of George Herbert, for example, and Hooker and Donne— but he lives by *The Compleat Angler*, of which the first parts appeared in 1653, and were so well received that in 1676 a fifth edition was published, containing Cotton's essay on fly-fishing. Is there in our literature a happier masterpiece or one more consistently suffused with what George Saintsbury called 'the golden simplicity of Walton's style'? Fishing techniques have changed; the fish, too, have changed or at any rate have been poisoned by industry; but men have not yet forsworn their allegiance to Walton's handbook of happiness, humour, and what Robert Burton defined as 'a kind of hunting by water, be it with nets, wheeles, baits, angling, or otherwise'. When you open *The Compleat Angler* you begin to smell the hay, to feel the sun, to hear the lark, and thereafter to share Piscator's regret that you cannot both have your fish and eat it: 'this trout looks lovely, it was twenty-two inches long when it was taken . . . and yet, methinks, it looks better in this good sauce.' The Compleat Angler is at all times a sober man: 'I would you were a brother of the Angle, for a companion that is cheerful and free from swearing and scurrilous discourse, is worth gold.' He is also a grateful man, settled yet not set in his ways; an open air person, who enjoys the song of birds, the murmur of brooks, the frisk of lambs 'sporting themselves in the cheerful sun'. Above all, he loves a good song and a good singer: 'As I left this place and entered into the next field, a second pleasure entertained me, 'twas a handsome Milk-maid, that had cast away all care, and sang like a nightingale; her voice was good, and the ditty fitted for it; 'twas that smooth song which was made by Kit Marlow, now at least fifty years ago; and the Milk-maid's mother sung an answer to it, which was made by Sir Walter Raleigh in his younger days. They were old fashioned poetry, but choicely good, I think much better than now in fashion in this critical age.' Would you know what 'smooth song' it was that Christopher Marlowe made 'now at least fifty years ago'? It began and ended like this:

> Come live with me and be my Love,
> And we will all the pleasures prove
> That hills and valleys, dales and fields,
> Or woods or steepy mountain yields.

> The shepherd swains shall dance and sing
> For thy delight each May morning:
> If these delights thy mind may move,
> Then live with me and be my Love.

To that invitation, 'Sir Walter Raleigh in his younger days' replied with this beginning and this ending:

> If all the world and love were young,
> And truth in every shepherd's tongue,
> These pretty pleasures might me move
> To live with thee and be thy Love.
>
> But could youth last, and love still breed,
> Had joys no date, nor age no need,
> Then these delights my mind might move
> To live with thee and be thy Love.

Not often has one nightingale improvised upon another; and never with such mastery of art. Small wonder, therefore, that when Piscator next saw the milk-maid and her mother, he said to his friend: 'I will give her the chub and perswade them to sing those two songs to us.'

With those songs to cheer me, and the music of Walton's prose, I continued my journey in complete solitude, across peat and boulders, to an eerie massif of fractured rock called Kinder Downfall. The pastoral beauty of Edale lay far below and out of sight. Even the present grim prospect grew fainter as a pall of cloud dimmed the sun. Once again, only the mist was visible.

I relieved the gloom by reminding myself that the Peak District is the first of all British National Parks, designated in 1950, covering 542 square miles, and containing within a seventy-mile radius of itself half the population of England. Peak, however, is a misleading name. The Langdales are peaks and so are the Himalayas but most of these Derbyshire summits are rounded hills. The Pennine Range, in fact, is a plateau whose domes are an aftermath of denudation by wind, rain, and extremes of temperature which contracted and expanded the rocks.

The Way itself cannot be understood without some knowledge of those rocks. To return to the first day of Creation is neither necessary nor possible. It will suffice to know that Britain arose like Venus from the water, being then part of what is now the continent of Europe; that phases of bitter cold and of intense heat came and went, through periods of time which are measurable but scarcely imaginable; that the land we see today was spewed up and hewn and chiselled by many violent forces—volcano, ocean, sunlight, frost—whose sequence and effects are sometimes clear, sometimes blurred. As a result of those upheavals the Derbyshire Way is based upon Mountain (or Carboniferous) Limestone, supporting a layer of shale which itself supports four separate beds of grit or Millstone. Shale, being softer than grit, wears away to reveal grit cliffs, here known as Edges. Derbyshire Millstone was deposited by rivers flowing from Scandinavia. In the Peak District the stone is 4000 feet deep. Misled by its hardness, Charlotte Brontë called it granite. This Millstone has played a leading role in English history. As millers know, it ranks next after the millstones that are found only at Epernon and La Ferté-sous-Jouarre near Paris. A few miles to the east of the Way, Sheffield grew rich on Millstone, using it to whet a famous cutlery trade. The stone forms its own monument at Holbeach in Lincolnshire, where a Peak Millstone bears the following inscription: 'East Elloe RDC. The Prime Meridian of Greenwich, longitude o degrees. This mill-stone was erected over this spot 6 June, 1959.'

What does the word 'peak' mean? Some people believe that it means *Peacs*, a Pictish tribe who are said to have migrated to Derbyshire; but I prefer a simpler interpretation, for the Old English word *peac* means a hill, and when the Anglo-Saxon Chronicle described these parts as *Peaclond* it seems likely that the name meant 'a land of hills' rather than 'the land of Picts'. The meaning of the word Derbyshire is less controversial. The Saxons called these parts Northworthy, but when the Danes arrived, and carved the kingdom of their Danelagh, they called the county Deoraby, from a Scandinavian word for deer. In Domesday Book the name became Derbyshire. A jingle illustrates the extent to which the facts of life are sometimes misrepresented by the demands of rhyme:

> Derbyshire born and Derbyshire bred,
> Strong in the arm and weak in the head.

At Glossop one day I met a parson who assured me that the

couplet's second line was originally 'wacken in the head', meaning 'wide-awake in the head'.

Between thinking those thoughts and watching my step, I came to Kinder River, which plunges a hundred feet—or may plunge, for if you come here during a drought the water is no more than a trickle. I came during a deluge, when the spate appeared to bounce back upon itself, upward to the summit. They say that the spray can be seen from Stockport in Cheshire. Kinder is a realm of rock and of nothing else, unless you happen to glance at the sky. It is a place where sight-seeing becomes site-seeing; the site (one supposes) of a derelict civilization—fractured, forgotten, forlorn—such as the Incas carved long ago on the roof of the world. Carved it had been, but not by human hands. This unpeopled city was founded when the land rose above the sea, to be cracked into fragments by the heat of the sun and by the ice of innumerable nights. Rain washed away the debris, then seeped into crevices and became ice that probed and fissured. A wind blew, day and night, century after century; and with the wind came sharp particles of sand, whittling the surface abrasively, until the summits crumbled and slithered downhill. And when glaciers had scooped a way for rivers, men of the Atomic Age created a land of reservoirs slaking industrial thirst. Far below, the Ladybower Reservoir resembles a Scottish loch with conifers sloping steeply to the water.

Until quite recent times the public had very little access to these heights. In 1905 J. B. Firth remarked: 'Most of the High Peak is private. . . . consequently, rights of way are scarce, and this stretch of Derbyshire reminds one more of the Highlands of Scotland, where the peasants have been hunted out of certain glens by the landlords to make room for sheep and then for deer. The High Peak is similarly sacred to grouse.' During the 1890s a number of village Hampdens formed the Northern Counties Footpaths Preservation Society, not in vain. Notices like this one began to appear: 'F. J. Summer, Esq. and others have conceded permission and right for the public in perpetuity to traverse on foot this moorland by the route indicated by posts . . .' But a *caveat* added: '. . . on the understanding that this is the only route to be followed and that there be no divergence therefrom or trespass upon any part of the moor.' Forty years later the battle was still being waged. In 1932, dissatisfied with the landowners' concessions, a party of belligerents did invade Kinder Scout, and six of them went to prison, not for trespassing but for assaulting the gamekeepers who barred their way.

After twelve miles' hard labour I reached Bleaklow Head, two thousand feet up, which some people regard as the wildest part of the Way. All is empty moorland; dun, dark, dank. Northward the Glossop factories wear their own halo of smoke, but the town itself lies far below and out of sight. The rest is silence, spoken by the wind. Men have died on Bleaklow—and children, too—caught by a blizzard or trapped in a bog: how many, no one knows, because not all the corpses are found. During the 1920s a Bog-Trotters Club took pleasure in wading through this country, covering seventy-five miles in thirty hours. Celia Fiennes, who rode from the Peaks to the Pennines in 1698, did not share their enthusiasm; these bogs, she complained, 'stagnate the aire and holde miste and raines almost perpetually'. She noted, too, the solitude, the steepness, the limestone walls in place of southern hedgerows: 'All Derbyshire is full of steep hills, and nothing but the peakes of hills as thick one by another is seen . . . neither hedge nor tree but only low drye stone walls . . .'

Suddenly, in the midst of 'miste and raines', I was amazed to hear a motor-cycle. I had quite forgotten that the Way here crosses the road between Glossop and Sheffield by the Snake Inn, which was built in 1821. The name of this high and lonely tavern does not refer to the snakelike winding of the road; it recalls an armorial device of the Cavendish family, Dukes of Devonshire, who own considerable property in the Peaks, but none at all in Devonshire. Why then did the family assume a West Country title? Tradition says that the patent of nobility was prepared by a clerk who mistakenly wrote Devonshire in place of Derbyshire. There is, of course, a famous earldom of Derby, whose holder in 1780 founded the Derby Stakes; but the earldom has no connection with the county, for it was bestowed, in 1485, on the Stanleys, who took their title from West Derby, now a suburb of Liverpool.

Shakespeare recorded the Stanleys' treachery to Richard III at
the Battle of Bosworth. The king cries: 'Call up Lord Stanley, bid
him bring his power.' But Stanley had already sold himself to
Henry Tudor, and, by turning coats when the battle was already
under way, he helped to kill Richard and to crown Henry. It is
not often that Shakespeare nods, but in *Richard III* he did make a
mistake, both in the text and in the *dramatis personae*, where Stanley
is described as 'Lord Stanley, call'd also Earl of Derby'. In fact, the
family's traitor was Sir William Stanley; and he came to a traitor's
end, having plotted against his new master.

In 1904 the Duke of Devonshire helped to present this countryside with a railway line whose object was to resurrect the disused
lead mines at Ecton. Part of the railway was a narrow-gauge line
from Waterhouse to Holme End; part was a loop line to the North
Staffordshire Railway at Leek. Elderly people still remember the
yellow saloon carriages and the chocolate-coloured locomotives.
Unfortunately, the loop line was not ready to receive the narrow
gauge, so a steam omnibus filled the breach. This coke-burning
vehicle was shod with iron tyres so vibrant that they shook wares
from the shelves of Leek shops. However, the two lines did meet
at last, in time to catch the post, for the loop carriage contained
a letter-box that could be used by people at intermediate stations.
On reaching Leek, the guard re-posted the letters in the town
pillar-box.

The Romans came this way, and built a road from Glossop to
Brough-in-Noedale, which they named Melandra—surely from
the Greek *melas*, meaning black—though nowadays it is called
Doctor's Gate, after a certain Doctor Talbot, concerning whom
nothing is known except that in the seventeenth century the
road was called Doctor Talbotes Gate. In 1955 the course of this
road was excavated near Hope Church. Three feet below the
surface they found a layer of flat sandstones, paved with smaller
stones.

Presently the mist cleared, the rain stopped, and I saw the full
desolation of treeless bog speckled with heather and grass; an
utter absence of human life; no bird-song, no flower, not even
a sheep. And all this was something more than an aesthetic

impression; it was an aspect of the essence of the Way, and one to be examined more closely, for it confirmed that I had entered the north of England.

Now Dr Ernest Jones said of Freud that 'he had in him a dichotomy, not a rare one, between the call of the North and that of the South. The high ideals of duty spoke for the North . . . but for pleasure, happiness and pure interest the South was pre-eminent. . . . Its softness and beauty, its warm and azure skies . . .' That dichotomy divides many Englishmen, and Derbyshire is its frontier.

This frontier can be described via buildings, landscape, climate, dialect. Yet the difference between the north and the south of England is not simply that the brick houses give way to stone—stone houses abound in the Cotswolds; nor that the hills become steep—in Devonshire they are more consistently steep; nor that the climate grows colder—the elements on Bodmin Moor can be at least as elementary as those on Kinder Scout; nor that the dialect differs—that will change throughout the Way, and never so markedly as at the end of it. Where then does lie the ultimate and irreducible difference which begins northward of Edale? I would express it with one word—'hard'—used as a collective noun to include harshness, brusqueness, independence. Those qualities, of course, can be distributed between the people *and* the places of the north. If, like myself, you happen to spend a large part of each year in the north and also in the west of England, you will recognize the landscape of each, even before you have quizzed its parts. There are innumerable skylines in England; yet I fancy I could detect Exmoor from among all other horizons. In England there are countless cottages; yet I could say which of them were of Westmorland stone and which of Cotswold.

Landscape and climate interact. Every winter the Derbyshire Way suffers the kind of blizzard that seldom visits Cornwall or the Isle of Wight, and never stays there above a few days. More-over the wettest place in England is in the north; so is the windiest; so is the foggiest. Peakland is one of those regions which Gilbert White had in mind when he said: 'The effects of heat are seldom very remarkable in the northern climate of England.' To that extent, therefore, the people of the north are hardier than those in the south; and if an Exmoor shepherd protests against the imputation of milk-sloppiness, then let us allow that northerners are more accustomed to snow and wind and rain. In the towns their resilience is being sapped, but elsewhere it abounds. To some people it will be the hero of this book.

Another kind of hero—a young German pastor, Carl Philip Moritz—wrote a travelogue, *Journeys of a German in England in 1782*, which contains an up-to-date portrait of these parts: 'Often I made my way by narrow mountain tracks at astonishing heights, seeing a few small cottages nestling deep down in the dale beneath. The grey stone walls that bounded the fields gave the whole district a wild aspect. The hills were mostly bare of trees and in the distance one could see the herds feeding their summits.' Wildness and astonishment . . . that was the German's first impression of these hills. It is also the impression of a southern Englishman seeing them for the first time. Nor is the impression mere fancy. From start to finish the Pennine Way seldom descends to the level of the highest land in Rutland or in Suffolk; and an Essex man finds himself a thousand feet above the roof of his own county, on an apparently endless backbone—the rump of a heaving whale—which either recedes into mist or advances from clarity.

There are no houses on these heights, though a few people live within a few miles of them. How do they earn their living? There is only one general answer: farming. And there is only one general farming: sheep. Rarely indeed between Edale and Kirk Yetholm does the Way follow a wheatfield, or even a crop of oats. The breed of sheep will vary—Swaledale, Herdwick, Cheviot—but only they can scrounge a living from land above fifteen hundred feet. On this part of the Way the sheep are chiefly Derbyshire Gritstones, a breed of great antiquity. Writing half a century ago, Dr William Fream remarked on the Gritstones 'having been bred without introduction of outside blood for considerably over a hundred and fifty years'. Nowadays the breed is mixed with alien stock—Limestone, for instance, and Scotch Blackface—but their dominant characteristics testify to the many generations of pure-bred originals. These Derbyshire sheep produce excellent lean mutton. Their wool used to be rated among the best in Britain.

Pastures at the foot of the Way yield a notable harvest of barley for ale and of milk for cheese. At Welbeck the medieval monks had their own brewery, but, being Premonstratensians, were not allowed to eat meat. Such meagre diet seems to have disagreed with such a cold climate. According to Joseph Tilley, the historian of Derbyshire, Pope Pius II agreed that the brethren should 'have a knowledge of beef steak and mutton chops'. Tilley adds that another Peakland monastery supplied one parish priest with nearly five hundred gallons of ale each year. Thomas Fuller, that worthy Doctor of Divinity, set Derbyshire ale before all others: 'Never,' he declared, 'was the wine of Sarepta better known to the Syrians . . . than the Canary of Darby to the English hereabouts.' In 1577 the county contained 276 ale houses; but a century later, in 1691, the English brewers, alarmed by the popularity of claret, issued a pamphlet, *A Dialogue between Claret and Darby Ale*. Needless to say, the Ales had it.

The local cheese was made from a mixture of the morning and evening milk, with full cream content; four cheeses weighing one hundredweight. At the beginning of the nineteenth century more than two thousand tons of Derbyshire cheese went by wagon to London and to the east coast ports. In 1870 Derbyshire built the first English cheese factory, at Longford; and it is significant that an American was imported to supervise the administration. There must have been something amiss with the Derbyshire farmwives' cheese-making, because people soon came to prefer the factory product. In 1874 the best Derbyshire factory cheese cost more than the best farmhouse cheese. Even the cheapest factory cheese cost thirty-five shillings more per hundredweight than its farmhouse equivalent. The modern Derbyshire cheese is flat-shaped and quick-ripening, larger than a Single Gloucester, drier than Cheddar.

For many centuries the Pennines were honeycombed by mines. Celia Fiennes called them '. . . those craggy hills whose bowells are full of Mines of all kinds . . . some have mines of Copper, others Tinn and Leaden mines in which is a great deale of Silver'. Derbyshire lead miners held their own Barmote Courts at Mony-ash, Wirksworth and Ashford. A miner staked his claim by cutting a cross in the turf and by sinking a shaft in an angle of the cross. If a fortnight's work yielded enough ore to fill the Barmaster's official Standa'rd Dish, the miner received a 'freeing note', and his claim was registered by the Court. In 1852 the various local laws and customs gave way to the Derbyshire Mining Customs and Minerals Act; and within a century the industry itself disappeared. I have met old miners who believe that it will reappear. Hitherto, they argue, the mines have been hindered by the level or water-table at which water ceases to sink away; but the level itself appears to be sinking, and technology may one day speed the process. Yet neither lead nor cheese nor ale was the principal Derbyshire product. That title belonged to the sheep. Centuries before Derby and Glossop glowered with Blake's 'dark Satanic mills', these Pennine people grew rich on wool. In the churchyard at Darley Dale you will find a weaver's tomb, carved with a loom, a spinning jenny, and the frame or tenter from which the cloth was suspended. The word 'tenterhooks' first appeared in 1480, and is still used to suggest suspense and wonderment.

Wonderment, too, was the response of Pastor Moritz: 'In Derbyshire they tell of the Seven Wonders of Nature, of which Eldon Hole is one; another is Mam Tor (Shivering Mountain) and a third the Great Peak Cavern which goes locally by the rather dirty name of The Devil's Arse. The remaining Wonders of Nature are Poole's Cavern (at Buxton) and St Ann's Well (also at Buxton), where two springs emerge quite close to each other, the one boiling hot and the other ice-cold. Next wonder is a spring called Tide's Well because for most of the time the water flows almost unnoticed and then, all at once, makes a mighty rumbling but not unmusical noise as it gushes up and overflows its banks. The last of the Seven Wonders is Chatsworth, a mansion at the foot of snow-covered mountains.'

Pastor Moritz's contemporary, Jean-Jacques Rousseau, never saw those wonders, though for more than a year he lived close to them, self-exiled from France. But Rousseau could not tear himself away from his mistress and his manuscript. The former was Thérèse le Vasseur; the latter, his *Confessions*. The National Gallery has a portrait, by a Derby artist, of a Peakland baronet, Sir Brooke Boothby, which shows him clasping a volume called *Rousseau*; a better title for the book would have been *Dialogues* because Rousseau presented the manuscript of it to Sir Brooke.

And what of the people themselves; not only those who dwell on the heights but also those others who delve in the depths; the miners and the quarrymen? You have only to talk with them in order to recognize the sons of forefathers who were gentle as well as warlike. The Derbyshire Regiment, for example, marches to a martial tune with tender words: 'The young May moon is beaming.' But some deeds sound louder than words. Thus, when the Prince of Wales led an expedition against Guienne in 1355, his shock troops included a detachment of Peakland archers. Two centuries later Derbyshire responded to the Queen's general muster by offering to train five hundred soldiers (Surrey, a more populous county, offered only three hundred).

This northern self-help did not always support the Establishment; on the contrary, the Court of the King's Bench under Edward I was greatly troubled by a Pennine landowner who, because he dwelt above the thousand-feet contour, assumed that he lived above the law also. The High Sheriff of Derbyshire complained to the Court that 'Sir Thomas Folejambe was accustomed to offer resistance to the king's ministers and bailiffs who wished to distrain him for debts. . . .' The royal bailiff of the Peaks therefore went again to Sir Thomas, and was again unable to secure payment. The bailiff then '. . . caused the sheep which he found there to be taken. And while he was elsewhere, there came people, who are still unknown, and rescued the said sheep and drove them away no one knows where'.

Presently Sir Thomas himself appeared, demanding of the sheriff '. . . by what warrant he had done this, and the sheriff showed him the king's writ under the privy seal. And Sir Thomas, biting his nails on his palfrey, read the writ and looked at the seal and said, "A fig for that!"'

The sheriff's reply was a hue and cry by horn and mouth,

whereupon the debtor surrendered himself with his three shepherds and their sheep. None of the culprits came to harm, for after two years a jury found them not guilty.

All that, of course, was long ago. But not so long ago the Way overlooked an industrial revolution; and it was a Derbyshire man, James Brindley, who played a leading part in that dreary transformation. Brindley was born near Wormhill, in 1716, in a cottage whose floor was suddenly pierced by a sprouting ash tree, as though Fate wished to mark the place; indeed, the tree grew so tall that the cottage was demolished in order to make way for it. Brindley's other local monument is a drinking trough, erected in 1875.

Brindley himself received nothing that we would now call an education, though it seems likely that he graduated after the manner of another self-taught genius, Thomas Bewick, who awaits us in Northumberland. Having served under a wheelwright, Brindley set up as a freelance inventor whose schemes proved so successful that his rivals dubbed him 'The Schemer'. He it was who built the canal which joined the Duke of Bridgewater's collieries at Wormsley with the factories at Manchester; and as soon as the canal was opened, the price of coal in Manchester fell from sevenpence to threepence per hundredweight. Between 1776 and 1792 the revenue from goods traffic rose from £12,500 to £80,000. Another of his achievements was to bore the longest tunnel in England—three miles and nine hundred yards—through the Pennines between Totley and Dore.

Brindley never learned how to spell conventionally. Perhaps he never wished to learn. His notebooks refer to 'logg o' deal', meaning a 'log of deal wood', and to 'ochiler servey', meaning 'ocular survey'. Neither reading nor writing was to Brindley's taste; and he seems not to have thought much of talking either. Thomas Carlyle remarked: 'The rugged Brindley has little to say for himself.' Calculations he took to bed with him, and declined to get up until he had solved them. No matter how grand the design, he never neglected its details. He invented a method of building watertight embankments and then of underpinning them to prevent subsidence. He set the example which now makes the

Limestone cliffs, Malham, West Riding

Storm over Ribblesdale, West Riding

British Rail, Horton-in-Ribblesdale,
West Riding

The lane to Arncliffe, West Riding

last sector of a new road carry reinforcements to the next. He designed floating forges and carpenters' shops. He trained the first of the labourers who in 1832 became known as navigators or 'navvies' because they built canals. At one time Brindley was working simultaneously on so many projects that he delegated some of the responsibility to other engineers, not always with the approval of his employers. Birmingham businessmen complained that 'Mr Brindley hath frequently passed by, and sometimes come into Town, without giving an opportunity of meeting to confer with him upon the progress of the undertaking'. Coventry capitalists were even more displeased; in fact, they sacked him.

Brindley died of overwork while still in his fifties. He was fortunate to have lived so long, being a diabetic who contracted nephritis during a survey for the Trent and Mersey Canal. His epitaph was pronounced by Carlyle: 'He has chained seas together. His ships do visibly float over valleys, and invisibly through the hearts of the mountains; the Mersey and the Thames, the Humber and the Severn, have shaken hands.'

Forty years later, on 19 April 1826, the *Derby Mercury* reported what must surely be the strangest of all cargoes travelling through the Pennines by canal: 'On Saturday arrived in this town by canal, a fine Llama, a Kangaroo, a Ram with four horns, and a female Goat with two kids, remarkably handsome animals, as a present from Lord Byron to a Gentleman whose residence is in this neighbourhood.'

Meantime, the Way descends from Bleaklow to Torside, and so passes out of Derbyshire, having travelled fourteen lonely miles from Edale. That the journey was impressive cannot be denied; that it was northern need not be emphasized. But was it uniquely of Derbyshire? It was. The sheep, the houses, the Bakewell tarts (they really are baked well in that pleasant town), the collieries, the quarries, the dialect . . . these things create a county imprimatur. Even so, the Peakland Way walks alone. Solitary, inhospitable, barren; one seeks in vain a single epithet. Perhaps the best description is 'aloof', for its remotest parts remain untouched by men except where the vegetation has been poisoned with soot from distant towns. For weeks at a time in winter no one ventures up here. During my own journey I learned again the truth of Landor's saying: 'A solitude is the audience-chamber of God.' Exploring such solitude for the first time, a stranger will conclude that the Way is a perambulation and not after all a pageant. And yet—if only with an inward eye— even the stranger can look down upon Derbyshire eminences who knew these heights: Florence Nightingale, for example, the most famous woman of her time, who took train to Derbyshire, and resumed the life she had led as a girl in the village of Holloway . . . Herbert Spencer, who was born at Derby, and went fishing by moonlight at Swarkeston . . . Thomas Hobbes (he wrote a poem praising the Wonder of the Peak) who served as tutor at Hardwick Hall, and was buried at Ault Huckenall . . . the Sitwells of Renishaw Hall . . . Judge Anthony FitzHerbert (his descendant still lives at Tissington Hall), novelist Samuel Richardson, progenitor Erasmus Darwin . . . all were Pennine people, nursed in the north. Hills that to others seem inhospitable, were to them a home which they loved with the loyalty enshrined by Walter de la Mare:

> No lovelier hills than thine have laid
> My tired thoughts to rest:
> No peace of lovelier valleys made
> Like peace within my breast.

Among those hills you will understand why Thomas Fuller composed a regional Te Deum: 'God, who is truly thaumaturgus, the only worker of wonders, hath more manifested his might in this than in any other county of England.'

3 Cheshire

M ANY people are surprised when they learn that the Way enters Cheshire, for rumour dies hard, and this county is commonly dismissed as flat despite one summit which, if it were ninety feet higher, would become a mountain. Even so, it does seem strange that a relatively small county should extend from the Irish Sea to the Pennine Hills. The cause of such a wide span is a spearhead which Cheshire thrusts into Derbyshire, Lancashire, Yorkshire. Within that spearhead the bleak and hilly landscape is most unlike the rest of the county.

Only about six miles of the Way are in Cheshire, yet the task of finding them confronts you with the dilemma of Mary Webb's pious abbot: 'One says "Come through the brake fern there to the left" and another says "No, yonder by the great yew tree" and a third crieth that he must go through the deep heather.' Two thousand years ago the poet Martial complained *quae fuerat semita* . . . 'What used to be a footpath is now a main road.' Only the most professional athlete could wish to see a cement 'walkerway' from Edale to Kirk Yetholm, but the journey thither would seem more enjoyable if it were marked by stakes, set perhaps half a mile apart, to save people the trouble of losing themselves in a maze of cairns, bogs, and sheepwalks. Similar guideposts lead a traveller to the summit of Plynlimmon. Such scattered courtesies obviate misadventure without impairing adventurousness. This sector, at all events, was the only one which I had never before visited; so, when I did arrive, it was with an eye refreshed by novelty, soon to be daunted by danger, and already aware of majesty, for the Cheshire Way is royal.

Cheshire became part-royal when, in order to contain the Welsh, William the Conqueror broke his custom of not granting too much land to any one subject in any one region. Along the Welsh border he placed four strong men in four great castles—

Montgomery, Hereford, Shrewsbury, Chester. The last of these
was entrusted to his own nephew, Hugh de Avranches, chief of
the Lords Marcher when Cheshire became a county palatine (Latin
palatinium or castle, first used to describe a high judicial officer
of the Merovingian Kings). There were three great counties
palatine—Chester, Durham, Lancashire—and the Way enters all
of them. Since they existed to maintain order in an unruly region,
they were granted autonomous courts: *regalem potestatem in
omnibus*, said Bracton. These courts could pardon treason, murder,
felony; all regional offences were held to be against the Courts'
peace and not, as elsewhere, against the King's, *contra pacem
domini regis*. It is interesting to note that parts of Wales were
surveyed by the English Domesday Book because they then lay
within the county palatine of Chester. The name of the county
was originally *Castra legionum*, the camp of the legions, which the
Saxons called *Legaceastir*.

Why then did Cheshire become wholly royal? The answer lies
deep in a maze of medieval genealogy. In 1232 the earldom of
Chester was inherited by John, Earl of Huntingdon, a nephew
of the Scottish King. When John died without issue the earldom
of Chester was held to lie with his eldest sister's elder daughter,
wife to William de Forze; but whether she and her husband could
inherit all the lands of the earldom was debated by lawyers. In
the end, the de Forze rights were quitclaimed, and then purchased
by the King of England; such was their strategic importance, not
only against the Welsh but also against rebellious English barons.
By long custom the Prince of Wales is also Earl of Chester, as the
Sovereign is also Duke of Lancaster. As though to emphasize
its royal associations, the Cheshire Regiment marches to the
tune of 'Wha wouldna' fecht for Charlie?' This old Scottish song
recalls the county's loyalty to Charles II when the rebels were
hunting him at Boscobel. One veteran told me that the Cheshires
wear an oak leaf on their caps . . . the Boscobel Oakleaf, no doubt.

Now the royal Way descends gradually to Torside Reservoir,
which, like Ladybower, resembles a loch among interlocking
spurs of treeless summits. And then—as though to confound the
traveller who supposes that he has discovered unspoiled England

—then Mammon appears, and Cheshire echoes Rilke's lament: 'The world has fallen into the hands of men' . . . men who clutter the Pennines with pylons, telephone wires, tin shacks, shunting yards, and bric-à-brac deposited by Manchester Corporation Waterworks. The fertility of the land is subordinate to the purity of its water. All farmers hereabouts must work to rule as laid down by Manchester. The numbers of their stock are severely limited; ploughing is either confined or prohibited; large tracts of grazing run to waste. No one would condemn Manchester to go thirstily unwashed, but some people do deplore the litter between Torside and Crowden, most of which was dumped before the many Pennine ways became a single Way. But let no one suppose that the Way itself is safe. Nothing is safe against the unholy alliance between Mammon and the State. Even Parliament becomes a bauble. Speaking as Chairman of the National Parks Commission, Lord Strang declared: 'Where a government department has had plans for erecting large installations of one kind or another in a National Park, I can remember no case where it has been diverted from its purpose by anything the Commission might say about the intentions of Parliament as embodied in the National Parks Act.'

This industrialism is, so to say, a straw in the wind, announcing both a national and a regional paradox, as follows: Britain is dangerously overpopulated, yet one-half of Britain carries a population of less than five persons per square mile, and in most of that half the average population is two persons per square mile. In 1968 the President of the Civic Trust estimated that within thirty years one-half of Britain would be a built-up area. And there is a second paradox, for although the Way follows many miles of the most intensely industrialized region in the kingdom, it seldom forsakes its own solitude, and never for more than a few hundred yards.

On then it plods, following the course of Crowden Great Brook, twisting snakelike among barren moorland, each skyline giving way to another, higher and bleaker. Laddow Rocks are here, a happy climbing ground for 'those in city pent'. Here, too, is Crowden Youth Hostel, emphasizing a feature of the Way. The youth hostel movement began in Germany, in 1910, when a schoolmaster, Robert Schirrman, opened a chalet for young holidaymakers. Not until 1928 did England follow his example, when the Northumbrian Trampers' Guild provided six 'shelters' for walkers. A year later the Merseyside Centre of the British Youth Hostels Association was formed, having 170 members, but no hostel. The Association's national office was a disused army hut at Welwyn Garden City in Hertfordshire. In 1968 the Youth Hostels Association of England and Wales had some three hundred hostels and nearly a quarter of a million members, with the right to use hostels in any of the countries belonging to the International Youth Hostels Federation.

This sector is as it were a sieve, and some pilgrims decline to pass through it. After two days of gruelling solitude they cannot believe that the going ever will become easier, the scenery softer, its hinterland more companionable. They foresee that to follow the Way from Derbyshire into Scotland is a very tedious task. The athlete may accept it as a challenge to his body, but an active mind soon wearies of such muscular monotony. Though I can still walk thirty miles a day, I should feel very aggrieved were I condemned to walk thirty days along these miles. Like a wide ocean, the narrow Way bears a remarkable resemblance to itself. And yet, after all, these heights gaze deep into Cheshire, whence cometh help to them that are everlastingly upon the hills. The mind's eye sees—or at any rate imagines—the village of Gawsworth, which has two Halls; the elder, a sixteenth-century masterpiece of Cheshire magpie, once had a jousting pitch two hundred yards long and sixty yards wide; the younger Hall was built by that Lord Mohun who fought a famous duel which Thackeray made more famous in *Henry Esmond*. Gawsworth church has a Tudor porch and the effigy of a Tudor knight, Sir Francis Fitton. Parts of the black-and-white rectory are *c.* 1470; its garden slopes to a lake.

This small village bred two poets, Samuel Johnson and Terence Armstrong. Johnson was a nonentity who wrote one successful opera, and then played the lead in it, as Lord Flame, a dancing fiddler. Gawsworth folk thereafter dubbed him Mr Flame. He composed the epitaph on his gravestone:

> Here, undisturbed, and hid from vulgar eyes,
> A wit, musician, poet, player lies.

The second poet, Terence Armstrong, was descended from the Tudor Fittons. I remember meeting him when he was a schoolboy at Merchant Taylors'. Writing as John Gawsworth, he attracted some notice during the 1930s, when he edited a collection of poems by Old Merchant Taylors, from Edmund Spenser and Thomas Lodge to Gilbert Murray and Edward Shanks. But Gawsworth is outshone by the reflection which comes eastward from Knutsford, the home of a woman whose novels are the very voice of the north.

Elizabeth Cleghorn Stevenson was the daughter of a farmer who became keeper of the records of the Treasury. She reached Knutsford as a motherless infant four weeks old, and lived there under the care of an aunt. When she was fifteen she went to school at Stratford-upon-Avon. Two years later her brother was drowned; two years after that her father died; and after another two years she became engaged to William Gaskell, a Unitarian minister at Manchester. Gaskell himself was a scholar whose brand of Unitarianism bore little resemblance to the zeal of Bethel. The Wedgwoods, the Darwins, and the Hollands were Unitarians. Their religion was rooted in an Anglican soil. Many of their churches were both beautiful and venerable. To J. A. Froude their intellectual heresy seemed '. . . the latest form of orthodoxy'.

Mrs Gaskell's *Cranford* is a portrait of Knutsford, in those years a feminine stronghold: 'Cranford is in the possession of the Amazons; all the holders of houses, above a certain rent, are women.' This well-loved book appeared as a series of weekly cameos in *Household Words*, which was edited by Dickens, who secured Mrs Gaskell as a regular contributor. Her later stories are riper and more resoundingly of the moors. In *The Moorland Cottage*, for example, she describes a scene that still exists along the Way: '. . . golden gorse and purple heather, which in summertime send out their warm scents into the quiet air. The swelling waves of the upland made a near horizon against the sky; the line is broken only by Scotch firs . . . the lark quivers and sings high upon the air.'

Two of her novels, *Mary Barton* and *North and South*, are documents of the industrial revolution, written with compassionate insight by an artist who lived among the poor and was acquainted with the rich (some of whom wrote to the *Manchester Guardian*, protesting that the artist was a subversive menace). In *Sylvia's Lovers* she ventured farther north, into Yorkshire; and there also she painted Wayside scenes which abide: 'on the bare swells of the highland you shiver at the scenery . . . moors enough for many a mile, here and there bleak enough, with the red freestone cropping out above the scanty herbage; then, perhaps, there was a brown tract of peat and bog.'

In 1850 Mrs Gaskell came to know the greatest of all Pennine people, the Brontës; and when Charlotte Brontë died, the bereaved father invited Mrs Gaskell to write a biography. Her *Life of Charlotte Brontë* possesses merits which all other Brontë biographies lack. Quiller-Couch rated it 'among the two or three best biographies in our language'. Charlotte had always praised the work of her friendly rival. Of *North and South* she told the author: 'What has appeared I like well, and better and better each fresh number.' The summit of generosity was reached when Charlotte postponed publication of *Villette* lest it dim the appearance of Mrs Gaskell's *Ruth*. Another of the northern tales, *Cousin Phillis*, was regarded by Quiller-Couch as the 'most perfect small idyll ever written in English'—praise indeed from a professor of literature who was also a master of prose. Mrs Gaskell died at Holybourne, Hampshire, in 1865, in a house which she had lately built as a gift to her husband.

In Mrs Gaskell's day the people of Appleton Thorn, away to the west, observed the custom of Bawming the Thorn on May Day. The 'bawming' was local dialect for 'adorning'; the Thorn was one of a succession that gave the village its second name. After a pageant, garlanded children decorated the Thorn, but the custom lapsed because it had grown disorderly. During the 1930s it was soberly revived, this time in July.

One year before Mrs Gaskell's death, Knutsford inaugurated

a May Day Festival which became Royal when it was witnessed by the Prince and Princess of Wales in 1887. The modern pageant begins with a parade led by the Town Crier and a mounted Marshal. Among the motley are Robin Hood, Maid Marian, Jack-in-the-Green, and King Canute, who, they say, gave his name to Knutsford (Cnut's ford). Mechanical vehicles are banned from the parade, but a sedan chair takes part, to remind spectators that Knutsford was Cranford.

This festival recalls another, far older, when the Knutsford streets were sprinkled with sand. Sanding occurred, too, on wedding days, as a local jingle tells:

> Then the lads and the lassies their tun dishes handling
> Before all the doors for a wedding were sanding.
> I asked Nan to wed and she answered with ease,
> 'You may sand for my wedding whenever you please.'

The heirs of Cranford will assure you that sanding is as old as King Canute, for they believe that he crossed a local stream, the Lily, on his way south from trouncing the Scots. Having crossed, the King was shaking sand from his shoes at the very moment when a bridal procession passed by. Seeing it, the King scattered some grains of sand on the ground, declaring that the couple must beget as many children.

And they observe another custom in this part of the Pennines, the ghostly rites of All Hallows' Eve, which falls on 31 October. Like several other Christian customs, this was of pagan origin, a lighting of fires to revive the dying year. On All Hallows' Eve families sat up late, eating small cakes, called Soul Cakes. As the clock chimed midnight, candles were lit to guide the spirits of the departed returning briefly to their earthly home. Yeats made a poem about it:

> Midnight has come, and the great Christ Church Bell
> And many a lesser bell sound through the room;
> And it is All Souls' Night,
> And two long glasses brimmed with muscatel
> Bubble upon the table. A ghost may come.

The self-styled realist will dismiss these traditions as archaic superstition. But reality itself is less blinkered than some of its observers. Many customs are echoes from an England that was merrie, not in a tipsy but in the sober meaning of that word, which implies a willingness to take both the rough and the smooth without being bowled over by either. The best of these customs add tuppenceworth of colour to the penny-plainness of urban life. They recall the deliverance from disaster, the munificence of a king or of a cottager, man's dependence upon seedtime and harvest, things temporal and things spiritual, matters of high estate and those other matters that are unknown except among the villagers whom they concern. Each has its place in the index to the story of England.

Meanwhile the Way swings east towards Black Hill, which appears so mountainous that the traveller asks why it should have been excluded from the *corps d'élite* of high places. The reason for its exclusion is inevitable and arbitrary; inevitable because the word 'mountain' must somehow be defined; arbitrary because custom in England and Wales has set the minimum height of a mountain at two thousand feet. There are 612 such summits. Scotland, however, is more exacting; there a mountain must reach at least three thousand feet, that being the level chosen by Sir Hugh Munro, who discovered 538 summits above three thousand feet (and scaled all but two of them). Scotland, in fact, out-tops the rest of the kingdom. England has only seven summits above three thousand feet; Ireland has eleven; Wales has sixteen. Some high places still defy Munro's conventions. For example, Cairn Hill in Northumberland is, as we shall ultimately discover, a mountain (2,545 feet), but Parys Mountain in Anglesey is a hill (450 feet).

Black Hill itself is ninety-two feet short of a mountain. If you do climb it, you will discover why mountaineering is a relatively modern cult. The word 'mountaineer' was not minted until 1610; and by describing a people as 'ignorant and mountainous', Francis Bacon assumed that ignorance walks hand-in-hand with altitude. The Augustans shunned the Pennines because they feared them. Though he lived almost into the nineteenth century, Gilbert White could still describe the Sussex Downs as 'that chain of majestic mountains'. It was Wordsworth who first put mountains on the fashionable map, obliquely via his poems, directly in his guidebook to Lakeland.

And yet some stalwart people did make their home on these heights. The earliest of them were Neolithic men, who—encouraged by a respite from a Glacial period—came from the Continent, not a great while after the Channel had islanded this country. By analysing the pollen in peat bogs, botanists have dated the beginnings of British agriculture as it was practised by men who felled and burned a clearing in the forest, and cultivated it, and then moved on, to repeat the process elsewhere. The earliest farmers were followed by Bronze or metal peoples who sowed more cereals. About the year 500 B.C. the British climate became colder and wetter; peat multiplied in bogs and fens; the Bronze Age gave way to the Iron Age or Sub-Atlantic period. During the Bronze Age, trees in the far north grew at a height of 3,000 feet, which is 700 feet higher than their present maximum level. When the Romans arrived they found much cultivation on the chalk and the loam soils of south-east England; but elsewhere the land was chiefly forest, inhabited by wolf, lynx, deer, bear. Place-names prove that woods on the limestone Pennines were mostly of ash: Ashbourne, Ashford, Ashton, Ashopton, Ashover.

Meanwhile, what about modern men along the Way? So few of them ever came *my* way that there are moments when I feel guilty for not having invented them—or at any rate their conversation—as the incomparable George Borrow did invent them. Some of Borrow's dialogue inclines one to ask which was the more improbable: that any such conversations could have occurred, or that, having occurred, any man should have been able to repeat them verbatim. Borrow, of course, did not repeat them verbatim; he prolonged them verbosely. No Welshman— nor any gipsy either—ever spoke as Borrow sometimes wrote. But Borrow was obliged to fill a given number of pages; so, his method has it. Whenever a sight-seer or jog-trotter comes to halt, he needs only, like Dickens, to 'think of' a Mr Pickwick, and lo, fair stands the wind for fantasy. Some people enjoy that sort of thing. Presumably they enjoy reading 'William the Conqueror, 1067' or 'Magna Carta, 1214'. You may protest that my attitude is pedantic, which it is, in so far as pedants pursue precision. You may protest that it robs a book of much of its charm, which it does, in so far as that sort of charm is a conjuror's trick. If a writer must mix fact with fiction, let him show us his recipe so that we may know when the turtle soup is mock. To say that his imaginary conversations are done well is no defence; it simply brands the soup as 'real mock turtle'.

In any event, only one of my Wayside conversations cannot be paraphrased, and that was a monologue. It occurred within sight of Black Hill, when a youth emerged from misty rain, so bent by his portable mattress, frying-pan, haversack, jack-knife, transistor, and groundsheet—so snail-like, so camelesque, so bowed by the burdens of Atlas—that I supposed him to be travelling like Traherne's corn 'from everlasting to everlasting'. As the domesticated apparition loomed alongside, he exclaimed —I have his words by heart—'Bloody awful weather.' And before I could agree, the mist had shrouded everything except the tinkle of his tinware.

On this sector the average traveller may fail to notice any life at all; yet many birds and beasts have prospered here; stoat, fox, grouse, weasel, whinchat, polecat, raven, deer. A naturalist will detect the difference between the lowland stoat of Knutsford and the highland stoat along the Way. The former seldom achieves the white and wintry covering which the latter wears as camouflage against snow; and in summer the latter always sheds its own camouflage, unlike the stoat of Ben Nevis, where snow may fall in August.

Some of these natives have disappeared; notably the wild cat and the golden eagle, which retreated to the far north. At Glengarry, between 1837 and 1840, 198 wild cats were trapped. In the Lowlands the last recorded killing occurred in Berwickshire in 1849. But with the decline of great estates and an army of gamekeepers, wild cats more than held their own. I have seen them on the mountains west of Braemar. They have bushy tails, and are camouflaged by grey and black stripes. A queen may bear fifteen kittens in one year; each kitten leaving to hunt in its own territory.

Two centuries ago the golden eagles were common here. Now they have gone. In the Scottish Highlands the eagle is *an t'eun*, the bird of birds; and in those Highlands the bird abides.

Polecats, on the other hand, are creeping south. They have been reported in Yorkshire and in Cumberland. The creature's evil smell is a defence mechanism, emitted by musk glands under its tail. Polecats will attack rabbits, geese, turkeys; but their staple diet is field-mice and fish and frogs.

And yet, as I say, the non-naturalist hereabouts may fail to detect any kind of company as he plods from Dun Hill to the summit of Black Hill, which I take to be the most desolate spot in all the Way, and the most dangerous. I came here only once, and that will last my lifetime. Through heavy rain I came, when the sky grazed the land in mutual animosity. Dampness, dourness, drudgery, desolation; that was how humanity translated the scene. If there were any trees, I did not notice them; neither did I observe any bird, beast, or creeping thing that might have ventured out on such a day in such a place. At Edale they had assured me that from the summit I would see a television mast, scarcely a mile away. I saw no such thing, and felt the better for it.

The summit of Black Hill is called Soldiers' Lump because of the military surveys that have been made from it. In 1841 some excavators uncovered the timbers which had supported the theodolite of a survey in 1784. The instrument itself was presented to the South Kensington Science Museum. During a survey in the 1930s many of the soldiers complained that the peat would not hold their tent pegs. As at Bleaklow, so on Black Hill; people have perished in the bog. Now the word 'bog' is commonly used of any marshy ground, but botanists reserve it for marshes bearing bog moss and its plants. Alas, the botany of Black Hill lies out of my bounds. I did read about it, but got bogged-down in a Graeco-Latinity of *Zyogonium ericetorum, Rhynchospara alba,*

Eriophorum angustifolium. Even so, the amateur botanist must persevere, for he may yet amaze the academicians, as David Davies amazed them during the 1914 war. This Davies was a Welsh collier. By collecting and classifying plant remains from each seam of his coal pit, he proved that different seams yielded different harvests; therefore there must have been mineral differences between each habitat. For his pioneer work in paeloecology, which helped to confirm the age of coal seams, Davies received the degree of Master of Science *honoris causae* from the University of Wales.

In order to reach Soldiers' Lump you must wade through the black bog which baptized the place. In that bog I went up to my knees, which means down to my knees, trying to discover where they were; and when at last I did discover them, I got what I believe is called the Hell out of it, lest I found myself seeking my waist, and after that my shoulders, and then my chin and finally my soul as seen by St Peter. So, I am one with those other self-preservers who may claim that they never reached the summit of Black Hill. Twenty yards short was quite long enough for me. In any event, you need not scale the Lump in order to share its loneliness. Twenty yards will make no difference to a solitude which encompasses the universe. I doubt that even the sunniest day could relieve the oppressiveness of Black Hill. On it you feel that you have entered

> A land where no man comes,
> Nor hath come since the making of the world.

From that dark desolation I looked towards Macclesfield Forest, which was the home of William Buckley, who also experienced loneliness. His story is the most amazing of its kind along the Way.

Buckley was born towards the end of the eighteenth century. Perhaps because he stood six feet tall, he enlisted as a soldier. While serving at Gibraltar he nearly finished the Victorian era before it began, for in 1803 he led a mutiny that was to have killed his commanding officer, who soon afterwards begat Queen Victoria. Transported to Australia, Buckley and three other convicts escaped from Melbourne, which was then called Port Phillip. One of the convicts was shot by the guards, two others went their own ways, and Buckley found himself alone in the desert. He had a kettle, a tin can, and nothing else.

While wandering through the bush, dying of thirst, he noticed a rough grave, surmounted by a spear. He took the spear, to help his own stumbling; and then he went on, knowing that he must soon perish. However, he had not wandered far, before a party of aboriginals arrived. Buckley assumed that they would kill him. But they did not kill him. They fell down and worshipped him, in the belief that he was the chief whom they had lately buried, returned to life with his old spear and a new complexion. To cut a short story shorter, Buckley ruled over the aboriginal tribe for thirty-two years.

Then one day a tribesman produced a pocket handkerchief, which must have seemed to Buckley rather as though a rabbit had produced the conjuror. Asked where he had found such a thing, the native replied that he had picked it up near by. Having recovered from his surprise, Buckley went tracking. After a few miles he discovered the camp of John Bateman, an explorer from Van Diemen's Land. At first Buckley could not make himself understood. He had forgotten his own language. In the end he decided to return to civilization, even though it would mean returning to prison. The Queen, however, was graciously pleased to pardon the man who had tried to murder her father. Indeed, she not only pardoned Buckley but also pensioned him. He retired to Hobart, in a blaze of publicity, and died there when he was seventy-six; having many times dined and wined on his skill as a raconteur of one of history's tallest true tales.

But William Buckley was among the least of the Cheshire men who left their mark on history. There was John Speed, for instance, a pioneer of English cartographers. By trade a tailor—and, in his spare time, father of eighteen children—Speed was nearly fifty years old before the generosity of Fulke Greville enabled him to put himself on the map. Fifty-four of Speed's maps embellished his *Theatre of the Empire of Great Britain*, in which he wrote a paean worthy of Shakespeare: 'England,' he declared, 'is the Granary of the Western World, the fortunate Island, the Paradise of Pleasure, and the Garden of God.' Speed's fellow-traveller, John Stow, was also a tailor; and Aubrey presented the pair with a punning posy: 'We are beholding to Mr Speed and Stow for *stitching* up for us our English history.'

A second Cheshire historian was Raphael Holinshed or Hollingshead, born *c*. 1520 in the village of Sutton. According to Aubrey, he went up to Cambridge, and became 'a minister of God's word'. Holinshed edited and wrote a great part of *Chronicles of Englande, Scotlande and Irelande*. He was a riper scholar than Speed: 'The histories,' he says, modestly enough, 'I have gathered according to my skill . . .' Having taken most of his plots from Holinshed, Shakespeare might have uttered Spenser's gratitude: 'Master Holinshed hath much furthered and advantaged me.' Shakespeare himself transmuted Holinshed's history into poetry:

> . . . let us sit upon the ground
> And tell sad stories of the death of kings:
> How some have been depos'd, some slain in war,
> Some haunted by the ghosts they have deposed,
> Some poison'd by their wives, some sleeping kill'd;
> All murder'd; for within the hollow crown
> That rounds the mortal temples of a king
> Keeps Death his court, and there the antick sits,
> Scoffing his state and grinning at his pomp . . .

A third local notable was John Gerard whose book about herbs is commonly accepted as the first of its kind in English. But Master Gerard deserveth a debunk. Born at Nantwich, in 1545, he practised as a barber-surgeon. For his knowledge of plants he was given the task of tending Lord Burghley's gardens in the Strand. In 1587 he published a *Herball or Generall Historie of Plants*, which he passed off as his own, though he had cribbed much of it from Dodeon's Latin textbook of 1583. In 1947 Professor Raven, Master of Christ's College, Cambridge, dismissed Gerard as 'a relatively ignorant rogue'.

Long indeed is the litany of Cheshire's eminence: Heber, son of the rector of Malpas (or, rather, of one of its rectors, for there were two until the beginning of this century). Heber was born at his father's rectory, in a room where a plaque records his arrival. Himself the Bishop of Calcutta, he wrote the missionaries' marching song, *From Greenland's icy mountains, From India's coral strand*. Then there was Charles Lutwidge Dodgson, alias Lewis Carroll; and after him Wilfrid Owen, a walker of the Way, who died on active service a week before the 1918 Armistice. Tormented by the carnage and incompetence, Owen forgot that he and his kind were indeed fighting for a purpose, and that if they had not won their fight, a large part of the world would have sunk in the German Ocean. Owen probably knew that he had written his own epitaph:

> Under his helmet, against his pack,
> After many days of work and waking,
> Sleep took him by the brow and laid him back,
> And in the happy-no-time of his sleeping,
> Death took him by the heart.

Another war arose to dim Wilfrid Owen's, and after it another generation of poets, for whom even that second war seemed stale. But to those of us who were left, and did grow old, neither the morning nor the going-down of the sun has forgotten them.

Unforgotten, too, is the Stockport cobbler's apprentice, named Shovell, who ran away to sea, served as a cabin boy, and became Admiral Sir Clowdisley Shovell. In 1704 he took part in the capture of Gibraltar, and went down when his ship foundered with all hands off the Scillies (in 1968 the hulk was found, and some of its valuables salvaged).

Finally, there was George Mallory, who was born in the beautiful village of Mobberley, and died near the summit of Mount Everest. A window in Mobberley church bears his epitaph: 'All his life he sought after whatsoever things are pure and high and eternal. At last in the flower of his perfect manhood he was lost to human sight between earth and heaven on the topmost peak of Everest.'

A homelier fame may be seen at the farms and shops which sell Cheshire cheese, a product second only to Cheddar in its economic importance—chiefly for the home market because its friable texture deteriorates during long and jolted journeys. A Cheshire farmer told me that the cheese owes something of its flavour to the local water, which is tinged with Cheshire salt. Penninefolk, he added, favour a friable and uncoloured cheese; the southrons prefer a riper and coloured variety. Celia Fiennes noted the farmers' communal enterprises: 'This Shire is remarkable for the great deale of greate Cheese and Dairys. On Enquiry I find the customs of the country to joyne their milking together of a whole village and so to make their great Cheeses. . . .'

These Pennine farmers maintained the traditions of northern self-help. In 1868, for example, they formed the Cheshire Chamber of Agriculture; eight years later several of the county families were paying the fees of youngsters at technical schools; and in 1885 the Cheshire Chamber of Commerce asked the Privy Council to finance evening classes for farmhands. Britain's first Dairy School was founded by private enterprise along the Cheshire Way—at Worleston, in 1886—and was taken over ten years later by the County Council, to become the genesis of the Cheshire School of Agriculture at Reasenheath.

Some Cheshire cheeses are stamped with the face of a Cheshire Cat, but nobody along the Way could tell me why. Is there a breed of Cheshire Cat? And, if there is, does the creature grin more broadly than the rest? The answers are No. Whence then the tradition? Two sources seem plausible. First, the Norman Earl of Cheshire, Hugh the Wolf or Lupus, had for his device a wolf's head which could have been taken for a cat's (the grin being more likely a growl of bared teeth). Second, the arms of the City of Chester impales the lions of England, and since the old armorists drew the device to resemble a leopard full-face or affront, that too may have been taken for a cat.

What, meanwhile, is the Cheshire Way like? It is remarkably like the Derbyshire Way—bleak, daunting, and therefore impressive—but much of the land beside the Cheshire Way is unlike

Derbyshire's, which was pastoral, fertile, wooded. At Edale you were in deep country; from Glossop only the outposts of industry appeared, and only from a distance. But in Cheshire the scene begins to change; and when, beyond Wessenden, you enter Yorkshire, you meet something more than a change of scene. You take part in a revolution.

4 Yorkshire: West Riding (1)

WHAT is this revolution? Where is this revolution? You can see it all around, through binoculars or with the naked eye. It is marked on the map: Oldham, Rochdale, Todmorden. It follows the map for miles: Halifax, Bradford, Keighley.

What does the revolution look like? It looks like nothing that ever was on earth before. William Blake, who saw more deeply and more widely than most men, described it as a Golgotha of 'dark Satanic mills'.

Why did the revolution occur? No one knows why, though many have their answer pat. The dynamics of human destiny elude us because they are a quilt, patched with climate and latitude (factors utterly beyond control) and with those other factors (call them our instincts) that are slowly coming under control, by entering into our conscious understanding of them. Unfortunately, many of the modern revolutionaries exploit their own self-knowledge in order to condition the uninitiated by evil communications.

How do you describe the revolution? You describe it according to the bias of your temperament; and if your temperament is able to detect and somewhat to reduce its bias, then your description will become considerably more accurate than those of the people who either praise the revolution as untarnished Progress or curse it as the ultimate catastrophe.

So, while the Way wanders westward, more than a thousand feet up, unaware that its *ancien régime* has perished, let us consider the redoubts of revolution, the industrial towns that lie along the Pennine Way. Now at the beginning of the eighteenth century those places were either villages or country towns. In other words, they were wholly rural and largely self-sufficient. They did not buy their daily bread from the wheatfields of Canada; they bought it from the wheatfields beyond their own windows, and then baked it in their own ovens. Nothing, of course, remained precisely as it used to be. During the later Middle Ages a primitive form of farmed-out factory-work had begun to undermine the even more primitive form of total self-sufficiency. Subsistence farming, too, had waned. Nevertheless, England was predominantly a nation of farmfolk, if only because the nation had either to feed itself or starve. Then came the revolution.

It was unique; its speed and scope without parallel. Our latest technology is an extension of it; and—to make the point once again—it was born beside the Pennine Way. The leaders of the revolution believed that they were guiding men along the road to Progress. Here and there, no doubt, some social misfit—a poet, a housewife, a mystic—did point out that the road was already congested and might one day grow so chaotic that it ceased to be a road at all, and became a cul-de-sac, crammed with the fossils of mass-produced Dodos buried beneath the debris of their own ingenuity. But such voices were dismissed by men intent on transforming England into an industrial wilderness. Like a snow-ball, the revolution gathered mass from momentum, and momentum from mass. In 1733 Kay, Arkwright's famous assistant, invented the flying shuttle. In 1759 the Duke of Bridgewater employed James Brindley to build what was virtually the first British canal. In 1764 Hargreaves invented the spinning jenny. Soon afterwards came Crompton's 'mule' and Cartwright's power loom. Thirty years later Davy invented the miner's safety lamp. Weaving and spinning began to leave their cottage homes and move into mills. Few of the immigrants benefited from the change. Dr Isaac Watts winced at what he saw:

> How many children in the street
> Half naked I behold!
> When I am clothed from head to feet,
> And cover'd from the cold.

So it went on, and never more swiftly than along the Pennine Way. A child born in 1750 joined a population of six million; a man dying in 1830 left a population of thirteen million. Roads,

canals, railways, factories, machines: Blake's England grew vastly
less green without becoming noticeably more pleasant. When
good men from all classes protested that children ought not to
crawl through the pits for twelve hours a day, the cry went up,
'The Constitution in danger!' When the Whig plutocracy produced
more machines, the hungry robots destroyed them, as though a
tinderbox might thaw Mont Blanc. And still the spate continued.
Between 1796 and 1801 Trevithick designed a steam tram. In 1821
Stephenson became engineer to the Stockton and Darlington
Railway. In 1834 few places south of Durham were more than
ten miles from a canal. Within nine years the number of power
looms leapt from thirty thousand to one hundred thousand.
Towns bulged and burst, fouling the countryside. England was
building the ground from under her feet.

The immediate lesson of all this is, none of it can be assessed
from the Way itself, which walks alone, high above the workaday
world, in a daydream of clear skies, loud larks, dumb rocks.
If you do wish to discover what life is like along this part of the
Way, you must take the road from Oldham through Rochdale to
Halifax, which traverses two centuries of what Sir Kenneth
Clark called 'the spiritual bankruptcy of a prosperous democracy'.
In its earlier phases, among the mean houses, the malaise seems
rather to be greed than a congenital lack of finer values; but in the
new car parks, chain stores, and other glossy garishness, you perceive at last that the old unwillingness to avoid squalor has
become a modern inability to create beauty. What a madman's
ménage it is, this hinterland of shining cars belonging to dingy
houses; of chapels which, having served as fish bars and auction
rooms, are now so unprofitable that no one bothers even to
demolish them. Here loom provincial skyscrapers (incorporating
someone's cement or someone else's mutual benefit), dumped
willy-nilly alongside Victorian villas, 1920 stucco, and the ruins
of a Bevanite shanty town. Press your thumb against a leaf or a
blade of grass, if you can find one; your thumb will turn black
with two centuries of export drive. Try to hear the birds that
peck the parks; you never will hear them, for only Mammon
has the gift of tongues, roaring through a world without peace,

without dignity, without anything at all that money cannot buy. Here began that process which transformed England from a farm to a factory. Here lived the men whose havoc caused Ruskin to cry: 'Every perfect and lovely spot which they can touch, they defile.' Was it all inevitable? Again, no one knows. Was it hideous and unhealthy? Everyone can see. A countryman walking here shares Hilaire Belloc's horror of a land buried beneath buildings:

> And never a ploughman under the Sun.
> Never a ploughman. Never a one.

Yet this county of Yorkshire is so vast that it swallows the factories without disturbing the rhythm of its rural digestion. The vastness is symbolized by an old Pennine saying, that there are as many acres in Yorkshire as there are words in the Bible. In fact, Yorkshire contains nearly four million acres. Its eastern border is the North Sea; its western border lies within a dozen miles of the Irish Sea. Yorkshire straddles England. From its northern heights you see Scotland; from the south, the Midlands. Yorkshire has fifteen thousand parishes; a population twice that of Wales, and a million more than Denmark's; in all, about five million. Because of its size the county has from time immemorial been divided into three administrative parts—North, East, West —called Ridings, a corruption of the Old English *thing* or judicial assembly. The smallest Riding, East, is twice the size of Bedfordshire; the North Riding is bigger than Norfolk, our fourth largest county; the West Riding contains seventy thousand acres more than Lincolnshire, our second largest county. More than one hundred miles of the Way lie in Yorkshire.

If you follow this sector by car as well as on foot, switching from loud roads to quiet tracks, you will marvel at the contrast. Once or twice you will not need to switch; as, for example, at Standedge Cutting, where the Way ventures within a few yards of the Huddersfield road. Under that road are three tunnels—two for railways, one for a canal—designed to carry coals from Newcastle and to bring bread to the cornfields. But away on the moors, beyond Holmfirth, you see another feat of engineering, the Famine Road, a melancholy memorial raised by John Fielden, who employed unemployed cotton spinners to lay a track from his home in Todmorden to the ridge at Stoodley Pike. Thus was philanthropy gotten out of business by pleasure.

The road across Standedge reaches 1300 feet. Below, near the seething River Colne, lies Marsden, birthplace of Henrietta Thompson, wife to Colonel Wolfe of Westerham in Kent. At Westerham, while staying in the vicarage, Mrs Wolfe gave birth to James Wolfe, who, though he stormed the Heights of Abraham, confessed that he would rather have composed Gray's *Elegy*. General Wolfe was killed in action on those Heights, and is remembered by a monument: *Here Died Wolfe Victorious*. His larger memorial is Canada.

Meanwhile the Pennine heights plod on; and again one must report a kind of impressive monotony. There are, of course, many curious sights . . . near Millstone Edge a plaque to Ammon Wright (*obiit* 1946), a Pennine minor poet; on all sides a maze of pack-horse tracks, left high and dry by Stephenson's *Rocket*, Telford's roads, Brindley's canals; on Windy Hill a radio mast; at Cattleshaw some traces of two Roman camps. But the Way itself is boulders or bog. If a man has walked hither from Edale, without knowing that the scene will soon change dramatically, he must feel weary indeed, for variety is a notable spice, and although that spice has been sprinkled, the ingredients remain unchanged; bald hills, bleak moors, and from the hinterland a perennial soot which darkens the face of the rocks.

The Pennines have been dubbed the backbone of England. They are an inland range. Yet the old men hereabouts heard their grandfathers sing a north country seafaring song:

> It's I've got a ship in the north country,
> Down in the Lowlands low,
> And I fear she may be took by the Spanish enemy,
> As she sails on the Lowland sea,
> As she sails in the Lowlands low.

That was a pre-industrial echo, recalling cabin-boy Shovell, who also ran from the Pennines to a port:

And up then stepped a little cabin-boy,
Down in the Lowlands low.
Saying: 'What'll you give me if I do them destroy,
And sink them in the Lowland sea,
And sink them in the Lowlands low?'

What a legacy of homely tunes was bequeathed by men whose heirs decline it.

At this point the Way begins to dither, uncertain whether it should enter Lancashire or remain with Yorkshire. In the end, it achieves the best of both worlds by jumping from one to the other and then back again. However, it does remain in Lancashire for about three consecutive miles, and since it never afterwards returns thither, both courtesy and convenience invite us to regard the next sector as though it were wholly Lancastrian.

In that sector the Way passes one of its classic places, Blackstone Edge.

5 *Lancashire*

BLACKSTONE EDGE so daunted Defoe that he called
it 'The English Andes'. A century earlier, in or about 1696,
Celia Fiennes, granddaughter of the eighth baron Saye and
Sele, had greeted the Malvern Hills as 'the English Alps'. She
greeted these hills, too, and described her journey across them:
'. . . then I came to Blackstone Edge noted all over England for a
dismal high precipice . . . that which adds to the formidableness
of Blackstone Edge is that on the one hand you have a vast precipice almost the whole way both as one ascends and descends and
in some places the precipice is on either hand. . . .'

The climate here is keen, even in summer, but when Defoe
arrived he was either unlucky with the weather or mistaken in
his dates: '. . . though we were but at the middle of August, and
in some places the harvest was hardly got in, we saw the mountains
covered with snow, and felt the wind very acute and piercing. . . .'
Happily, he discovered that the natives knew how to keep warm:
'the store of ale which flows plentifully in the most mountainous
parts of this country, seems abundantly to make up for all the
inclemencies of the season. . . .' Like the Way itself, Defoe went
up and down: 'From Blackstone Edge to Hallifax is eight miles,
and all the way, except from Sorby to Hallifax, is thus up hill
and down; so that, I suppose, we mounted to the clouds and
descended to the water level about eight times, in that little part
of the journey.'

Altogether he had a rough passage: 'It is not easy to express the
consternation we were in when we came up near the top of the
mountain; the wind blew exceeding hard, and blew snow so
directly in our faces, and that so thick, that it was impossible to
keep our eyes open to see the way.' Nor did the people please
him; the miners especially he disliked, describing them in almost
exactly the same words as Herrick had dismissed his Devonians:

'a rude boorish kind of people'. However, Defoe did notice a skill which the Lancashire colliers still possess: '. . . they are a bold, daring, and even desperate kind of fellows in their search into the bowels of the earth; for no people in the world can outdo them; and therefore they are entertained by our engineers in the wars to carry on the sap, and other such works, at the seiges of strong fortified places.' Captain Fluellen would have understood, though without yielding Rhondda's precedence to the Pennine pits. Like the heirs of Defoe's 'desperate kind of fellows'—the Royal Lancashire Regiment—the Cheshire Regiment choose Scottish song as their regimental march: 'Corn Briggs are bonnie.'

In the main, however, Defoe complained chiefly against the Pennine climate: and modern statistics justify his complaint. Away to the south-west, the Manchester district receives an average of only 967 hours of annual sunshine, which is half that of Eastbourne. Nowhere along the Way does the average July temperature exceed sixty degrees, compared with an average of sixty-two degrees at Great Malvern and sixty-three degrees in parts of Essex. Farther north, the Wayside July average sinks to fifty-four degrees. What Wordsworth remarked of Lakeland is true of most of the Pennine Way: 'The country is indeed subject to much bad weather, and it has been ascertained that twice as much rain falls here as in many parts of this island.' Defoe dismissed Blackstone with ten words: 'the most desolate, wild, and abandoned country in all England.'

Nevertheless, Blackstone Edge stands foursquare to the wind of change, for it reveals a Roman road—Celia Fiennes called it 'a Causey'—which ran from Manchester to Ilkley, a distance of twenty-seven miles. Some people deny that the road is Roman; but most archaeologists agree that it is. Climbing a gradient of nearly one in four, the road appears as a pavement of stone setts, sixteen feet wide, supported by kerbs, and reinforced with a rib of millstone grit. This grit is grooved, and the groove is worn (very likely by the brake-rods of descending wagons). This very ancient monument belongs to the National Trust. Our own roads need to be repaired every year, even in the mild south; but this road was so constructed that not even a northern climate has destroyed it; the surface is as strong as when they made it two thousand years ago. However, even the undeviating Romans flinched from a one in four gradient, so they built a by-pass, which remains visible as a green outline north of the original road. And they built a second road hereabouts, seven miles long, from Ripponden to Rastrick; and parts of that, too, are discernible; notably as an *agger* east of Back Shaw on Harden Moor.

Many people forget that European civilization is rooted in Rome. The names of our popular novels are Roman, *romances*. Latin itself is least esteemed by those who most use it—the people who scorn a Saxon word while they wander through a maze of Latinized circumlocution. On the simplest as on the subtlest things Rome laid her finger. The extent to which English jurists imbibed the spirit of Roman law is proven by the assurance with which they modified its letter. As engineers, the English either languished or laboured through more than a millennium before they equalled Rome's expertise. The soldiers on Hadrian's Wall used a kind of lavatory and bathroom which some British cottages still lack. Brindley himself was hailed as a pioneer for doing what Rome had done. Not until Victoria became Queen were the majority of British main roads comparable with the highways that led the Legions from Cumberland to Cornwall, from Wales to the Wash. As late as 1734 the Pennine high road from Rochdale to Littleborough was closed by Act of Parliament because 'it has become so exceedingly deep and ruinous that in winter season, and often in summer, many parts thereof are impassable for wagons . . . and very dangerous to travellers'. We cannot say 'There's the bus' nor 'Where's the office?' without we echo a Latin word. All of us are *heredes necessarii* of Rome; and Kipling put those words into her mouth:

> Under their feet in the grasses
> My clinging magic runs,
> They shall return as strangers,
> They shall remain as sons.

On this part of the Way those sons and strangers wear a red

rose, and have been known to flaunt it, thorn-foremost, at the white rose of York. The red rose is the smaller (Lancashire ranks fifth in size after Yorkshire), but it is also the more prolific (Lancashire is Britain's most densely populated county). The Wars of the Roses, said Sir Winston Churchill, were the 'most ferocious and implacable quarrel of which there is factual record'. That quarrel was finally resolved when the Yorkists won the Battle of Tewkesbury in 1471, but it was revived and, as we now say, sublimated, in 1864 when the Lancashire County Cricket Club was founded. Those were the days indeed; the days of Barlow and A. N. Hornby. When Hornby won his place in the Harrow Eleven he weighed less than six stone, yet he became Lancashire's greatest captain. When Barlow and W. G. Grace opened for England the bowlers were shut-down at lavish cost to themselves. Hornby and Barlow are among the select band of cricketers whom a famous poet praised. That poet was Francis Thompson, himself a Lancastrian, who, as he drew near 'the shadowy coast' of death, remembered the years when the sun stood high, lighting a pitch whose players were now among the shades:

> For the field is full of shades as I near the shadowy coast,
> And a ghostly batsman plays to the bowling of a ghost,
> And I look through my tears on a soundless-clapping host
> As the run-stealers flicker to and fro,
> To and fro . . .
> O my Hornby and my Barlow long ago!

A later generation, as they too approach 'the shadowy coast', rewrite that famous last line:

> O my Paynter and my Washbrook long ago!

But on the Lancastrian Way one is aware rather of work than of play. Those cotton mills, for example; they did not come to Lancashire by chance; they came because the Way at this point, being relatively near to the Atlantic, breathes the humid air which cotton spinning requires. The Four Magi of the revolution were born along the Lancastrian Way: John Kay of Bury, James Hargreaves of Blackburn, Samuel Crompton of Bolton, Richard

Arkwright of Preston (and their sons lived to see Lancashire's cotton trade grow by four hundred per cent). Near or far, the towns tell the tale: Oldham, with 200,000 citizens, still spinning and weaving; Salford, with more than 200,000, likewise spinning (and dyeing and bleaching, too); Bolton, a hub of cotton, mining, tanning, iron-founding; Rochdale, Wigan, Bury, whose 300,000 citizens cluster 3000 to a square mile. The litany can be recited figuratively; thus, in the year 1800 some eighty per cent of the population of northern England was rural; in 1900 only twenty per cent; in 1969 less than ten per cent.

And what a roll-call answers to this red rose: De Quincey, Gladstone, Peel, Dalton, Romney. Lancashire was the first home of Edmund Spenser, and the last of John Ruskin. In Lancashire the Brontës went to school. At a village near Bury lived the Grant Brothers whom Dickens re-created as the Cheerybles ('A cheque for £20 . . . God bless you . . . come and dine with us.') They say, too, that Robin Hood came here with Little John, whom we remembered at Edale. An old Pennine song tells how a merchant fell in and then out with John and Robin:

> By chance he met two troublesome men,
> Two troublesome men they chanced to be,
> And one of them was bold Robin Hood,
> And the other was Little John so free.

Fortunately, the taverns that sustained Defoe were able to restore the peace:

> They sheathed their sword with friendly words,
> So merrily did they agree,
> They went to a tavern and there they dined,
> And cracked the bottles most merrily.

In those taverns the Way overhears a new tone of talk, which to many southrons sounds comic, though Beatrix Potter was not among them: 'To me,' she wrote, 'no tongue can be as musical as Lancashire.' But the author of *Peter Rabbit* had made her home near Coniston Water, where Lancashire's accent is leavened by the deeper notes of Westmorland and Cumberland. Nevertheless, country talk is a reliable sound-post; and the traveller who translates its nuances can say whether they echo Edale, or Blackstone, or Cross Fell, or Wooler.

Soon after Blackstone the Way passes an ancient guidepost, the Aiggin Stone, and then crosses Chelburn Moor, through rather tedious scenery. Thereafter it meets the Halifax highroad near the White Horse Inn. Here for a while the Way becomes a road; and very strange it feels, if you have walked a dozen miles among boulders and bog. This is reservoirland, the realm of Oldham Waterworks and of many mallard also. More reservoirs appear, with Lancashire falling away to the left, and Yorkshire on the right. Here, too, the Way is a road, or at any rate a waterworks track. Ahead looms Stoodley Pike on the Yorkshire side of the border.

This Pike or stone plinth stands 120 feet high. Its history seems more interesting than its appearance. They built it by way of congratulating Napoleon on his abdication in 1814. Forty years later, at the outbreak of the Crimean War, the Pike fell down. They rebuilt it when the war ended; and when the Boer War began they added a lightning conductor, as though to placate their rational superstition. A few hours before the Great War ended in 1918, the Pike again fell down and was again repaired.

Stoodley Pike is 1,400 feet above the sea. From it a whole bookful can be gathered, beginning two miles to the south-west, over the Yorkshire border, at Hebden Bridge, a milling and foundry town, cupped in a combe where Hebden Water joins the River Calder. Hither came the Brontës' black sheep, their only brother, Branwell, to take up a new post as Clerk-in-Charge at Luddenden Foot, a small station on the line to Sowerby Bridge. That was on All Fools' Day, 1841. Next morning Charlotte Brontë wrote to her sister, Emily: 'It is to be hoped that his removal to another station will turn out for the best.' It did not. With very few passengers to handle, and only one porter to talk with (his name was Walton), Branwell spent much time at the Lord Nelson. In bad verse he sympathized with his own self-pity at not being able to write better:

> The bustle of the approaching train
> Was all I hoped to rouse the brain
> From stealthy apathy . . .

Branwell soon extended his custom to the White Horse at Hebden Bridge. Although he fell far short of Aristotle's hero confronting vast odds, his notebooks contain the names of great men who did vanquish adversity . . . Galileo, Milton, Cowper, Burns. Thoughts too deep for tears float upon the pages of Branwell's Luddenden notebooks; and the best of them anticipate a therapy which had not yet been devised:

> Grant me the stern, sustaining power
> To look into the past,
> And see the darkly shadowed hour
> Which I must meet at last.

It is difficult to decide which fate is the more terrible; to rebel because one knows that one never could have been a major poet, or to rebel because one knows that one ought to have been.

At the end of his first year at Luddenden, Branwell's accounts were found wanting. In plain language, £11 1s. 4d. was missing. When auditors examined his ledger, they were shocked by the sketches and caricatures in its margin. The Company did not suspect him of theft—the money had been stolen by Walton while Branwell went tippling—but they did dismiss him for negligence. He returned to Haworth, a broken man, and died there, six years later, of a malady which his death certificate described as 'Chronic bronchitis-Marasmus' or general emaciation. Charlotte shed no tears. Four days after the funeral she wrote to a friend: 'The removal of our only brother must necessarily be regarded by us rather in the light of a mercy than a chastisement.' But Emily felt otherwise. Two years before Branwell died, she wrote his epitaph:

> Do I despise the timid deer
> Because his limbs are fleet with fear?
> Or, would I mock the wolf's death-howl,
> Because his form is gaunt and foul?

> No! Then above his memory
> Let Pity's heart as tender be;
> Say 'Earth lie lightly on that breast,
> And, kind Heaven, grant that spirit rest.'

Hebden, however, has another and more joyful tale to tell, for its children observe the ancient Pace Egg Play. Now Pace is a corruption of Pasch, the Jewish Passover, which became the Christians' name for Easter. At that season the people decorated the very symbol of birth, which is an egg. Then they ate the egg, and relished it all the more because it had been forbidden them during Lent. On Easter Day 1307, 450 hard-boiled eggs, decorated with gold leaf, were presented to members of Edward I's household. The Church, in short, co-opted a pagan custom, and paganism has won it back at last, as a Carnival of Chocolate.

The Pace Egg Play is still performed at places along the Pennine Way from Derbyshire to Northumberland, but its genesis remains as mysterious as the egg's. Sir Edmund Chambers derived it from Jonson's *Seven Champions of Christendom*; other scholars find comparable plays in the fourteenth century. Sometimes the Play is acted at Christmas, with Father in the lead:

> In comes I, old Father Christmas,
> Welcome or welcome not.
> I hope old Father Christmas
> Will never be forgot.

The point is, these customs kindle the ashes of wonder among a generation to whom only machines are miraculous.

The industrial town of Todmorden lies a few miles northward from Hebden Bridge. Its Town Hall was formerly bisected by the Lancashire–Yorkshire border; its commercial ugliness still is haunted by remembrance of John Wesley, who lived and died a priest of the Church of England. You cannot walk this Way—nor anywhere else in England—without you soon follow the footsteps and the horse-shoes of that tireless Tory radical. Wesley's followers now call themselves Methodists, which suggests that all other kinds of Christianity are somehow less methodical, but Wesley himself did not use that word in that way.

He first chose it when he was an undergraduate at Oxford, to denote, as he put it, 'the method of study prescribed by the Statutes of the University'.

Throughout a long life he arose before the winter sun, and soon after sunrise in summer. His mission was to bestir the Church of England in particular and the people of Britain in general (to whom he afterwards added the Americans). Misguided men impeded him; the dregs of the mob pelted and sometimes almost killed him; yet he bore his life and limbs so well that, at the age of eighty, he could in one day ride fifty miles, and preach a brace of sermons *en route,* and afterwards find time for writing his *Journal* and saying his prayers.

At Todmorden Edge the first Wesleyan Quarterly Meeting took place. Not a great way off, at Colne, you can see a chapel in which Wesley preached; its façade is the same, but the contents are now an engineering works. In that chapel, so large was Wesley's congregation, the gallery once collapsed. Blackburn, Bolton, Rochdale, Wigan, Halifax, Bradford; he knew them all. Near Hebden Bridge, on the wild heights of Heptonstall, where the wind bends the trees at birth, there too he preached, in a chapel built by local craftsmen. The house in which he stayed, 4 Northgate, is called The Preacher's House.

One of the last sermons he ever did preach was at Warrington, on his twentieth visit there, in the eighty-eighth year of his life, when the body was at last weaker than the will. An eye-witness described the event: 'He stood in the wide pulpit, and on each side of him stood two friends, and the two held him up. . . . His feeble voice was barely audible, but his revered countenance formed a picture never to be forgotten.' Wesley did not rest after that sermon, but took coach to Liverpool and more work. In his age he was so loved that people gathered at cross-roads to see him pass, and held up their children that he might bless them. John Wesley was the most influential Englishman in the history of religion.

This part of the Way is royal in so far as the Sovereign has for centuries been Duke of Lancaster. Like Chester and Durham, Lancashire became a county palatine, though not until the reign of Edward III. Its capital, Lancaster, was formerly *Loncastra* or the Roman camp near the River Lune. The most colourful Duke of Lancaster was John of Gaunt, Shakespeare's 'time-honoured Lancaster', who was born at Ghent, fourth son of Edward III. Gaunt acquired his duchy by marrying its heiress, Blanche, patron of Chaucer, who composed her elegy, *The Deth of Blaunche the Duchesse*. When Blanche died, Lancaster married a second heiress, Constance, daughter of the King of Castile; and when Constance became Queen, Lancaster ruled as King. In 1387 he abdicated in favour of his daughter. When John of Gaunt's son dethroned Richard II, and so became Henry IV, he was careful to separate the Crown lands from his own duchy of Lancaster. Indeed, he caused Parliament to decree that the duchy was no part of those lands. Sir Edward Coke observed: 'he knew he had the duchy of Lancaster by sure and indefeasible title, but that his title to the crown was not so assured . . .' Edward IV's Parliament agreed that the duchy should retain its '. . . separate guiding and governance from the other inheritances of the crown'. This county palatine administered its own courts until the nineteenth century, and still retains a Chancery Court under its Vice-Chancellor. The Chancellor himself is nowadays a member of the government, ranking next after the Chancellor of the Exchequer. Since his only Lancastrian duties are to appoint regional county court judgeships, the Chancellor is commonly entrusted with non-departmental aspects of government policy.

There is another way in which Lancashire perpetuates its royalty, for the Counts of Lancaster are a branch of the royal house of Portugal via George de Lancastre, bastard son of King John II. The name de Lancastre is a legacy from John of Gaunt, Duke of Lancaster and sometime King of Portugal.

The capital of the Lancastrian Way is Rochdale, a place made famous by John Bright and the Co-operatives.

Bright, the son of a Quaker cotton merchant, joined with Richard Cobden to achieve the repeal of the laws which ensured that the price of corn did not fall below about £3 per quarter. Those laws helped agriculture, but they lay heavily on the poor to whom bread was a staff of life. Bright himself became Member of

Parliament for three industrial constituencies—Durham, Manchester, Birmingham—and was appointed Chancellor of the Duchy of Lancaster. His speeches prove that he had been bred upon the Bible. He once said that by studying Milton he discovered that oratory expresses 'the serious and hearty love of truth' (which was over-kind because Milton often begged Pilate's question with vicious abuse). Many have detested Bright's politics, but all admire his integrity. He died in 1890, and was buried among his Friends at Rochdale.

The Co-operative Movement is sometimes fathered on a Welshman, Robert Owen, but its true founders were a group of weavers who, on 24 October 1844, formally registered the Rochdale Equitable Pioneers. Not Wall Street itself could have sharpened their business acumen. The Pioneers were out to make money, and their prospectus said so: 'The objects of this Society are to form arrangements for pecuniary benefit . . . by raising a sufficient amount of capital in shares . . .' Many of the capitalists were devout dissenters and patriotic Liberals, at all times on the side of those austere ideals which, they believed, were practised by the angels. Thus, their prospectus proposed 'That for the promotion of sobriety, a Temperance Hotel be opened in one of the Society's houses as soon as convenient.' Temperance of any kind will raise a snigger from a generation intent upon smoking and drugging itself into juvenile decay; yet the fact remains, Victorian temperance shone like a good deed in a world of publicans so indifferent to decency that their placards said 'Come and get drunk for a penny'. At the end of its first year the Society had twenty-eight members and a capital of £28; thirteen years later the membership had increased to 1,800, and the capital to £15.142 1s. 2d. Today the Co-op weaves its own materials, makes its own shoes, grinds its own corn, buys its own tea, sugar, and meat. Truly those Rochdale Pioneers might have taken for their motto some words from the Epistle of St James: 'Behold, how great a matter a little fire kindleth.'

Although Rochdale folk love their town, and are proud of its prosperity, they would not, I think, present it as beautiful. At times it becomes invisible, for it lies on the fringe of a fog-belt, in which, on at least ten days every year, and sometimes for several weeks, visibility is reduced to less than two hundred and twenty yards. The air was cleaner when Celia Fiennes visited Rochdale: 'A pretty neate town,' she found it, 'built all over stone . . .'

Less than a century later, Defoe discovered the smoke. Rochdale, he reported, was noted for 'two sort of course goods, called half-thicks or kersies, and the market for them is very great . . .' Traffic problems, however, differed from our own. Were it not for its mills, said Defoe, '. . . the town is situated so remote, so out of the way, and so at the very foot of the mountains, that we may suppose it would be but little frequented.'

The Way also is little frequented, at any rate whenever I explore it, which is out-of-season on a working day. Even at Hebden Bridge I walk alone, along that lovely track through Callis Wood. How refreshing it is to be greeted by trees, after so many miles of unrustling moorland. There are some silver birches in Callis Wood, and among them you hear what you have scarcely heard since Edale, the songs of many birds. Perhaps because the going is so green, you forget the complaint which you have shared with many other travellers, both past and present, that the farther north you go, the longer its miles become. Nowadays, of course, that lengthening of length is an illusion, induced by steep hills, sharp stones, inclement climate. But there was a time when northern miles were indeed longer than southern, for at many places above Edale the so-called 'old British mile' was still in use, which meant that in order to cover one mile you had to walk nearly one mile and a half (to be precise, 2,428 yards). What we now call a mile had been devised in 1593, but it did not appear on any map until 1675, when Ogilby used it for his *Britannia*. So, John Taylor of Gloucester—that vagrant Caroline jingler—was justified when he complained: 'The further I travelled northward the more the miles were lengthened.'

That lengthening will not seem an illusion to a stranger walking here for the first time. There will be moments when he asks himself whether he has made any progress at all since pastoral Edale gave way to moorish Bleaklow. And there will be other moments when, seeing or remembering the skyline of factories, he asks whether he really is on the Way, or whether he has not wandered on to some other Way, some Elysian height, maybe, an inexplicable frontier between sanity and a mechanized nightmare.

But already the Way has re-entered Yorkshire, and will remain there for nearly seventy miles.

6 Yorkshire: West Riding (2)

RE-ENTRY into Yorkshire does not imply release from industry. For another fifteen miles or so the Way is flanked by a hive of factories whose hub is Halifax, 'the holy field of flax'. Camden came here four centuries ago, and reported what the townfolk had told him about that flax: 'A certain priest, as they call him, had long been in love with a young woman without success, and finding her virtue proof against all his solicitations, his love suddenly changed to madness. The villain cut off her head, which, being afterwards hung upon a yew tree, was reverenced and visited by the common people till it began to grow corrupt, every person pulling off some twigs of the tree. The tree, stripped of its branches, maintained its reputation for sanctity among the credulous, and the vulgar fancied the little veins spread like hair or threads between the back and body of the yew tree were the maiden's identical hair. A pilgrimage was established from the neighbourhood hither, and such a concourse came that the village of Horton grew to a large town, and took the name of Hali-fex—Holy Hair.'

By whatsoever name, Halifax was certainly large. Camden reckoned the population at 12,000, but he was wide of the mark. In 1566 Halifax had about 2,600 inhabitants; in 1801 it had 9,000; in 1841, 20,000; in 1891, 82,000; in 1969, nearly 100,000. Even so, Halifax in Camden's day possessed more rich men than square miles: '. . . the inhabitants often say this their parish maintains more men than any kind of animals; whereas, elsewhere in England in the more fruitful places, you will see a thousand sheep and but a few people, as if men had given place to cattle or sheep, or had been devoured by them.' Camden acknowledged the town's self-help: 'The industry of the inhabitants here is also surprising, who, possessing a soil which can scarce maintain them at all, much less in a comfortable manner, have carried on such woollen manufacture, first established about seventy years ago, as to raise themselves great fortunes and bear the prize from all the observation that men's industry is often whetted by the barrenness of the soil.'

Another visitor, the ubiquitous Defoe, reminded his readers of the town's 'Engine' or guillotine, an early example of automation, devised expressly to reduce the number of thieves in the wool market. The 'Engine' was itself axed, in or about 1650, but some Frenchmen are said to have seen it, as a result of which, Dr Guillotine is said to have copied it. Defoe was shown some plans of the machine, but declined to admit them as evidence: 'The whole thing,' he scoffed, 'is a little Yorkshire. . . .'

Halifax received a third distinguished visitor, Charles Dickens, who disliked the town ('It is as horrible a place as ever I saw') but approved the mill-hands who came to hear him read ('They were really worth reading to for nothing'). Dickens, however, rated them above their worth by charging so much that on a single night he took, in modern currency, about £700. However, the ultimate equity lay with Halifax, for Dickens had presented five pages of the manuscript of *Pickwick Papers* to a member of his audience, Mr Whiteley, whose descendants sold them for £7,500.

The town's chief merit is its situation on a slope above the River Calder. Most of the old houses have gone, but everywhere the moors encroach, and some of the meanest dwellings enjoy the finest views. On the outskirts of the town are Shibden Hall (1420, timber-framed and cross-gabled) and Branwell Brontë's Lord Nelson Inn (1654). I like, too, Old Hall (1690), Holy Trinity Church (1798), and the former Mechanics' Institute (1857). What I do not like is the absence of any guidance to the Way near Calder Valley. On this tract not even the hiking manuals can navigate a stranger among the maze of moor, road, track, path, bridge, stile, gate, field, wall. It is probable that I never have followed this part of the Way, but only steered across the map. However, at Colden Water I did achieve a feat of fishmanship by finding, first, a length of string, and after that a slice of bread, and after the bread a pin (it was in my lapel) with which I fixed the one to the other. Thus equipped—having made certain that no Izaak Walton was present—I cast my bread upon the water. Nor had I to wait many days, for in less than three minutes the bread returned to me in the form of a fish, which rose thrice before accepting the fact that it had (as we say) had it. At Colden therefore I avoided what Leigh Hunt called 'the angler's infinite non-success'.

But that was in holiday mood, before I had undertaken to explore one hundred miles of a Yorkshire skyscape so sprinkled with so many sorts of star that each seemed a lode, on no account to be overlooked. Alas, time was shorter than eternity. I had therefore to select from among these White Roses and those others, the Red, that were still within sight. It was a woman, I remembered, who first gave the White Rose to York, for the flower came north via the Duke's marriage with the Clifford family, who had themselves taken it as their emblem in memory of Rosamund, mistress to Henry III. Anthony à Wood stated: 'We rede that in Englonde was a king that had a concubine whose name was Rose, and for her great bewty he cleped her Rose a monde, that is to saye, the Rose of the World.' This celebrated lady was born in a manor house, now a farm, at Frampton-on-Severn. Part of the house is still called Rosamund's Bower, though the lady's real name was Jane.

I thought, too, of another and dissimilar lady, Mrs Aaron Stock, who came striding here from Wigan, covering thirty-six miles in one day. This nineteenth-century Wayfarer rushed in where Defoe had feared to tread: 'I can,' she boasted, 'skip like a lamb amongst rocks, and enjoy the sport after a ten or twelve miles walk.' When Mrs Stock ventured farther along the Way, into Cumberland, she skipped *in excelsis*: 'A fine, noble, lofty, rugged mountain, has more charms for me than a fine, formal, artificial walk . . .' Mrs Stock's adjectives were compiled with some care, for she kept a diary, and wrote many letters, with both eyes on posterity.

Abraham Wood, by contrast, was not a literary person, though he did once run forty miles so quickly that some of the accompanying horsemen failed to keep up. A contemporary noticed that this inexhaustible Yorkshireman was 'possessed of good WIND and a great BOTTOM'.

These were more or less private persons, but there were also public appointments which neither time nor space could keep unless by breathless proxy: Blackburn, for example, a weaving Wem, redeemed by its moors (here the spinning jenny was born, and so was John Morley, editor, historian, Cabinet Minister). Eastward lay Bradford, city of the smoky Fleece and of cotton and silk and engineering. Bradford has memorials to a Prime Minister, Sir Robert Peel, and to an actor, Irving, who made his farewell appearance at the Bradford theatre, and died an hour afterwards, saying, 'Into thy hands, O Lord, into thy hands.'

And then, as I approached a place called Withens, all fell silent —the spinning jennys, the power-houses, the kings, the conquerors, the capitalists—not one among them could be heard, for a wind had risen, out of the heather and down from the sky.

Now when De Quincey described his first visit to Grasmere, he began by confessing that Wordsworth was '. . . the man who, of all others since the beginning of time, I most fervently desired to see'. Within a few yards of the Way stands Wuthering Heights, the place which, of all others that adorn English fiction, I most fervently desired to see. I first came from Westmorland, where the morning had been bright and blue, but when I entered Gargrave the autumn clouds overtook me, and at Keighley the streets were awash. I left the car near Scar Top, and then walked into the heart of the Brontë moors. The wind was up in arms now, flaying whatever opposed it. Black clouds really did seem to race overhead, though whether fleeing or pursuing I could not say. Sometimes their bellies grazed the earth and were ripped open like bottomless buckets. A crow floundered by, struggling for steerage way, and then gave up, and walked to wherever it was going. This was the type of country which Wordsworth knew:

> Where earth is quiet and her face unchanged
> Save by the simplest toil of human hands
> Or season's differences . . .

Presently a covey of trees appeared, and some of them Emily Brontë had seen: 'One may guess,' she wrote, 'the power of the north wind blowing over the edge, by the excessive slant of a few stunted firs at the end of the house; and by a range of gaunt thorns all stretching their limbs one way, as if craving alms of the sun.' Alongside those trees lay the ruins which Emily Brontë's genius rebuilt as Wuthering Heights. I say 'rebuilt' because the Heights in the novel was a substantial home, having a kitchen on the ground floor, but the Heights on the Way (they call it Top Withens) has only one sizeable room on the ground floor. Again, Wuthering Heights had several bedrooms, but Top Withens only two. Even so, this is very probably the site which Emily Brontë chose for her tale.

Until the 1930s Top Withens was occupied. Now, year by year, it falls to bits. The roof has collapsed, the walls are defiled, the grass is a graveyard of sight-seeing litter. It was some consolation to discover that no one had yet desecrated a plaque, erected by the Brontë Society, which confirms that this situation may have been in Emily's mind when she wrote her epic of the Pennine Way.

Wuthering Heights stands apart from all other of our novels. It is a kind of *Macbeth* and a sort of *Othello*. 'Imagination,' said Blake, 'is not a state, it is human existence itself.' Emily Brontë's masterpiece of human existence had a hard fight to get published, and in the end it fell flat. Did she know that it would one day rise? Consciously she may not have known, and, having delivered herself of it, she may have ceased greatly to care. But unconsciously she may indeed have foreseen that *Wuthering Heights* would haunt the future; for, at the very end of the tale, when Cathy is dead, and Heathcliff has joined her, a little boy is found near Wuthering Heights, in tears. They ask him why he weeps. And he replies: 'There's Heathcliff and a woman, yonder, under t'nab . . . un I darnut pass 'em.'

Before visiting the Brontës' home at Haworth, it may seem interesting to glance at their destinies. The father of this remarkable family, Patrick Brontë—alias Brunty, alias Prunty—was born on St Patrick's Day, 1777, in County Down, Ireland. Their mother, Maria, was a Cornish gentlewoman. Thus a Celtic dawn broke upon the Yorkshire moors. In 1820 the family moved to Haworth Vicarage, and there they were outlived by their father.

Maria and Elizabeth Brontë died in childhood.

Branwell, who drank himself to death, was a clever failure, whaling among the minnows in a beer house. With such a father, in such a setting, at such a time, Branwell may have been fore-doomed from infancy.

Charlotte is the best-known, as the author of *Jane Eyre*, an idyll of young love with both feet planted in elderly reality. Her greater novels are less popular. She outlived her mother, her brother, and her sisters; dying when she was thirty-nine, a few months after marrying her father's curate.

Anne Brontë was buried at Scarborough, where the inscription on her tombstone contains five errors, including one about her age (she was twenty-nine when she died, not twenty-eight). Anne left two agreeable novels, and one poem—to her dead fiancé—which is among the most beautiful things ever written by a woman to a man:

> Life seems more sweet that thou didst live,
> And men more true that thou wert one;
> Nothing is lost that thou didst give,
> Nothing destroyed that thou hast done.

Emily, also a spinster, died of consumption when she was thirty. Only two hours before the end, she had refused to see a doctor. She wished to die standing up. But her fate was swifter than her will, and she died on a sofa in the parlour. Emily Brontë outshone the rest because, unlike them, she was first and last a poet. Even her novel is a poem, though she wrote it in prose. When her poems did appear, under a pen-name, two copies were sold; yet those two copies contained the kind of art that transcends a merely literary criticism. Charlotte recognized the quality of her sister's poetry: 'Of its startling excellence I am deeply convinced. . . . The pieces are short but very genuine . . . they stirred my heart like the sound of a trumpet.' To seek dazzling word-play in Emily Brontë is as idle as to seek corruption in Bunyan, or health in

Baudelaire. Her voice was the wind's voice, which has no need of effects. She was neither an innovator nor an imitator; she was an artist; and her genius sprang from an eye that could detect 'eternity in a grain of sand', or the universe on a Yorkshire moor. Some poetry may be likened to a rare wine. Emily Brontë's poetry resembles a moorland beck. Each of those two draughts has its excellence, and both subserve different needs.

'Stronger than a man, simpler than a child, her nature stood alone.' That was how Emily Brontë appeared to a great novelist, her own sister, Charlotte. Yet there was one form of aloneness which not even Emily could withstand. When she did leave the Pennine Way, to become a governess in Brussels, she wilted. 'Day by day,' wrote Charlotte, 'I watched her sinking, a captive of captivity.' She longed always

> For the moors, for the moors, where the long grass
> Like velvet beneath us should lie:
> For the moors, for the moors, where each high pass
> Rose sunny against the clear sky.

Beethoven once wrote four sentences on a slip of paper which he framed and kept always on his desk. The fourth sentence was: 'He is alone by Himself, and to Him alone do all things owe their being.' The first of those propositions can be interpreted (or misinterpreted) as Beethoven's self-identification with God. But not even Beethoven believed that Ludwig had created the universe. The sentence, in fact, is the first and almost the only Article of a creed which Emily Brontë recited in the last and greatest of her poems:

> No coward soul is mine,
> No trembler in the world's storm-troubled sphere:
> I see Heaven's glories shine,
> And faith shines equal, arming me from fear.
>
> O God within my breast,
> Almighty, ever-present Deity!
> Life—that in me has rest,
> As I—undying Life—have power in Thee!

> Though earth and man were gone,
> And suns and universes ceased to be,
> And thou wert left alone,
> Every existence would exist in Thee.

That was the wind I heard from Haworth moor; the wind without need of effects; that bloweth seldom and only upon the summit.

Haworth itself, about four miles west of the Way, is nowadays a suburb of Keighley (they call it Keethley), a weaving town on the rivers Aire and Worth. Here the Brontës went shopping. The local stationer would walk twenty miles to Halifax and back lest at any time he lacked the writing paper which Charlotte Brontë bought from him by the half-ream. And from Keighley station Charlotte travelled to London, to astound her publisher and the world (though not the insightful Dickens) by revealing that the author of *Jane Eyre* was not, after all, Mr Currer Bell, under whose name the book first appeared. Her luggage had reached Keighley by cart, but she herself walked the four steep miles through a thunderstorm.

Haworth village is of dour gritstone, set on the slope of a hill whose gradient Mrs Gaskell recorded: 'so steep that the flagstones with which it is paved are placed end-ways, so that the horses' feet may have something to cling to, and not slip backwards.' In Emily Brontë's time those flagstones led towards

> A little and a lone green lane
> That opened on a common wide . . .

Nowadays the common is a summer car park, and Main Street a Pennine Polperro, obstructed by amiable queues gazing at inappropriate shop windows. Mid-week in winter is the season when you are most likely to find the Brontës at home to imagination.

Patrick Brontë would scarcely recognize his old church, for in 1880 it was rebuilt, and only the west tower survives. It is a dark place, hemmed in by iron railings. Some of the gravestones are paving stones. Charlotte remembered them vividly: 'the church-yard so filled with graves that the rank weeds and coarse grass scarce had room to shoot between the monuments.'

. The Brontë parsonage is a museum, filled with treasures and trinkets: the dog's collar, the lock of hair, the sampler, the tea caddy, a copy of Wesley's edition of Thomas à Kempis, presented to Charlotte by an aunt, and inscribed *Charlotte Brontë—Her book*. The shrine at Haworth parsonage is the sisters' nursery, adorned with their childish murals. That, too, Charlotte remembered, but then wavered, even she, the professional describer: 'Pen cannot portray the deep interest of the scenes I have witnessed in that little bedroom . . .' But we know them already, for this was the room where Gondal and Angria grew up, to become *Wuthering Heights* and *Shirley*.

There has been no English family like the Brontës. Half-orphaned in childhood; cooped in a remote place with an aloof father; tormented by a wastrel brother; exiled from their home and one another, to serve as governesses; all dying young, all but one unmarried, and she to die soon after. Yet from that barren soil the Brontë sisters arose and shone. I do not know of any other birthplace so steeped in so many recollections of such untranquil emotion; nor any so resoundingly triumphant.

After Haworth the miles seem dull as they cross Ickornshaw Moor, *en route* for the Keighley road at Cowling, within a few hundred yards of Middleton, the birthplace of Philip Snowden. A plaque at Middleton states: 'In this cottage was born, on July 16th, 1864, the Right Honourable Philip Snowden, PC, First Viscount of Ickornshaw, three times Chancellor of the Exchequer of Great Britain.' *De mortuis nil nisi bonum*; but the good implies the truth; and the truth is, Snowden and his fellow-travellers disarmed not only our defences but also our willingness to see what really was afoot in Germany.

After Cowling the Way becomes so wooded that one of its heights is named Wood Hill. Below lies Lothersdale and Stone Gappe, an eighteenth-century house which became the prototype of Gateshead Hall in *Jane Eyre*. Jane was unhappy at Gateshead, and in expressing her misery Charlotte Brontë spoke for many Victorian governesses: 'I was a discord in Gateshead Hall; I was like nobody there; I had nothing in harmony with Mrs Reed or her children . . .'

Now Pinhaw Beacon appears, 1,200 feet up; and when you have reached it you look down upon a Promised Land, the land of Craven, whose name—from the Old Welsh *craf* or garlic—is indeed a place-name because garlic thrives on Carboniferous limestone. Hitherto since Edale the Way has followed a region of Millstone grit, but now at last it walks upon limestone. The moors give way to pastures; the heather is supplanted by primrose and cowslip. Here you may say with John Clare:

> The shepherd on thy pasture Walks
> The first fair cowslip finds,
> Whose tufted flowers on slender stalks
> Keep nodding to the winds.

The next dozen miles are a delight, unlike anything that has gone before. The stony Way becomes a necklace of footpaths beside a stream and the Leeds and Liverpool Canal (forty-six years in the making). Directness, however, it never does achieve, for, after wandering east, it suddenly heads north through Thornton-in-Craven. The village of Thornton is altogether agreeable, having an ancient church and a comely almshouse of 1815. Here was born that masterful Mistress Barbara who awaits us over the skyline near Gargrave. Meanwhile the pastoral progress continues, through a herbage which nourished the famous Craven Heifer, bred in 1807 by the Reverend William Carr, for fifty-four years the parson at Bolton in Wharfedale. Carr's heifer weighed 150 stone, and fetched (in modern currency) about £5000. At Arches Farm you can still see the enormous barn door that was built for the heifer.

Craven is a country of Shorthorns, a breed whose origins are unknown except in so far as the animals became popular during the 1770s, largely through the skill of two breeders, Charles and Robert Colling of County Durham. Even fifty years ago Shorthorns were known overseas as Durhams. During the present century the stock was improved by two Yorkshire breeders, Thomas Booth and Thomas Bates. The colour of Shorthorns varies from red to white, but their physique is unmistakable—straight back, broad chest, short horns. In the distant days of my

Dent Town, West Riding

Leeds and Liverpool Canal at Gargrave,
West Riding

Springtime in Swaledale, North Riding

High in the North Riding

own farm pupilage Shorthorns formed three-quarters of the entire milking cattle of Great Britain and Eire. Six gallons daily was common, and nearly three pounds of butter within twenty-four hours.

Here the hills grow green, gentle, low; and beyond them, to the west, lies a sheep town or Skipton, the bright and breezy capital of Craven, a market and a meeting-place for Pennine farmers. Of its Norman castle only one gateway remains; the rest is a blend of the fourteenth and seventeenth centuries. From 1311 until 1676 Skipton Castle was the principal seat of the Cliffords, a family dominating the Way from mid-Yorkshire to north Westmorland. When the Cliffords became Earls of Cumberland it was said that they could ride from Skipton to Brough without leaving their own lands. The most colourful Clifford was a lady whom we have yet to meet, Lady Anne, Countess of Dorset and of Pembroke and of Montgomery.

Skipton is one of those ruins which the Cromwellians knocked about a bit. It received a market in 1203; a canal to Bradford in 1773; a railway to London in 1847. High, wide, and handsome is the main street; and the best visiting hours are early in the morning, when chaff glistens in the gutter, and sparrows peck at what we will call the crumbs from a rich man's stable. At noon the town bustles with no-nonsense farmwives; with gaitered and macintoshed men whose last testament will nudge its noughts across the column of the local newspaper; and high-hobbling nylonized nymphs who, an hour ago, were gumbooted in acres of rougeless muck; and soap-sheen scholars from the Grammar School (alas, too many of them dream of ICI and other white-faced collars); and massive men in shiny serge, the grandsons of farmhands who fetched, carried, hewed, hoed, and raised six healthy hulkers on the price of a present packet of cigarettes per day. Here, then, they are. Here they always have been. Happen they will not soon depart.

But now the Way enters Airedale, a new feature of the journey. The word 'dale' (Old English *dael*) means a deep place. However, what went down must have come from up; and in Yorkshire a dale connotes both high and low. Wordsworth for example wrote of 'That part of those dales which runs far up into the mountains'. The word 'dalesman' was first recorded in 1769, when it referred especially to Westmorland and Cumberland. How many dales are there in Yorkshire? The answer is 'Too many to be cited'. Most Yorkists will agree that the principal dales are Wharfedale, Littondale, Upper Airedale, Dentdale, North Ribblesdale, Wensleydale, Coverdale, Bishopdale, Arkengarthdale, Swaledale, Garsdale. The Way overlooks all of them, and each has its *differentiae*. Swaledale is slender, wild, steep. Wharfedale is softer and sinuous. Wensleydale is wooded, winsome. Dentdale is a miniature of the whole.

Airedale took its name from the river and then gave it to a dog, the largest of all terriers, which was first bred in 1865 from ancestors that are said to have been hybrids, part otterhound, part terrier.

Soon the Way makes one of its very few entries into a town, Gargrave, formerly the central parish of Craven, with its own market. If you care for such things, you will find the remains of a Roman villa and of a prehistoric camp near the town. In 1318 the Scots raided Gargrave and, it is said, destroyed six of its churches, but spared the seventh because it was dedicated to St Andrew: a religious form of nationalism. The town was raided again, in 1826, when armed Luddites destroyed the new power looms at Mason's cotton mill. Traffic has made Gargrave an unmelodious place. No longer can you hear the river flowing quietly under the bridge. On the far side of the street things are better; notably at the canal, which now harbours some pleasure craft whose masts and anchors seem nostalgically out of their depth amid these 'Andes of England'.

North-east of Gargrave the Way skirts a plantation, follows a wooded waterscape grazed by cattle, and so reaches Airton, which has a village green, a post office (1666), a manor house (1686), a Friends' Meeting House (1700), and an old cottage or squatter's home—that is, the house of a homeless man who received from Quarter Sessions the right to build a garden and a house on common land.

Near Airton, at Calton Hall, lived Major-General and Mrs

John Lambert. In 1516 the original Hall (destroyed by fire during the 1660s) was acquired from John Malham by a lawyer, John Lambert, whose descendant served under Cromwell at Marston Moor. In 1647 he was promoted Major-General in command of the rebels in the north and thereafter in Scotland. In 1651 he led the right wing of Cromwell's army at Worcester. Unlike Cromwell, General Lambert was a republican. Having opposed Cromwell's assumption of the style of Highness and Lord Protector, he retreated to a house at Wimbledon, there to repent leisurely of the haste with which he had supported the most ruthless dictatorship ever suffered by the English people. From Wimbledon he was recalled to serve on the ominous-sounding Committee of Safety under the dictator's son, Tumbledown Dick. When King Charles II returned to England he arrested Lambert, but allowed him to end his days on Guernsey.

Lambert's son married one of the Listers of Gisburn, known locally as Mistress Barbara, a rich widow, who established a kingdom of Independent saints in Craven. In 1704 she financed the building of a Congregational church at Winterburn. In 1880 the church was closed, but re-opened two years later as a chapel of ease to Gargrave church; which it still is.

Although the Lamberts were Republicans—or perhaps because of the fact—they belonged to the Whig oligarchy, and would hardly have approved the regimental march which the West Yorkshires borrowed from blood-stained France. Known as *Ça ira* or 'Murder the aristocrats', this tune was composed by a Paris lay-about named Ladre, and the French revolutionaries marched to it across Europe, conquering almost every nation which declined their offer of liberty. Very different was the choice of the men of the West Riding Regiment, the Duke of Wellington's. They preferred 'The Wellesley', recalling the fact that the Iron Duke, being then Colonel Wellesley, had led them against Tippoo Sahib.

Now the Way enters Malhamdale, which some people regard as the most dramatic corner of Yorkshire. The village of Malham is a haunt of artists who set up their easels among white cottages and scarlet honeysuckle festooned around a green beside a river.

It was here that the Pennine Way was officially opened by the Minister of Land and Natural Resources, on 24 April 1965. Among the speakers at the ceremony were Lord Strang, chairman of the National Parks Commission, and Tom Stephenson, of the Ramblers' Association, both of whom did much to create the Way. The three local wonders are a Scar, a Cove, and a Tarn. The Scar is the roof of a limestone cave which collapsed and became a rampart, rinsed by a waterfall. The poet Gray declared that the memory of Gordale Scar would last throughout his life.

The Cove is another limestone cliff, poised over a stream three hundred feet below. Here you will think yourself in Peakland, among green pastures and stone walls dazzling as sunlight.

The Tarn is a lake, the highest in the Pennines, thirteen hundred feet above the sea. Nowadays it forms part of a nature reserve, barred to motorists but at home to walkers. In 1745 the land here was reserved for a different purpose; five thousand head of cattle grazed 730 acres of pasture beside the lake. They belonged to John Birtwhistle, a grazier who specialized in the Scottish market. Financed by the British Linen Bank, he would sometimes have ten thousand animals on the road to Carlisle. The Way follows the shore of the tarn, and enters the grounds of Malham Tarn House, built in 1850 by a northern millionaire, Walter Morrison, who occupied his highland fastness for sixty-four years. Among his callers were Ruskin, Darwin, Kingsley; of whom the last put Malham on the map by placing it in a book.

Kingsley's map-making began a few miles off the Way, at the village of Arncliffe. I first found Arncliffe by chance, while motoring leisurely over the hills, along a lane that ambled sans hedge or wall or house, switchbacking a skyscape speckled with sheep thick as mushrooms, and occasionally by cattle whose Highway Code contained one word only: yield. I saw a plover, I heard the lark; but of man himself I found no sign at all.

Presently the lane gave way under its own feet, and not even bottom gear seemed low enough. But in the core of the combe I sighted a seventeenth-century house, Darnbrook Farm, lone as a fallen star that had gathered itself together as a human habitation. Daffodils in the garden nodded their approval of the beck's

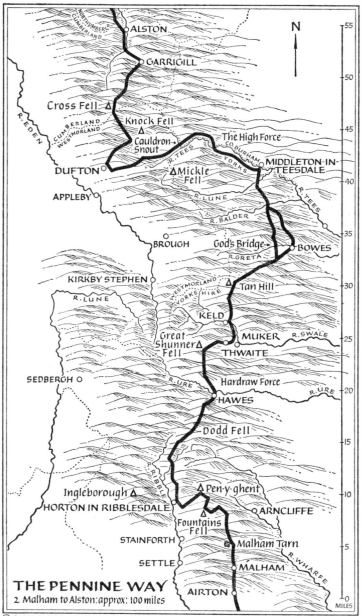

N

ALSTON

GARRIGILL

Cross Fell △

Knock Fell
△
Cauldron→
Snout

The High Force

R. EDEN

CUMBERLAND
WESTMORLAND

NORTHUMBERL
CUMBERLAND

CO. DURHAM
YORKS.

DUFTON

△Mickle
Fell

MIDDLETON-IN-
TEESDALE

APPLEBY

R. LUNE

R. TEES

R. BALDER

BROUGH

God's Bridge→

BOWES

R. GRETA

KIRKBY STEPHEN

WESTMORLAND
YORKSHIRE

△ Tan Hill

R. LUNE

KELD

Great
Shunner△
Fell

MUKER

R. SWALE

THWAITE

SEDBERGH O

R. URE

Hardraw Force

R. URE

HAWES

Dodd Fell

Ingleborough △

△ Pen-y-ghent

ARNCLIFFE

HORTON IN RIBBLESDALE

R. RIBBLE

△
Fountains
Fell

STAINFORTH

Malham Tarn

SETTLE

MALHAM

R. WHARFE

THE PENNINE WAY
2. Malham to Alston: approx: 100 miles

AIRTON

55

50

45

40

35

30

25

20

15

10

5

0
MILES

© CASSELL & CO. LTD. 1969

perennial sing-song. The world was so still that you could hear the silence. Then came three wise men, blakeying their boots across the cobbles; and at the sound thereof the welkin roused itself and rang. The wisest of the trio told me that for three years he had not left his valley, except to scale its heights in search of sheep. And then he told me why he had not left: 'Away in't towns 'tis nobbut bloody pandemonium.' I think, though, that the wise shepherd had strayed as far as his own town, the hamlet of Arncliffe, whose population is so small that no one has bothered to publish it. The stone houses are small, too, and most of them overlook a miniature green. At the inn I found a pamphlet of poems by a Yorkshirewoman, Gwen Wade, and came on a dialect verse which told how Noah himself had first trisected Yorkshire into Ridings:

> Mi lads, Ah've hed a vision
> Of what ahr lahf'll be
> When all this flood is owered
> For which wes'll put to sea—
> Wes'll hev all t'pick o' t'pastur,
> For t'wo'ld 'll be wer awn,
> Soa frame to big yon ark wi me
> Wi blessins at ye're born!
> Ther'll be no competition
> For land, but—fair is fair—
> Ah'll split awk Yorkshire inti three,
> An gi yer each a share!

A path across the green leads to a river, a church, a bridge, a house; all four composing a portrait of actively still life.

Arncliffe church stands so close to the River Skirfare that from its porch you hear the stream in spate. The first church here was Saxon, made of timber. The first rector arrived c. 1180. He and his successors, some of whom became vicars, are recorded in the church, which was rebuilt in 1793 except for the sixteenth-century tower. Another scroll recalls the Arncliffe men who in 1513 followed the Pennine Way northward to fight at Flodden Field. Their numbers exactly equal those of the villagers who served in 1914 and in 1939.

Bridge End House, on the far side of the river, has a garden sloping to the water. It was here that Charles Kingsley wrote part of an English classic. Kingsley himself was a Devon man, born at Holne Vicarage in 1819. He became rector of Eversley in Hampshire, chaplain-in-ordinary to Queen Victoria, Canon of Chester and of Westminster, Regius Professor of History at Cambridge. As a young man he supported F. D. Maurice, the founder of Christian Socialism. In 1844, the year that rent Europe, he published *Yeast, a Problem*, a novel indicting the hardships of the poor. But he wearied of his aggressive Socialist friends, and ultimately disowned them.

In 1863 Kingsley was staying at Bridge End with his family. He knew the Pennines well and had intended to use them as the setting for two novels, neither of which got under way. At Bridge End his three older children one day reminded him of an unfulfilled promise that he would write a book for his baby son, Grenville. To this, said Mrs Kingsley, 'He made no answer, but got up at once and went into his study, locking the door. In half an hour he returned with the story of Little Tom. This was the first chapter of the *Water-Babies*, written without correction.' The story, she added, 'was a pure labour of love'. The book's full title is *The Water-Babies, a Fairy Tale for a Land-Baby*. It appeared monthly in *Macmillan's Magazine*, having been written in what Kingsley described as 'white hot heat'.

According to his wife, Kingsley was wholly unprepared for the fervour with which the nation responded to the ordeals of young chimney-sweeps. Yet the fervour seems in character, for another eminent Victorian, Matthew Arnold, described the era as one of '. . . unsettlement and of impatience with authority, convention, routine. . . .' Times had changed since Charles Lamb, that kindliest of men, wrote an essay, *The Praise of Chimney-Sweeps*, whose opening sentence reveals a national blindness: 'I like to meet a sweep . . . one of those tender novices, blooming through their first nigritude, the maternal washings not quite effaced from the cheek. . . .' Although Kingsley's fairy tale for Grenville, a Land-Baby, is now regarded as a sociological tract, it was written as a theological fantasy, depicting the regeneration of an old, albeit very young, Adam. Its moral is a profound psychic truth, which the wicked Grimes denied: 'Foul I would be and foul I am,' he cries, 'it's all my fault; it's too late.' But the good fairy tells him: 'Never too late. . . .' Kingsley embellished the book with his own brand of politics and religion. 'He is a Scotchman,' says one character, 'and fears God but not the priest.' Another character—echoing the author's disillusioned Socialism—is described as being 'as good an Englishman as ever coveted his neighbour's goods'. Some parts of the book are beyond a child's understanding; other parts echo the poetry of childhood: 'The shadows of the clouds ran races over the bright blue bay, and yet never caught each other up; and the breakers plunged merrily upon the wide white sands, and jumped over the rocks, to see what the green fields inside were like . . .'

Kingsley came late into the lists, for Blake had long ago written a chimney-sweep poem—'A little black thing among the snow'. Others had campaigned less lyrically. In 1785, for example, Jonas Hanway published an indictment of cruelty to chimney-sweeps. Two years later Parliament required *inter alia* that at least once a week the children '. . . be thoroughly washed and cleansed from soot and dirt'. Despite legislation, young sweeps were still at work in Kingsley's day, crippled by rheumatism, killed by cancer. *The Water-Babies* appeared when the national conscience was ready to receive it. In 1878, two years after Kingsley's death, Lord Shaftesbury's Act forbade children to be sent up chimneys.

Arncliffe, or the eagle's cliff, was sometimes called Amberdale, the dale beside the river:

> The White Doe followed up the Vale
> In the deep fork of Amberdale.

So wrote Wordsworth in his poem about the Doe of Rylstone, which, he said, was founded on a tradition that the Cliffords had joined a rebellion by Roman Catholics. Only a daughter and one son disapproved the rising. The son was killed, having tried to protect his father and brothers; but the daughter survived and lived in pious seclusion, attended by a doe which seemed able to perceive her sorrow:

> So to her feet the Creature came,
> And laid its head upon her knee,
> And looked into the Lady's face,
> A look of pure benignity.

In Malhamdale and Littondale there is no need to utter Charles Lamb's plea: 'Will no kindly earthquake swallow up those accursed cotton mills?' These limestone pastures resemble a vast golf course, intersected with drystone walls. Andrew Marvell, who lived beside the Wharfe, as tutor to Lord Fairfax's daughter at Nun Appleton Hall, set the hayfields to music:

> The tawny mowers enter next,
> Who seem like Israelites to be
> Walking on foot through a green sea.

Green indeed, and still surprising after the bogs and boulders of Blackstone Edge. Yet this remains a hill country; the mountains wait northward, visibly formidable. Near Dale Head a track leads south into the village of Stainforth-under-Bargh and the hamlet of Knight Stainforth, between which the Ribble flows, under a graceful pack-horse bridge, a gift from the Maudsleys of Stainforth to the National Trust. Stainforth Hall was built *c.* 1670 by a Quaker, Samuel Watson, who obtained licence to hold meetings there. Stainforth-under-Bargh is steep, wooded, watered. I once took the temperature of its telephone kiosk, and found that it was 96° F.

Now at last comes Pen-y-Ghent, a mountain of 2273 feet, whose name is Welsh, *pen y cant*, the hill of the border country (*cant* meaning a rim). Some philologists prefer *caint* or open country; others deny that the word *caint* ever existed. Either name seems appropriate because the mountain overlooks both the open country and the border with Lancashire and Westmorland near Cowan Bridge. From this high plateau you are on a par with Great Whernside (2,419 feet) and Ingleborough (2,373 feet).

I have an old acquaintance with Ingleborough, for it greets me when I climb from Over Kellett to my *pied-à-terre* in Westmorland. Ingleborough is Yorkshire's most-climbed mountain. They run up it. They play hockey on it. They used to hold horse races over it. You may say of Ingleborough what the Lakelanders said of Skiddaw, that the man who climbs it has little cause to brag:

> Lile brag it is for any man
> To clim oop Skidder side;
> Auld wives and bairns and jackasses
> To twippy top ma' ride.

Ingleborough and Pen-y-Ghent reach the summit of their splendour by snow-light. They confirm Dorothy Wordsworth's remark: '. . . it is a pleasure to a real lover of Nature to give winter all the glory he can, for the summer *will* make its own way, and speak its own praise.' Yet winter, too, will speak for itself; and never so eloquently as from these Pennine peaks. While Bournemouth basks in sunshine, Ingleborough may wear the white crown of winter. There is nothing magical nor haphazard in this division of labour. Snowfall is conditioned by the lowest altitude or line at which snow will lie perpetually. Near the equator the snow-line is 17,000 feet; therefore snow lies perpetually on the highest tropical mountains. The snow-line for the northern half of Britain is 5,000 feet and for the southern 7,000 feet; therefore snow does not lie perpetually in Britain. Altitude, however, is only one of the relevant influences; situation also plays a part. Thus, the Westmorland fells above Kirkby Lonsdale may be snowless while Great Whernside remains snowbound. Snow tends to diminish as it moves south, or towards the coast.

Having climbed Pen-y-Ghent, the Way turns south to Horton-in-Ribblesdale, like a man in search of an inn. King Henry VI came to Ribblesdale, hiding from his enemies during the Wars of the Roses. At Waddow Hall he was recognized by a monk named Cantlow, who betrayed him. The King, in fact, was ambushed while trying to cross the Ribble at Bungerley Hipping-stones. His captors carried him to the Tower of London, where he languished for several years, and then died—some say, of grief—while Edward IV entered London in triumph.

Horton is a hub of many tracks over the dales. Its church of St Oswald has a Norman door and a Norman herringbone font.

Adjacent is a house that was part of the grammar school founded by John Armistead in 1725.

A railway climbs this way, from St Pancras to Scotland. The Horton stationmaster used to command two clerks, three porters, ten signalmen, thirteen plate-layers; and in 1938 he shouldered a new responsibility, for at ten minutes to the hour throughout the day he was required to send a coded weather analysis to Dishford airport near York, whence the news reached the Air Ministry in London. Some of that news was daunting. In 1954, for example, the stationmaster recorded nearly 110 inches of rain, or four times the annual rainfall at Cromer. And when it was not wet, it grew so windy that on 15 January 1954, three trains, each with a full head of steam, were halted by an eighty-mile-an-hour gale. Until the 1950s the Vicar of Ingleton held a monthly Evensong in the booking-hall at Horton station; such was the size and, one assumes, the piety of a community serving the era of steam. During the 1960s this once-important station became a down-at-heel do-it-yourself-diesel-halt.

Now for a dozen miles the Way once more turns its back upon mankind, following its own devices, which are partly a walled lane, partly a track, sometimes a footpath. Yet always it eschews the damp monotony of Black Hill. The white walls glint, the grass glows green. There are no Brontës hereabouts, neither Kingsley, nor Wordsworth, nor Walton. The land belongs to sheep and rabbits and curlews; and beneath it are the pot-holes whose unprofitable darkness attracts people who creep like serpents on their belly. Every year they come. Every year they get stuck. Every year someone risks his life in order to retrieve them. Ingleborough itself may refer to the *burgh* or underground city, glistening with stalactites, honeycombed with caves.

This green solitude echoes the voice of Kipling when he spoke to Britain as the Romans might have spoken:

> I weave an incantation
> And draw them to their knees.

From Ingleton the Romans built a road to their fort at Bainbridge, nineteen miles northward. You can trace its exit from Ingleton via a hill between Kingsdale beck and the River Greta. North-east it climbs, over Cam Fell; and at Dodd Hill it falls only a few feet short of being mountainous. To follow it is to discover the skill with which the Romans steered a middle way between excessive gradient and lazy deviation therefrom. It is unlikely that you will meet any natives on this sector, but if a shepherd does pass by, his voice alone will remind you how far you have travelled since Edale—even since Rochdale and Beatrix Potter's favourite accent. When an Ingleton farmer says, 'Ah light seem' he means, 'So I believe.' When a spring-cleaning housewife complains that all is 'hankled', she means that her parlour is upside-down. When a sexton remarks that the new curate is 'a kysty lile chap', he means 'rather finicky'. When a roadman says 'Aye, 'tis mannerly,' he means, 'Yes, it's a lovely morning.' All that, of course, is a kind of poetry, uttered in prose by men who, though they may appear stolid as oxen, are nevertheless evidence supporting a belief which Robert Bridges expounded with the modesty of self-assurance: 'There must,' he said, 'be thousands and thousands of persons alive at this very moment in England, who, if they could only give poetic expression to those mysterious feelings with which they are moved in the presence of natural beauty, would be one and all of them greater poets than have ever yet been.' Such men, or their masters, did sometimes give poetic expression to emotion. Among them was a sixteenth-century squire, Sir Timothy Hutton of Marske in Swaledale, who, when his infant daughter died, wrote upon her tomb:

> Into this world, as strangers to an inn,
> This infant came guest-wise, where when 't had been,
> And found no entertainment worth her stay,
> She only broke her fast and went away.

The appearance of this land has not greatly changed since those words were written. Woods have been razed, it is true, and many of the cottages have disappeared, yet the churches remain and are accompanied by not a few farms and manor houses. Four facts help to set the scene at Craven and beyond. First, the land is high; the highest since Edale. Second, it is green; the gayest since Callis Wood. Third, it is fertile; a seedbed for flowers, fruit, fleece. Fourth, it is unsullied; only the prospect of more motor-cars seems vile.

Soon the Way enters a wilder country, topped by a famous water-shed. Within a few miles of each other, the Ribble, the Wharfe, and the Ure arise like blue ribands. Here, after a journey of seventy miles, broken only by a brief entry into Lancashire, the West Riding hands its baton to another.

At Cold Keld Gate, by a drystone wall, the Way enters the North Riding.

7 Yorkshire: North Riding

THE North Riding of Yorkshire is seventy-eight miles wide and forty-five miles long. It could swallow Rutland and Westmorland, and still find room for itself. The Danes divided it into a dozen wapentakes or weapon-takes, and the Way follows it for about forty miles, keeping well to the western half, where the mountains grow taller. This Riding, in fact, contains fifteen summits above 2,000 feet, and their effect on the climate can be gauged by the mean annual rainfall, which is sixty-three inches at Hawes in the west, but only thirty inches at Guisborough in the east. So far, nearly every mile of the Way has been rural, many were magnificent, most were solitary; yet none of them can vie with the summits which here mount up like eagles. The North is the highest and the wildest of the Ridings.

The Way begins by entering Wensleydale, formerly called Yoredale, after the River Ure, though in Leland's day that name had lapsed. There was no place, he reported, 'caullid Uresdale . . . Wensedale, as some say, taketh the name of Wensela market'. The dale, in short, was re-named after its only market town, Wensley, with a charter of 1202. But Wensley is now a hamlet, long since superseded by Hawes. On Saxton's map (1577) Hawes appears as Horsehouse, a tautological version of *hals*, the Old Norse word for a narrow spit of land—in this instance, a spit between two heights. Not far away, under the shadow of Great Whernside, a hamlet still is called Horse House.

The little town of Hawes has leased itself to the tourist trade. In summer the teashops and trinketries overflow. In winter, however, when the visitors have gone, Hawes is more truly at home to guests. It never was a beautiful place, but the main street looks decently weathered. The best parts of the town are by the beck, where the road becomes narrow.

Throughout Wensleydale you will see posters praising Real

Wensleydale Cheese. Bolder than philosophers, the advertising trade has no difficulty in defining reality. But the real Real Wensleydale Cheese—the old Blue Wensleydale—is a dream from the past. It first became popular during the 1880s when the Hawes farmers founded their own cheese fair, at which they made an extra profit of ten shillings per hundredweight by excluding the middlemen. A local farmer, Thomas Nuttall, soon afterwards persuaded the dalesfolk to rennet their milk while it was still warm, to use a standard amount of rennet, and to improve the drainage of whey by cutting the curd instead of pressing it by hand.

Hawes has an endearing hamlet, Gayle, whose name recalls the Danish invaders; *geil* being their word for a ravine. Through that ravine swirls Duerley Beck, under a bridge beside a cluster of cottages. During the 1780s they built a cotton-mill at Gayle, which soon turned to the traditional Yorkshire wool-spinning. In 1969 the mill sawed wood.

On a still night at Gayle a curious sound may be heard, causing you to wonder whether Robin Hood and Little John—those 'two troublesome men'—are on the warpath again. But your fears will be groundless, for the sound comes from Bainbridge, three miles or so to the east, where the hornblower calls curfew at 9 p.m. from September until February (in local terms, from Hawes backend fair until Pancake Tuesday). For a village wedding three blasts are sounded. The horn itself—a buffalo's—was presented in 1864. Curfew, from the Norman-French meaning 'cover your fire', was of especial importance when houses were built of timber. Though it never became a law in England, curfew did remain a common custom for many centuries. John Masefield, who died in 1967, could remember the years when several Herefordshire villages sounded curfew, and it was not simply an anachronism.

Some people say that curfew has been sounded at Bainbridge since the thirteenth century. Others go back further, claiming that the curfew began when Roman sentries blew a trumpet to guide any soldier who had lost himself in the forest. Certainly the remains of a Roman fort can be seen on Brough Hill, across the River Bain, and at Cravenholme Farm they collected Roman coins, glass, pottery, ornaments. The look-out post is nearly 1,600 feet above the sea.

A hornblower story was told to me by Jonty Wilson, the blacksmith at Kirkby Lonsdale in Westmorland, who once rode over to Bainbridge and demanded to hear the curfew out of hours.

'Impossible,' he was told. 'It would be contrary to custom. In any event the hornblower is old and infirm. He couldn't coax even a whimper from the horn.'

But Jonty Wilson is not the man to accept No when he has come to receive Yes. So, the hornblower is summoned, the barrel is tapped, and, after a period of prolonged preparation, the blower finds himself in a mood to sound his horn. And sound it he does; not, like T. S. Eliot, with a whimper, but Wesley-wise with a welkin-rousing roar, whereat the shepherd forsakes his sheep, the housewife her hearth, and the inn is besieged by anxious inquirers after the second Armada or another blitz.

The Way meanwhile keeps slightly to the north of Hawes, marked by a signpost pointing across two meadows and thence into the hamlet of Hardraw, where the Green Dragon Inn has a waterfall and a bandstand in its back garden, viewable on payment. The waterfall is described as the highest in England, but it is not the highest. The bridge over a shallow stream recalls Celia Fiennes' remark that dalesmen were skilled at 'catching Salmon by speares when they leap. . . .'

Beyond Hardraw the Way becomes a grassy track between stone walls and past some fir plantations which Dorothy Wordsworth noted in her *Journal* for October, 1802: 'Before we got upon the bare hills, there was a hunting lodge on our right, exactly like Greta Hall, with fir plantations about.' At Bluebell Hill, a thousand feet high, the walls disappear, and a cairn crops up, and another, then a third, and thereafter so many that I have never counted them. But the going is good, over firm turf, with the world falling away from either side . . . pastoral on the left, moorish on the right. Having climbed 1,600 feet, I once made a detour from Bluebell Hill, scrambling across fields and a stream, down into Cotterdale, which contains a farmhouse, two

Quaker Meeting House at Brigflatts, near
Sedbergh, West Riding

The road to Keld, North Riding

A beck near Muker, North Riding

Tan Hill Inn, North Riding: the highest
in England

or three cottages, four or five ruins, a dissenting chapel built by miners, and a seventeenth-century idyll named Shepherd's Cottage. Looking up at the encircling hills, I understood the astonishment of Bishop Pococke when he passed by in 1751: 'The prospect from the top is the most awful and grand I ever beheld.'

Back on its pedestal, the Way passes some derelict lead-workings and many peat-pits. At Crag End Beacon it becomes mountainous, and at Great Shunner Fell it pauses for breath, 2,340 feet up, astride the highest summit since Edale. Many Yorkshiremen regard this as their finest viewpoint. In clear weather the Lakeland peaks flash a greeting southward to Ingleborough. Away to the north-east, England's highest inn shines like a miniature mushroom. And beyond it, in silent majesty, Cross Fell appears, the very summit of the Way.

The Way itself makes no Roman effort to go straight. On the contrary, it sheers north-west and then south-east, all the while nearly 2,000 feet in the clouds, crossing Thwaite Common. Horton and Hawes seem suddenly to have become faint memories, mere exceptions to the rule that the Way walks alone. Although I have been on this sector several times, and beside it many times, I can never wholly remember what lies below and near at hand. Always I resign myself to hard labour in solitary confinement, seeking what comfort I may from my own company: *nunquam minus solus quam cum solus*. With each revisitation, therefore, I am surprised when the Way slides into Thwaite.

Built at a bend in the road, Thwaite is a handful of houses, one of which is called Kearton, after the two famous natives, Richard and Cherry Kearton, the naturalist photographers. One of the Kearton family, a gamekeeper, had the task of catching trout for his master's table. When a new master appeared, Keeper Kearton went as usual to the river, where, as he cast his line, he uttered a prayer: 'O Lord, if t'new maister's a good 'un, hook 'em on fast. But if he isna', then gie t' trout a chance.'

In Thwaite the Kearton brothers practised what was then a new method of photography—from a hide—and learned, as they put it, 'to imitate the call-notes of most of the wild creatures inhabiting the hills around our home'. Among those creatures are the Swaledale sheep, known locally as Swardles. Although less sturdy than the Lakeland Herdwicks, these sheep thrive on high ground in cold weather. They are horned, black-faced, grey-nosed, mottle-legged. Some farmers cross them with Wensley-dales to produce hybrids or Mashams.

There is no school at Thwaite, so the Keartons went to Muker, a mile away. Cherry Kearton cycled thither, but Richard, having a slight deformity, could not ride, and was obliged to limp. Muker is built in terraces above the River Swale. Every house looks either pleasant or old or both; and the post office serves as a shop. For centuries this small village was a local capital. It acquired a school in 1678, and a market soon afterwards. The present school bears memorial plaques to the Keartons.

Muker church stands half-way up a knoll, on the site of an earlier church (1580) that had a thatched roof, and was used as a chapel of ease to the parish of Grinton. In 1761 they enlarged the church and destroyed its thatch. In 1890 they restored the church again, this time destroying the musicians' gallery. A Victorian literary institute stands near the church, but reading has acquired a rival nowadays, which may be one reason why the institute became a part-time bank.

A guidebook of my childhood describes Muker as 'a village as completely shut out from the world as any, perhaps, in England'. Muker is no longer shut out from the world; it welcomes the world, and sometimes has difficulty in parking the world's traffic. Come, therefore, out of season, or, better still, before sunrise in June; then, as you stand on the topmost terrace, surrounded by hills, you will say with Rimbaud that you have embraced the summer dawn: *J'ai embrassé l'aube d'été.*

Muker and Thwaite are good measure indeed, pressed down and overflowing with their own unexpectedness. Alone on the heights, who could have guessed that two such havens lay below? Who could have guessed that they were part of a trio, and that the third member would outshine them? The Way itself certainly gives no hint of what waits ahead. From Thwaite it steers east and then north-west through a slow arc, more than a thousand feet up, skirting the summit of Kisdon, another 600 feet up. Presently you hear thunder, or what sounds like thunder, until a detour leads you to its source, which is a waterfall, Kisdon Force. The water is never still, but the pastures beside it are always green; and many a wise man, lying here in the sun, has lacked the courage of the convictions of George Sturt, a Victorian country-man, who said: 'People talk of the waste of life by war, disease, calamities of all sorts: but what is it all, in comparison with the waste due to Business, that ever-raging epidemic?' I, too, have lain here in the sun, or sheltered from a storm; and at every season it has occurred to me that Sturt, a busy timber merchant, did not daydream of a Golden Age which spent its life supine in sunlight. More likely, I thought, Sturt rebelled against that obsessive multiplication of un-necessities which calls itself Trade, and is propagated by slaves at a treadmill, who live only from Friday evening until Sunday night, and are dead to the rest of the week. Everyone, I reasoned, must often perform tasks that are tedious. Somebody must empty our dustbins, proof-read our telephone directory, criticize our television playwrights, compute our overdraft, and thank Dear Sir for his esteemed order. But must quite so many people squander quite so much of their lives quite so tediously? W. H. Davies looked—or at any rate hoped— for a more lyrical standard of living:

> When will it come, that golden time,
> When every heart must sing?
> The power to choose the work we love
> Makes every man a king.

From the waterfall a pleasant footbridge leads to a footpath which climbs between two hills, past a meadow of hay. In spring I watch the grass growing; in summer I see the men mowing; and both autumn and winter persuade me that Virgil was telling the truth when he described the farmer as a man fortunate in his vocation.

The hamlet of Keld is certainly fortunate in its location, and the place seems to please the people, too, for I have never seen a Kelder frowning. To remark that they sometimes weep and often wince, is simply to say that they are human beings; but whenever I come among them, there is no sign of a face long as the interval between Sunday night and Friday evening. Keld is my favourite hamlet along the Way, for although it has neither a church nor a pub, it does contain one shop and a multitude of blackbirds.

This *celde*, or hamlet beside a beck, is scooped in a hollow half-way down a skyful of hills. You can walk the length of it in thirty brisk seconds. Some of the cottages are so small and so squeezed that you might mistake two of them for one room. Like Muker, Keld has a Victorian literary institute, which now serves as an occasional bank. In that institute the shepherds and the ploughboys would recite Tennyson, discuss Dickens, and compose their own thoughts concerning the nature of things.

Keld Congregational chapel was built in 1789 and rebuilt in 1860. It has a handsome timber gallery and a 1914–18 memorial to the Keld men who died defending England: R. Alderson, T. Clarkson, W. Hutchinson, R. Rukin.

Keld Post Office is also Keld shop, an endearing example of things ancient blending with things modern to achieve the best of both worlds. At this old-style village store you may buy wares from a new-style deep-freeze. Keld, by the way, is fortunate to have Earl Peel *in loco parentis*. The keepers' cottages which he built near by were designed to harmonize with the other houses. If you come here at holiday time you may find the place cluttered with traffic, for Keld, like Hawes, is not truly at home on summer weekends. But at all other seasons it becomes a haven whose human conflicts are often steadied and sometimes resolved by the peace and strength of its hills. Keld is a place which Wordsworth knew:

> He had trudged through Yorkshire dales,
> Among the rocks and winding scars,
> Where deep and low the hamlets lie
> Beneath their little patch of sky
> And little lot of stars.

Now for a while the Way follows another of those tracts of solitude which heighten the brief encounters with mankind.

Due north it goes, over Stonesdale Moor, nearly two thousand feet up. Suddenly the trees disappear. The cottages disappear. Everything disappears except the sky and the next summit. And this disappearing act emphasizes that the Way has its *longueurs*, not all of which are boulders and bogs, for the architecture, too, begins to pall; the north being a stony ground, and nine-tenths of its buildings made of that stone. Nowhere between Edale and Kirk Yetholm will you find a country town built, like Montgomery, of mellow Georgian brick; nowhere the thatched roofs of Devon, the brick-and-flint cottages of the Chilterns, the half-timbered farms of the Welsh Marches, the Weald's weatherboarding, the Fens' brickwork. The northern climate and a thin soil left our forefathers little time and less inclination for the graces of life. Many of these villages and country towns are comely, but where along the Pennine Way will you find a Lacock or a Lavenham? The typical parish church is small; a Norfolk or a Somerset church would seem like a cathedral were it transplanted to Arncliffe or Garrigill. Nowhere else in England can you travel so far amid so little variety. If you travel half as far—say, from Suffolk to Yorkshire—you pass from a cattle country and a seafaring country to the cornfields of Norfolk; from the cornfields to the flowers and vegetables of the Fens; and from the Fens to a grazing country. You meet seamen and wildfowlers and maltsters and graziers and market gardeners and foresters and thatchers. You pass seaports, windmills, hillscapes, flatscapes. The temperature changes, the rainfall changes, the sunshine changes. 'What came ye forth to see?' cried John the Baptist. No man ever came this Way hoping to see a cross-section of England, for it offers only a hill's-eye view of part of the North. And in England as in France the North breeds a weariness, which Madame de Staël called *cette fatigue du nord*. But having said as much, one must report that scenes lie ahead which shall make a southron feel as though he were beside the Thames, or at a Wiltshire village with a chalk stream in the sun.

So near and yet so far: that is the motto of Tan Hill and its elusive tavern. In all Britain I know only one other destination so persistently unattainable, the little town of Moffat as seen from and interminably approached by the lane above Beattock. Moffat and Tan Hill; you sight them from afar, and then they disappear, and when you have already congratulated yourself on seeing a mirage, the phantom reappears and is found to be substantial though hardly at all nearer. On this sector the surface becomes dangerous as well as deceptive; this was an area of derelict coal-mines whose shafts were not filled in, though a few are now marked by poles. One of these days—or one of these nights—somebody will disappear into the earth, and not reappear alive. While you crick your neck by looking for these pitfalls, and sodden your socks by sinking in quagmire, the miles seem longer and more northerly than any others in the world. However, not even the longest mile makes two, and at last you cross a lonely road and confront the inn that has been confounding you.

I first approached Tan Hill on a summer day, along the hair-pin lane from Kirkby Stephen; and although as a rule I dislike the taste, the price and the effects of alcohol, this was the moment when a barrel seemed next best to a beck. James Boswell, a con-firmed alcoholist, had experienced a similar celebration on the Isle of Skye: 'I was in cordial humour,' he confessed, 'and pro-moted a cheerful glass.' In order to promote my own cheerful glass, I parked the car by some derelict out-buildings, and strolled across to the inn. It was shut despite opening time. A card on the door said: Closed For Decorations. A ladder leaned near by, so I climbed it and took a photograph of a plaque above the door, which stated that the inn stood 1,732 feet high, and was therefore the tallest in England. My later visits were less thirsty. On each occasion I arrived at tea-time for tourists, and found beneath the friendly but uninspired façade some traces of the old inn . . . a low ceiling, a stone floor, an open hearth where fires glowed, even in June.

Six centuries ago they were mining coal up here. It went to take the chill off Richmond Castle and the castles of Lady Anne Clifford at Appleby and Skipton. During the nineteenth century one of the shafts, called King's Pit, was leased (in modern cur-rency) at about £7000 yearly. Old dalesfolk remember seeing half a hundred coal wagons here. Celia Fiennes described the seventeenth-century method of mining: 'They have also engines that draw up their coale in sort of baskets in a well, for their mines are dug down through a sort of well and sometimes its pretty low before they come to the coales . . .' Most of the colliers lived in 'shops' or bothies near by, and returned home at weekends. The seams on which they worked were about four feet thick. Tan Hill pit was closed during the 1930s, but the inn retains its own shaft.

The present inn is an eighteenth-century building, formerly called King's Pit House. Two of its outbuildings were also inns. For several decades the publicans were members of the Pounder family. Down at Kirkby Stephen they told me about a Pounder who had renewed his licence at Richmond, but without stating the opening hours; an omission which the magistrate covered with a completely white sheet: 'Keep open day and night,' he said. Many a snowswept traveller on these heights must have toasted the memory of that totally non-abstaining magistrate.

After the Pounders came the Peacocks, who presided from 1903 until 1945. Jonty Wilson of Kirkby Lonsdale assured me that Mistress Susan Peacock was, as we say, a card who wore the pants, and would, if required, remove the same garment from unruly miners. She died in 1937, having given some BBC talks that made the place famous. Swaledale sheep breeders still hold an annual show here.

There is an outcrop of rock behind the inn, from which you can see Shunner Fell above Hawes; and eastward a dirty cloud no larger than a man's hand, though man's hand made it . . . the smoke stacks of Middlesbrough, nearly fifty miles away. What they call 'the season' at Tan Hill is mercifully short. I have come here in winter and seen nobody in three hours. I have come here in spring, and again nobody passed by. Even at noon in July I have had the place to myself. It is only during warm weekends that a wise man does not intrude upon the festivities. For most of the year Tan Hill is wind-worn, lonely, a speck in the interminable square mileage of moorland, occupied only by sheep and those other creatures that were before men, and may be after.

Once again the Way follows a familiar pattern by retreating into what Coleridge called 'the meek Sabbath of self-content'. North-east it goes, across Sleightholme Moor, at an average height of 1,200 feet, and then across Stainmore, which lives up to its formidable name, *Stanmoir* or stony land.

At Stainmore Gap the Way passes a curio known as God's Bridge, a natural limestone span across the River Greta, which here flows underground except after prolonged rain. Whenever I pass this way I think of another natural curio, Charles Lutwidge Dodgson, alias Lewis Carroll, who was born along the North Riding Way at the village of Croft, where his father was rector. Even as a child Dodgson had specialized in youthful entertainment. For his three brothers and seven sisters he built a model theatre, sponsored a family magazine and designed a toy railway. Dodgson became a deacon, but was too shy to be ordained priest. Instead, he taught mathematics at Christ Church, Oxford. On 4 July 1862, while boating on the Isis with a friend and three little girls, he began to tell them a story, making it up as he went along and afterwards writing it down. The heroine of that story was called Alice, and the fame of her Wonderland overwhelmed the author. He was offered preferment by the premier, Sir Robert Peel. He received letters addressed to 'Alice, Oxford'. And although it was conceived in Oxfordshire, his fantasy did owe something to the North Riding, for the March Hare was inspired by one of the gargoyles in the church of St Mary at Beverley.

A very different sort of fantasy came from Bowes, the next village *en route,* a straggling, wind-worried place on the main road to Appleby, only a short distance from the Way. Many visitors are perplexed when they fail to find the famous Bowes Museum. In fact, the museum is near Barnard Castle, a few miles eastward in County Durham. Its history is as vivid as its exhibits, and both were the work of a Pennine man, John Bowes, only son of the tenth Earl of Strathmore, who was denied his title by the Committee of Privileges, but did inherit large estates in Yorkshire and County Durham. Bowes, however, preferred to live in Paris. In 1854 he married Josephine, Countess of Montalbo, an amateur sculptor, who at that time disported herself as an actress with the

Théatre de Variétés. The husband used his wealth to indulge the wife's fondness for objects of art. Within a short time they had collected some Goyas, an El Greco, and so many valuable trinkets that John Bowes decided to build a public museum at Calais. However, the political situation in France caused him to remove his treasures to Durham, where he began to build the museum which he had withheld from Calais. In 1890 his wife laid the foundation stone, but five years later only the walls were ready, and at that point the lady died. Her husband then finished the work as a memorial to her. Built of stone from Streatlam and Stainton, Bowes Museum was designed as a princely château, three hundred feet long, occupying an acre of land, overlooking formal gardens and a large park. It is as though *l'ancien régime* had anticipated the deluge by escaping to the Pennines. In 1969 the Museum was administered by Durham County Council.

So much for what Bowes village does not contain; its own attributes outweigh the loss. First, along the south side of the street, is the site of a Roman camp, and on it the remains of a Norman castle whose walls are still higher than any house within sight. From it you can see the Way you have come and the Way you will go; the latter a blend of bleakness to the east and of fertility to the west—Teesdale, in fact, and the Eden Valley.

Bowes church, which stands near the castle, is basically Norman and partly Angevin. In the churchyard, in 1822, they buried a boy whose grave Charles Dickens saw when he came here after a blizzard: 'The first gravestone I stumbled on that dreary afternoon was over a boy who had died suddenly. I suppose his heart broke. He died in this wretched place, and I think his ghost put Smike into my mind on the spot.' So was born a book which, like Arncliffe's *Water-Babies*, seared the conscience of a nation; for the real boy was George Ashton Taylor, and the imaginary boy, Smike, was, as his creator admitted, as terrible as truth. The revelation of that truth began when, in his own childhood, Dickens overheard a story about another child, who had been sent home from his Yorkshire school because of an abscess which the headmaster gouged with an inky penknife. Twenty years later that story inspired part of *Nicholas Nickleby*. Dickens's friend and first biographer, John Forster, gave a bare outline of the process. Dickens, he said, 'went down into Yorkshire with Hablot Browne to look up the Cheap Schools in that county to which public attention had been painfully drawn by a law case in the previous year'. Yorkshire, in fact, was notorious for schools to which parents and guardians could send unwanted children. These schools, said Forster, were the ones which Dickens 'was bent upon destroying if he could'. Dickens and his illustrator therefore took the Glasgow coach as far as Barnard Castle. They carried a letter of introduction—from a solicitor whom Dickens knew, to another named Barnes—in which Dickens was described as the friend of a widow seeking a school for her sons. Barnes himself was honest. After some hesitation he warned Dickens that the local schools were dreadful places; their pupils went ill-clad and hungry; some had died of food poisoning. The worst offender, he added, was a certain William Shaw of Bowes Academy, who had several times paid heavy damages for maltreating his pupils.

Dickens and Browne called on William Shaw; but he, like most villains, was cunning; and on this occasion Dickens's indignation may have impaired his flair for acting. After five minutes' wary conversation the two visitors found themselves ordered off, instead of being conducted over, the premises. But Dickens had seen and surmised enough at Bowes and elsewhere in the district. So, William Shaw of Bowes Academy became Wackford Squeers of Dotheboys Hall, sounding the knell of a tribe which, in his preface to *Nicholas Nickleby*, Dickens arraigned as 'traders in the avarice, indifference, or imbecility of parents . . . ignorant, sordid, brutal men, to whom few considerate persons would have entrusted the board and lodging of a horse or a dog . . .' Dickens did not spoil his case by overstating it: 'Mr Squeers and his school,' he explained, 'are faint and feeble pictures of an existing reality, purposely subdued and kept down lest they should be deemed impossible.' We may therefore accept the picture of what Dickens saw in and around Bowes: 'Pale and haggard faces, lank and bony figures, children with the countenances of old men. . . .' Not every North Riding school resembled Dotheboys Hall. Some were of good repute. Yet Dickens was justified when he declared:

'These Yorkshire schoolmasters were the lowest and most rotten on the whole ladder'. And Forster, too, was justified when he said that *Nicholas Nickleby* had 'filled the world with pity for what cruelty, ignorance or neglect may inflict upon the young'.

For once in a while the pen was mightier than the sword, or at any rate it drew sufficient blood. Dotheboys Hall was ruined, and Shaw himself died prematurely, killed by chagrin or by remorse. The number of pupils in the district dropped from eight hundred to twenty, which caused many servants and tradesmen to revile the man who had slain a source of their income. What Dickens did not destroy was the school building. It still stands, facing the main road, and in 1969 was a teashop. Externally it remains much the same as when Nicholas Nickleby first saw it, on alighting from the London coach to take up his duties as the new usher, at a yearly salary of £5 'payable at indefinite periods'. Dotheboys Hall, he discovered, was 'a long, cold-looking house . . . with a few straggling outbuildings behind, and a barn and stable adjoining'. This is the keenest corner of England; Stainmore and snow are synonymous. Even in high summer I have seen a visitor's hat bowled down the road at a rate of knots. Yet when Nicholas Nickleby arrived in midwinter, only one fire warmed Dotheboys Hall—in the headmaster's kitchen. Small wonder that while the new usher gazed 'upon the wild country around, covered with snow, he felt a depression of heart and spirit which he had never experienced before'.

North of Bowes the Way again walks alone, and at Tute Hill it passes a number of prohibited areas, as described by the magazine *Cumbria* in 1966: '. . . northwards from Stainmore one encounters gathering grounds of the Tees Valley Water Board, infantry training ranges near Barnard Castle, grouse moors around Middleton-in-Teesdale, the Upper Teesdale Nature Reserve from about High Force onwards, the Army firing range on Mickle Fell, and then the Moor House Nature Reserve lying between the Eden Valley and the Tees—roughly a hundred square miles of country in which the humble walker is not particularly welcome.' Well, I have no objection to grouse moors, if only because they enable people to live and work in the open air. Nor have I any objection to being defended by an Army. I cannot complain, either, if a relatively small area of the kingdom is reserved for its oldest inhabitants. At least these prohibited areas have not been disfigured by factories and a latticework of pylons. In any event, what Sir Walter Scott called 'the shapeless swell' of Stainmore becomes softer as it approaches the Westmorland border. Parallel with the Appleby road, a disused railway feels sorry for those who never knew the joys of exploring England from a by-line. That was a colourful era indeed. Do you remember the olive-green engines of the Highland Railway, the pale blue of the North British, the light brown Caledonian, ebony North Western, rich-red Midland, apple-green Great Northern, red-and-green Great Central, mauve Somerset and Dorset? Disbelieve the people who tell you that a diesel demands as much footplatemanship as a steam locomotive. Such sophists were confounded by the historian of twentieth-century British railways, G. S. Knock: 'With diesels and electrics,' he declared, 'there are no half measures; you either get the standard, unvarying performance, or they fail outright and have to be towed away.' And what first-class comfort you found. On the Lancashire and Yorkshire Railway the Pennine merchants had their own saloons, painted a deep brown with yellow panelling. Inside, each member occupied his own arm-chair.

If a walker follows only one sector of the Way, he will misinterpret its system of communication, supposing that the rivers flow southward, whereas most of them flow to or from the east. He will suppose that the Way seldom crosses a road, whereas it is riddled with roads. Though I never counted them, I can remember more than twenty that are either on the Way or within two miles of it.

Meanwhile the Way at this point avoids any road at all. Bearing north-west, it follows a tedious moorland, never less than 1,200 feet high. From Wythes Hill you see the glint of a river and the roofs of a town. The river is the Tees, the town is Middleton; and there the Way enters County Durham.

8 County Durham

THE most dramatic approach to Middleton-in-Teesdale is not via the Way but by road from Brough, a solitary road, climbing and twisting over moorland wild as any in England, flanked by snowposts, and nowhere entering a village. It is a type of Bleaklow, transplanted among wider vistas. In all Britain I can recall only two other roads of comparable length and approximate loneliness: one is the single-line lane from Braemar to Tomintoul, the other is the single-line lane from Helmsdale to Dounreay. But when you have persuaded yourself that the solitude never will end, it does end, on the brow of a hill overlooking the kind of country which you had posted as lost without trace.

Middleton is a bonnie little town, an oasis on the edge of a desert. Its main street is tree-lined and green-banked. The church, rebuilt in 1866, has a detached belfry (1557) on a knoll near by, the only one in the county. I think I am right in saying that it was built at the behest of William Bele, to contain three bells. A townsman assured me that one of the original bells survives, and that the trio is played with two hands and one foot. What seems to be a clock-towered town hall is the Regency offices of the London Lead Company, which received its charter in 1652. These offices were administered by Quakers who built so well that their workpeople's cottages are the sturdiest in town. One of the Victorian miners, Richard Watson, wrote poems in the Teesdale dialect.

I pass through Middleton three or four times a year, and my last arrival was greeted by a thunderstorm, from which I sheltered in a teashop. The only other customer was an elderly Scotswoman; so there we both sat, serenely sedate, while a too-long-playing jukebox urged us to gather rosebuds ere the silvery strands had set them out of reach. Why do these establishments assume that all customers are adolescent, tone-deaf and disinclined to talk?

What a rumpus there would be if the youngsters were compelled willy-nilly to hear advice on preparing for retirement, or a choice of tombstones, or how to stoop without bending.

Then a sizzle of lightning dimmed the fluorescence, and my venerable co-customer leaned across and said to me: 'Did ye ken that folks are killed by lightning every year?' A second sizzle delayed my reply. She leaned closer. 'I was near killed mesel'.' I said that I was sorry to hear it, but glad that she had recovered. 'I've no' recovered. The doctors say I ne'er shall.' She paused during a third sizzle. 'Aye, it's terrible the number who dee in a storm.'

I returned to the car, and found some consolation in remembering that Durham itself had survived many storms. At one time it was part of the kingdom of Deira, whose capital, *Dunholm* or the island with a hill, is almost islanded by the River Wear. From Deira a group of pioneers moved north to Bamburgh, where they created the nucleus of the kingdom of Bernicia. Then Bernicia joined with Deira to form Northumbria, the kingdom north of the Humber, with Durham as its capital.

The Normans made Durham the greatest of all palatinates. Stephen's *Commentaries* emphasized the county's antiquity: 'Three counties, viz., Chester, Durham, Lancashire are counties palatine. The two former are such by prescription or immemorial custom, or at least as old as the Norman Conquest.' Unlike its peers, Durham was basically a spiritual power, having been granted to St Cuthbert and his successors. The prince bishops of Durham signed themselves in Latin and in Norman-French; one bishop was *Dunelm*, his successor was *Dunesm*, and the next bishop was *Dunelm*. Under the King, as tenants-in-chief, the bishops exercised quasi-regal power. They had their own army, their own mint, their own courts. In 1873 the jurisdiction of the Court of Pleas of Durham was transferred to the High Court of Justice in London; but the Court of Chancery of the County Palatine of Durham continues to assert its authority on behalf of the Crown. The last prince bishop was William van Mildert, who helped to found Durham University. Mighty indeed were the Bishops of Durham. Not even the Primate of England overawed them. In the year

1248, for example, the Warden and Scholars of Merton College, Oxford, appealed to the Archbishop of York because Anthony Bek, Bishop of Durham, had denied their claim to the church at Ponteland in Northumberland. Bek retorted that the Primates had never been known to exercise their protection against Durham. This same bishop Bek rode at the head of his army to subdue the Scots. Even in 1939 York dealt warily with Durham, for, when the See fell vacant, and York appointed the dean as its guardian, the Archbishop was careful to add 'without prejudice to the general question'.

The counties palatine confute those perverse persons who complain that the monarchy fleeces the taxpayer. The truth is otherwise, for the taxpayer fleeces the monarchy of revenues from so-called Crown lands, which in 1968 yielded £5,264,000 to the Treasury. Her present Majesty's privy purse of £60,000 yearly must seem half-empty to pop groups, TV personalities, property developers, and other more important people.

The Way avoids the collieries, factories and shipyards in the eastern half of the county; preferring a countryside that was known to St Cuthbert, the shepherd-boy Bishop of Holy Island, whose coffin was sheltered by a temporary wooden church that begat Durham Cathedral . . . a countryside known to Bede of Jarrow, who first translated the Gospel of St John into the vernacular . . . known also to Bonnie Bobby Shafto . . . to the Eden family, Earls of Auckland, one of whose descendants, Sir Timothy Eden, Bt., was the twentieth-century historian of the county . . . known to Mary Hutchinson, wife of William Wordsworth . . . to Elizabeth Barrett Browning, whose memorial at Kelloe says: 'A great poetess, a noble woman, a devoted wife' . . . to R. S. Surtees and his jaunty Jorrocks . . . Gertrude Bell, Arabian explorer and Oxford historian . . . Field-Marshal Viscount Gort, VC, a grandson of Surtees.

Beyond Middleton the Way enters the deepest solitude south of Northumberland. The next village lies twenty miles ahead, and the steep journey thither springs the greatest of all Wayside surprises by revealing a fairyland of riverside flowers and trees. This surprise springs from the soil itself: in general terms, the

Red Sandstone of Westmorland meets the older rocks of Durham. In less general terms, an igneous rock called Whin Sill has been compressed against carboniferous rocks; whence the lead mines and this pastoral path beside the Tees. Bleaklow, Black Hill, Shunner Fell . . . how faint they seem. We wish that this green path could carry us all the way to Scotland. But County Durham accompanies the Way for only five or six miles, and even then it reverts briefly into the North Riding. Here, therefore, as in Lancashire, it seems convenient to regard the next few miles as part of one county.

After an hour's ambling, beside meadows and the shining river, you reach a footbridge. The original structure was built in 1704 by miners who claimed it as England's first suspension bridge. Slung twenty feet above the water, the pair of planks (with only one handrail) must have sobered many nocturnal revellers. A local historian described the bridge as a hazard 'to which few strangers dare to trust themselves'. In 1820 a man was drowned when the bridge collapsed. Twenty years later the present bridge was built. Although it stands awash during floods, it does now possess two handrails.

This is *par excellence* a summer sector: flower-filled, bird-blithe, blossom-dappled. Rocky peninsulas wade into the water and wait there, as though hoping that you will walk the plinth. Trees lean towards one another, almost spanning the stream, like the gables of a by-street in Shrewsbury. Here indeed a Chiltern wayfarer may think himself at home beside Spenser's 'sweet Thames'. Alas, the waterscape soon gives way to wild country and the thunder of High Force, a waterfall plunging seventy feet through a narrow gorge. Sir Walter Scott heard the sound from a distance:

> The Tees itself, though far away.
> Threading its course through distance grey,
> Proclaims aloud with a mighty roll
> Its progress to a far-off goal;
> And rushing madly headlong o'er,
> At High Force leaps with a ceaseless roar.

As becomes a border region, Durham is a county of castles, the finest being Raby Castle at Staindrop, away to the north-east.

Market shelter, Kirkby Stephen,
Westmorland

Kirkby Stephen church, Westmorland

Tudor spinning gallery, Kirkby Stephen,
Westmorland

Gipsies near Appleby, Westmorland

The first Raby Castle was given to King Canute by Durham Priory. A century later the Nevilles rebuilt it so massively that Leland called it: 'the largest castel . . . in all the north country'. In 1569 the Nevilles rebelled, and their lands were forfeit to the Crown. In 1626 the castle was bought by Sir Henry Vane, chief secretary to Charles I, who turned traitor by joining the rebels. In 1698 the Vanes were created Barons of Barnard. In 1969 Raby was still their residence.

Staindrop has literary as well as warlike associations, for Christopher Smart spent several years at Raby Castle, his father being agent to Lord Barnard. When he was thirteen years old, the poet fell in love with Lady Anne Vane, who was about the same age. The children tried to elope but were hauled home. No one seems to have been disturbed by their precocity. Smart had first seen the Lady Anne in Staindrop church. Many years later, when he was mad, he recalled that Pennine idyll in a poem, *Jubilate Agno*:

> . . . I saw a blush in Staindrop church,
> which was of God's own colouring,
> For it was the benevolence of a virgin
> shown to me before the whole congregation.

Hither also came Wordsworth and his sister Dorothy. Her *Journal* describes the making of a poem: 'Just when William came to a well or trough, which there is in Lord Darlington's park, he began to write that poem of the Glow-Worm . . . interrupted in going through the town of Staindrop, finished about two miles and a half beyond Staindrop. He did not feel the jogging of the horse when he was writing; but, when he had done, he felt the effect of it, and his fingers were cold . . .' This poem, of five stanzas, tells how Wordsworth had presented a glow-worm as a gift:

> Among all lovely things my Love had been;
> Had noted well the stars, all flowers that grew
> About her home: but she had never seen
> A Glow-worm, never once, and this I knew.

Wordsworth was a Lakelander who soon returned home. Gilpin, on the other hand, was a Lakelander who came and remained. In the south his name is widely unknown, but in the north it is familiar even among those who have never heard of Bishop Bek nor Christopher Smart. Along this part of the Way, Gilpin is still called the Apostle of the North.

Bernard Gilpin was born in 1517, at Kentmere Hall by the foot of the fells near Staveley in Westmorland. The Hall still stands— indeed, I have been a guest there—at the end of a cul-de-sac, guarded by a peel tower. From Kentmere Hall Gilpin went up to the Queen's College, Oxford; in 1552 he accepted the living of Norton-on-Tees from his great-uncle, Bishop Tunstall, but soon afterwards declined it in order to study at Paris and Louvain. In 1556 he became Archdeacon of Durham and rector of Easington, a parish along the North Riding Way. In the following year he returned to County Durham, as rector of Houghton-le-Spring, one of the richest livings in the north. There, too, he found a peel tower, and set about enlarging it so that—on every Sunday between Michaelmas and Easter—he could give dinner to any who cared to come for it, and a simpler meal to twenty-four poor men. Gilpin was a shepherd who sought his flock among the byways. At a time when the Northumbrian Marches teemed with brigands, he dared to ride alone into their deepest dales, spreading the good news. Nor were brigands his only enemies, for under Mary Tudor the Roman Mass was said within the See of Durham, sponsored and protected by nobles and gentry of the Old Faith. Against them Gilpin evangelized for England, tireless as a friar, fearless as a Wesley. He had been offered the Bishopric of Carlisle, but chose rather to ride the rounds as a parish priest. At the age of sixty-six, weary with his exertions, he was injured by an ox at Durham market. A few months later he died, and was buried in his church, under the shadow of the grammar school that he had founded.

One agreeable Durham custom has died. It was observed at Croft, near Houghton-on-Tees, where a bridge with seven arches marks the border between County Durham and the North Riding. This custom recalled a Pennine Beowulf and a local Grendel,

Sir John Conyers, lord of the manor of Sockburn, who, they say, slew an unidentified monster that had terrorized the district. When a newly consecrated bishop crossed the bridge for the first time, he was greeted by the lord of Sockburn. Courtesies having been exchanged, the lord presented his bishop with the Conyers falchion or sword, saying: 'My Lord Bishop, I here present you with the falchion wherewith the champion Conyers slew the worm, dragon, or fiery flying serpent which destroyed man, woman, and child; in memory of which the King then reigning gave him the manor of Sockburn, to hold by this tenure, that upon the first entrance of every bishop into the county the falchion should be presented.' The falchion was last presented in 1826 to the last prince bishop, William van Mildert, who bequeathed it to Durham Cathedral.

In 1969 another kind of warfare was waged in these parts, against the rare Teesdale plants that have both a scientific and an aesthetic value. Naturalists and countryfolk wish to maintain such plants, but the philistines seek to destroy them by reservoirs and other industrial improvements. Clearly the basic welfare of humanity must precede the welfare of plants. But nobody's welfare will be injured if Upper Teesdale is left in peace. Water and work are to be had otherwhere in sufficient quantity. The plant life of this region is of outstanding interest. Once destroyed, it may never revive.

It is pleasant to observe the true stewardship with which the Vanes tend their own estates. Well-built farmsteads relieve the montony of this moonscape, and nearly all are whitewashed. At Middleton they will tell you about a Lord Barnard who once lost his way on the hills, and was given shelter by a farmer. Next morning the refugee repaid his host by inviting him to have his house renovated and to send the account to the Barnard land agent. The farmer thereupon delved deep into his guest's pocket, and in due time delivered the bill. Lord Barnard expressed surprise but not amusement when the agent informed him that the reno-vated farm was not part of his estate. By way of long-term insur-ance against similar risks, Lord Barnard ordered all his own farms to be whitewashed. It is a good story, but I doubt it.

There is no doubt at all about the debt which these Durham

farmers owe to modern convenience. Even twenty years ago many of them cooked on a coal stove, and went to bed by candle-light. Theirs was a colourful routine, but less reposeful than it appeared, for the garden privy stank; hot water was a luxury not to be splashed all over the body; and bad lighting scarcely encouraged the reading of good books.

At Sour Hill Farm I once discovered a good book—a copy of W. H. Davies's poems—which somebody had dropped by the Way. I picked it up—the cover was ruined, but the contents were readable—and found a foreword by Daniel George, with whose fame I was unacquainted: 'Poetry such as his will never be written again . . . or, if written, will remain unpublished.' I was not alone in rejecting such jubilant pessimism, for J. C. Trewin had lately declared that the future of English poetry will be 'not the hot ice and wondrous strange snow of that tottering New Order on Parnassus, but the great matter—the fadeless amaranth—of our English rhyme'. I therefore deleted Daniel, and revealed Davies by displaying him in a dry place, open for any to read:

> Sing for the sun your lyric, lark,
> Of twice ten thousand notes;
> Sing for the moon, you nightingales,
> Whose light shall kiss your throats;
> Sing sparrows, for the soft, warm rain,
> To wet your feathers through;
> And when a rainbow's in the sky,
> Sing you, cuckoo—'Cuckoo!'

And a cuckoo answered, for this was the eve of St George's Day, and the bird is so patriotic that it will make its home even near Falcon Clints, where the hills confirm the Durham diary of Celia Fiennes: 'you do ascend a great height and steepness which is full of rocky stony stepps . . .' Falcon Clints was baptized by the Middle English *faucon* and the Danish *klint* or flinty rock. Our place-namers were indeed practical poets. Within a few miles of Langdon Beck you will find Merrygill Moss, Nichol Hoople, the Isle of Man, Olde Folde, Dead Crook, Bleabeck Grains, Pegheart Lodge. My own prize for a Durham place-name goes to Pity Me, whose etymology will perplex even the multiple-linguist, for the name has nothing to do with compassion, but recalls the French monks who founded a monastery there, and called it after a small lake near by, *le petit mer*.

Meantime these isolated farms emphasize how difficult it is to sift truth from falsehood in history, even in recent history. Thus, an official inquiry of 1872 showed that the average farm worker's weekly wage in England and Wales was 14*s*. 8*d*. (it is idle to compare it with a pound whose value has ceased to be sterling), and that the average wage of a Durham farm worker was 30 per cent above the norm. During the next generation, while Durham still held its lead, Professor Atwater reported that not even a Durham farm worker earned 'sufficient to maintain a family of average size in a state of merely physical efficiency'. We know, too, that a high percentage of 1914 volunteers was ill-nourished. Yet, in a climate so harsh as Durham's, even moderate physical exercise required considerable physical efficiency. If you talk with Pennine farmfolk who do remember the last of Victorian England, they will tell you that life then was hard but never hungry. 'How else,' they will say, 'do you suppose we worked?' And they will very likely add, 'In those years work *was* work.'

The coldness of the climate was emphasized in a report by Joseph Granger, a Durham land-surveyor: the bean harvest, he said, lasts until the end of October 'and is sometimes not finished till the middle of November'. All crops, he added, are relatively poor, 'the weather in spring being either too harsh, or in the beginning of summer too cold and dry, and in the autumn too wet and windy; and the whole face of this county . . . is exposed to, and annoyed by, the north-east wind. . . .'

On another matter, however, the historians agree and are irrefutable. During the 1890s George Sturt kept a journal in which he recorded his impressions of the Surrey farmfolk: 'I believe it to be a fact of central importance in regard to the working people that they never have their Feelings touched except by Reality . . . little artificial experience of any kind is ever experienced.' Stuart then cited Oscar Wilde's belief that one of the functions of art is to produce sterile emotion—emotion about trivial matters—so that emotion itself can be sharpened by exercise. Such stimulation has invaded even the Durham moors. I remember passing some cottages and noticing that, despite the beauty of the evening, not one of the occupants was out of doors; each cottage window flickered with the glow of television. That night I took the trouble to discover what those screens had shown. The cottagers' choice lay between a play about sexual perversion and a film about louts conspiring to rob with murder. Now murder and robbery and sexual fixation are probably as old as mankind, and seem likely to live as long. To become aware of them, and to acquire some understanding of their dynamics, is a duty of all adults who do not seek to remain children. And television might always have been, as it sometimes still is, an ally of the general good. But were those programmes, and the multitudes like them, devised to further the general good? Is the generality itself made happier and healthier and more truly wise by watching such programmes, night after night through decades? Wordsworth was either right, or wrong, when he said: 'the human mind is capable of being excited without the application of gross and violent stimulants.' In other words, the soliloquies of *King Lear* are more exciting than the slaughter of *Titus Andronicus*.

So much for base entertainment: as for true re-creation, a transistor radio will sometimes become a congenial fellow-traveller, as I discovered while walking here one day, feeling very weary after several hours of rain. I sat down, while sheltering under the lee of a rock. I switched on the set, and out of it came the last movement of Bach's A Minor Violin Concerto. No physical stimulus could have produced such an effect; neither rest nor food nor alcohol. I felt as Edward Thomas when he also was weary: 'And I arose, and knew that I was tired, and continued my journey.' My own journey was prodded forward by those marching violins. And you will learn other things, too, from music by the Way, some of which may astonish you; for are there not moments when the song of a bird transcends even the depths of Beethoven's final fourfold harvest?

At other times the Way utters shriller sounds. The worst storm I ever encountered was on the lane to a hotel near High

Force, which used to be the Duke of Sutherland's shooting lodge. Rain fell so fast that the windscreen wipers could not cope with it. I saw nothing beyond the bonnet of the car; and when I halted with headlamps on, each gust of wind sent a shudder through the world. Within three minutes a dreary November afternoon wore the look of a wild midnight. Then a shepherd walked by, swathed in a sack. Seeing him, I opened the window, offering refuge. But he shook his head and shambled on. I may have kept the window open for ten seconds. When I shut it, my right side was soaked to the skin. Have you ever tried to undress in a small car on a narrow lane during a storm that has reduced visibility to three yards? I commend the feat to all who regard themselves as supple. While I lay on my side, trying to extricate a damp shirt from the gear lever, a pony careered down the lane, terrified by the thunder. Such was the roar of the gale, I did not hear hooves until they were alongside. The phantom vanished, but then reappeared, heading for the car. What happened to the pony, I do not know; but I have the clearest recollection of paying thirty shillings for a new headlamp. It was not the horse that hit it; it was a stone that the horse had hit.

Next morning broke blue and bright, and by the light of it I climbed Mickle Fell, overlooking the Moor House Nature Reserve across the Westmorland border. Away to the east, Langdon Beck flowed in spate, tumbling large stones as it went. Near by was an outcrop of Spring Gentian or *Gentiana verna*. At Cronkley Farm they told me that these rare plants were defended against vandals by a Gentian Patrol of naturalists who know the various habitats. They also told me of their fears that Cow Green would be flooded by a reservoir.

The Way meanwhile crosses and re-crosses the county border, here marked by the Tees, though at Holwick Beck Durham claims a few hundred yards of the western bank. Near Scorberry footbridge the Way re-enters the North Riding, and remains there while passing Low and High Forces, a riverside walk of great grandeur, for the Tees here is studded with rocky islets full of flowers against a Durham backcloth of woodland. Then the Way re-enters Durham, dips into Westmorland, and again returns to Durham. And all the while, from Mickle Fell, imagination peoples the present with the past, so that young Kit Smart appears, strolling hand-in-hand with Lady Anne of Raby Castle, along a lane which leads to an impossible destination. And her ladyship's maternal grandmother appears, Henrietta, Duchess of Cleveland, who was so impressed by Smart's classical scholarship that she sent him up to Pembroke Hall, Cambridge, where he became a Fellow, and received an allowance from the duchess until she died twenty years later. Smart gave thanks in an elegy:

> For her, who cherished with a mother's care,
> And fill'd the Orphan's mouth with praise and pray'r.

Indeed, he gave thanks to all who had befriended him in County Durham—the lord, the landscape, the castle:

> Can I forget fair Raby's towers,
> How awful and how great!
> Can I forget such blissful bowers,
> Such splendour in retreat?

Smart was not a native of Durham (he came from Kent) but he did spend the most impressionable years of his life in this county. Robert Browning's wife, by contrast, was a native of Durham, born at Coxhoe Hall in the parish of Kelloe (which her family leased from Sir Henry Vane Tempest) and sonorously baptized Elizabeth Barrett Moulton Barrett. Coxhoe Hall had been built in 1725, at a time when the gentry expected the butler and footmen to man the parapets, ready to aim their arrows at Turks, or Frenchmen, or some other improbable intruder. Lady Tempest herself owned a large estate in Herefordshire, called Hope End, which Edward Barrett had seen and approved. On 6 September 1809, he sent a letter to his three-year-old daughter, announcing that she might soon leave County Durham. He and his advisers, he said, were examining Hope End with a view to buying it: 'The more I see of the property the more I like it and the more I think I shall have it in my power to make yourself, Brother and Sister and dear Mama happy.' That same year he bought Hope End; and in the year following, his family took up residence there. But something of County Durham accompanied Elizabeth into Herefordshire, for Hope End was almost as stately as Coxhoe Hall (it had twenty bedrooms and five hundred acres of land) and was soon to become as curiously defensible. Many years later, in a letter to Robert Browning, Elizabeth described how her father had adorned Lady Tempest's former house with 'minarets and domes . . . with metal spires and crescents'. Time has tilted the fashion which once set Elizabeth Browning above Emily Brontë.

Like Lancashire and Yorkshire, the Durham Way claims a notable walker, Canon A. N. Hooper, sometime curate of Chester-le-Street. A memoir states that Hooper's 'pastoral duties involved him in a great deal of walking, for he had neither horse nor carriage . . .' Unlike the other Pennine walkers, Hooper specialized in foreign travel. By way of limbering-up for a pilgrimage to Rome he walked from Filey to London in one week, starting on Easter Monday, 1887. For his continental walk —via Antwerp, Strasbourg, Basle, Milan, Bologna—the Canon wore a dark knickerbocker suit, a wide-brimmed clerical hat, and (for Sunday churchgoing) a pair of white gloves. His longest day's march was forty-two miles. In some villages he paid no less than eighteenpence for supper, bed, and breakfast.

There is no record that Canon Hooper ever came to Cauldron Snout, yet one feels that he must have come, because this border-land is second only to that other where Lancashire joins Westmorland and Cumberland within sight of the Langdale Pikes. At Cauldron Snout the North Riding meets Westmorland and County Durham, to the music of several becks and the thunder of the Snout itself, a cataract of foam, seething headlong into a ravine of sculptured rocks. Here, in a horseshoe of mountainous water, the Maize Beck bends eastward to be joined by Langdon Beck flowing into the Tees. Such a symphony, set among such heights, composes a memorable finale to the Durham Way.

9 Westmorland

AFFECTION is wide-eyed. It perceives the Alps as higher than the Quantocks, yet may prefer to live among the latter. We love best the beauty that we know best. This Westmorland sector is the one best known to me; therefore I love it above the others.

The name Westmorland says what it means, which is 'the land west of the Yorkshire moors'. Its people were at one time called *Westmoringas*. The word 'Lakelander' did not appear until 1829. Although this beautiful and majestic county is small—twenty-eighth in size after Yorkshire—it contains either part or the whole of Windermere, Grasmere, Buttermere, Crummock Water, Rydal Water, and the smallest of them all, Brother's Water. Lakeland's most dramatic skyline—the Langdale Pikes—is in Westmorland; so also is a large part of Helvellyn, England's third highest mountain. Alone of English counties along the Way, Westmorland has no industrial town; Kendal, the largest, could slip into Manchester without being noticed. Only three other places can claim to be towns—Appleby, Kirkby Stephen, Kirkby Lonsdale—and to a southron they will seem no more than villages.

If Yorkshire claims the supreme poetess, then to Westmorland belongs the poet whom some have ranked next after Shakespeare, and supreme in his own domain, which is the English countryside. Much of Wordsworth's Westmorland stands in relation to Cumberland as Dorset to Devon; tourists race through the one in order to arrive at the other. Although the county contains several large estates, it has for centuries been a republic of peasant-landowners, known locally as Estatesmen, who share the independent spirit, but never the servile hunger, of those Dorset men who suffered transportation because they believed it was wrong that they should labour and starve while others grew idly fat. An eighteenth-century Bishop of Llandaff observed: 'Labour is dearer in Westmorland than it is in almost any of the counties either to the north of south of it. This probably is owing to the greater number of smallholders, or statesmen above-mentioned, who doing the work upon their own estates, with their own hands and those of their families, are perhaps disinclined to labour for other people.' The good old Bishop winced at one aspect of life hereabouts: 'It is painful to one, who has in his composition the least spark of knight-errantry, to behold the beautiful maidservants of this county toiling in the severe labours of the field.' The Landgirls of two world wars would have astounded him. Westmorland therefore is a community of farmers, chiefly of sheep farmers. From sheep comes their daily bread. The jam (and too many pips) is spread by tourists. Like every other county, this has partly changed beyond recognition. The beginnings of that change were dated by Dorothy Words-worth when she compared the crowds of tourists in 1802 with the relative scarcity of visitors in '. . . our mountain wilds 30 years ago'. Even during the twentieth century the main road over Shap to Scotland was so deeply rutted that motor-cyclists walked home, carrying the broken frame. Now that road is out of date, and will soon be by-passed. Beatrix Potter, the doughty Lakeland sheep farmer, once uttered a prophecy: 'Not even Hitler can damage the fells.' But Mammon rushes in where madness could not tread; and many of the Lakeland by-ways have become a summer car park. Fortunately, the Way avoids those congested regions, keeping closely to some of the least-sullied and seldom-seen splendour in England.

The entry into Westmorland is dramatic. Instead of continuing northward, the Way turns suddenly west, as though intent upon reaching Arnside, which is Westmorland's only seaside place; and having travelled fifteen miles from Langdon Beck, it actually reaches a point south of that Beck. Meanwhile, the Way becomes a track leading to Birkdale, one of the loneliest farms in England, sheltered by two (or is it three?) trees. Even the drystone walls are scarce. Bare moorland rises and falls, and again falls and rises, farther than the eye can see. A guidebook of 1920 described Birkdale as it was when motor-cars really were private: 'In this neighbourhood, close to the Yorkshire and Durham boundaries, are two small farm-houses called Birkdale, without so much as a cart track to them. To reach them and return to Dufton involves a long and hard day's journey across the desolate and trackless moors, while if it is desired to go by road from Birkdale to Dufton, forty miles would have to be traversed, by way of Middleton, Wemmergill, and Brough.' Speed, which robs distance of its dignity, and transforms tracks into highways, has set this once-secluded place within easy reach of Lamb's 'accursed cotton mills'. On summer weekends, they tell me, the track to Birkdale is cluttered with cars. I take their word for it. My own visits are made mid-week between October and May, which is one reason why I find Birkdale alone and at home in a solitude of sky and stillness. If I had another ten lives to live, I might choose to spend one of them at Birkdale.

And now begins a long and lonely voyage into the interior not only of Westmorland but also of your own self. For the best part of a day you neither see nor meet anyone unless by remote chance. Over the heather you go—up over the heather—past the rubble of a miner's cottage at Moss Shop, and then past Nichol's Chair, a basalt plinth, named after a cobbler who (so they will tell you at Dufton) sat astride it while he mended a pair of boots.

If you reach Maize Beck at spate-time you will be unable to cross it without wading hip-high; and even then the current may break your neck against a rock. All this while you are climbing—sometimes gradually, sometimes acutely—in a land as wild as any since Bleaklow, and farther from cities and factories. People tend either to forget or never to know what the act of climbing means. I have overheard middle-aged men challenge one another to scale Cross Fell in one hour. But Cross Fell is a mountain nearly three thousand feet high. An Alpine guide would tackle it at about 1,200 feet an hour. Three miles an hour is a workmanlike pace across steep country, plus half an hour for every thousand feet of ascent. Walkers carrying heavy equipment ought to be content with two and a half miles an hour, plus one hour for every 1,500 feet of ascent. Remember, you are not yet a disembodied spirit. You must carry your own weight uphill, and then prevent it from sliding downdale.

Along the less remote parts of the Way you will notice the kind of costumes that ask a question: 'Which of us is the most unsuitable?' In winter a city typist will climb Pen-y-Ghent wearing gym shoes and a macintosh that leaked before she set out. In summer a salesman approaches Cauldron Snout in a uniform that would cause Everest itself to bow down defeated. If anyone walks this part of the Way he must wear strong boots and two pairs of socks, carrying a dependable oilskin. In bad weather he will do well to take a light tent which he can pitch under the lee of rocks when rain or wind deter him. On the Westmorland Way a gale may exceed eighty miles an hour and snow can obliterate all tracks within twenty minutes. A man is therefore out of his wits if he walks alone in winter without telling someone where he has gone.

Like Lancashire and Yorkshire and Durham, this county had a band of famous walkers. Thomas de Quincey, for instance, walked from Manchester to Chester in two days, over rough roads. Despite his opium, he edited *The Westmorland Gazette*, a weekly newspaper which still flourishes. He once confessed that he never felt well unless he walked at least eight miles every day. Like Dickens, he was a compulsive night-walker: 'I took the very greatest delight in these nocturnal walks through the silent valleys of Cumberland and Westmorland.' In his seventy-first year he was still walking seven daily miles. 'Happier life,' he declared, 'I cannot imagine than this vagrancy.'

Another drug-addict, Samuel Taylor Coleridge, likewise shook off his lethargy when he came to Westmorland. Dorothy Wordsworth's *Journal* several times speaks of his walks from Keswick to Grasmere, a mountainous distance which few motorists would care to cover on foot. But the classic Westmorland walker was Wordsworth. When the poet was sixty-five, de Quincey did some arithmetic: 'I calculate,' he wrote, 'that Wordsworth must have traversed one hundred and eighty thousand English miles.' And Wordsworth lived to traverse thousands more. At sixty he was skating as fleetly as at sixteen. At seventy he climbed Helvellyn. 'For him,' said de Quincey, 'walking . . . stood in the stead of alcohol and other stimulants . . . to which, indeed, we are indebted for much that is most excellent in his writings.' To mix the metaphors, walking was Wordsworth's wine of life and midnight oil:

> . . . the lonely roads
> Were schools to me.

Even when you have learned them by heart, the surprises on this sector never seem stale. Toiling along the flanks of Murker Fell, all the while heading south-west, away from your ultimate destination, you surmount another skyline, and then you look up at the next. But it is not there. Instead, far away to the west, you sight the Lakeland mountains which tell their own homely tales . . . of Windermere and the road to Kirkstone Pass, capped by an inn that a vicar founded as a haven for weatherbound travellers . . . then Grasmere and another inn, the Dove and Olive Branch, which became Wordsworth's home . . . and Kendal, where Romney lived and died. But these faraway visions ought not to be over-indulged because, just north of the point where Murker Fell becomes a mountain, the Way approaches the brink of High Cup Nick, whose deep crater becomes a point of no return for anyone who falls therein. Here the scree trickles into a pit of the centuries' debris. What carved this grim horseshoe? Not, certainly, the beck that slips gently from its brim. High Cup Nick crater was scooped by a glacier, and crowned at its northern tip by a crag, called Narrowgate Beacon because in the old time men crouched there beside a brazier that blazed news of a raid by the Scots or a rising by the Catholics. Perhaps a posse of Tudor Estatesmen stood guard, peering southward lest Shunner Fell or Pen-y-Ghent had learned that the Armada was anchored off Dover, and Kent already in Spanish hands. So, even this desolate height played its part in Masefield's panorama of wars and the rumours thereof:

> Part of infinite procession hurled in fire through the sky,
> Bearing things that seem, and then seem to be not . . .

But not all the news was sombre. In farms and villages below the Way some of the old people remember a song which Ralph Vaughan Williams transcribed:

> Come all you cockers, far and near,
> I'll tell you of a cock-fight, when and where,
> At Tumbler's Hill, they all did say,
> Between the black and the bonny grey.
> With a hip and a ha, and a loud hooray,
> The charcoal black and the bonny grey?

I know a Westmorlander who lately brandished a pair of miniature cock-fighting spurs in the face of his friend the police sergeant, who exclaimed: 'What the devil are they?' Yet less than a century ago the sergeant's predecessors spent much time sleuthing that old and unlawful pastime, for many Wayside farms and manors had their own cockpits. I have seen certain remote hilltops where cock-fighting took place within living memory, and have heard of other remote places where it still does take place.

In Westmorland as everywhere else in England the dialect is dwindling. You no longer hear a dalesman say *lockerty* or globe-flower, *gale* or bog-myrtle, *late a lock* or beg a ration. But a few words do survive. In 1802, for example, Dorothy Wordsworth's *Journal* mentioned 'slacks of grassy ground'. When I asked a Westmorlander the meaning of 'slack', to discover whether the word were still in use, he answered, 'Slack? It's a hollow. Didn't you know?'

Meanwhile the Way has crept warily round the brink of High Cup's hollow, as though fascinated by the basalt cliffs below and the Lakeland peaks above. I usually hold a conversation with myself at High Cup, in which I discuss the obtuseness of people who suppose that to talk with oneself is the mark of a madman. It can be, of course. Perhaps Joan of Arc really was mad. Perhaps William Blake was mad, too, when he told his friend Butts: 'I have written this poem from immediate dictation, twelve or sometimes twenty or thirty lines at a time, without premeditation, and even against my will . . . I may praise it since I dare not pretend to be anything other than the secretary; the authors are in eternity.'

Wiser in our generation, we know now that authors speak through their unconscious mind. We know also that most people remain unaware of their unconscious, which is a paradoxical way of saying that most people never become fully self-conscious. They live in a dream. You have only to watch them—or, better still, to watch yourself—when they appear to be in full possession of their faculties. They scratch their noses, they jerk their knees, they tap their feet. Everyone does. But not everyone always rushes around in a dream of unrecognized impulses. Next time you pass this Way—or any other lonely place—have a chat with yourself. You will surprise you. You will alarm you. You will shock you. You may weep or curse or laugh, because self-communion dredges the channel between your selves. Along this sector of the Way, near the village of Knock, I once said to myself aloud, 'Hooray for the sun!' An old man peered over the wall, but instead of asking, 'Art thee barmy?' he said, 'Happen I was thinking on t' same thing.'

From the top of High Nick I always look back to the border between Westmorland and Yorkshire, thinking of Dentdale and its Long Drag. Dentdale is six miles from end to end, and more than 1,500 feet high. Its capital is the village of Dent, known as Dent Town, not ironically in view of its present smallness, but evocatively in view of its past importance. The high street is a cobbled lane just wide enough for one vehicle, and walkable in half a brisk minute. Hartley Coleridge etched Dent Town with a couplet:

> Narrow and winding are its rattling streets,
> Where cart with cart in cumbrous conflict meets . . .

Midway down the street, near the entrance to the church, a slab of Shap granite commemorates Adam Sedgwick, son of the vicar of Dent, who was born here in 1785, and attended Dent Grammar School (founded in 1603, closed in or about 1900, and still well cared for). In 1967 one of its Old Girls told me that at this comprehensively co-educational academy the boys were required to light the schoolroom fire. Sedgwick himself went from Dent to Sedbergh School and thence up to Cambridge, where he became

Seventeenth-century almshouse,
Appleby, Westmorland

Dufton, Westmorland

A corner of *Garrigill*, Cumberland

Professor of Geology. A tablet in Dent church says of him: 'His University claimed his life's labour, but though removed for the greater part of his life from his beloved birth-place, his love for it was always fresh, and he ever revisited it with increasing affection.'

Dentdale is wholly pastoral. Its green flanks shine with farmsteads white as sheep. But more and more of these farms are falling into the hands of fewer and fewer farmers, one of whom assured me that most of the land will soon belong to half a dozen dalesmen. Yet even a century ago many small-holders dibbled a living from a dozen acres, and their struggle for existence is recalled by a local saying, 'Do as they do in Dent' . . . in other words 'Go without'.

Have you, I wonder, heard of 'the terrible knitters o' Dent'? It was not the knitters who inspired terror; what startled the world was their energy. While they watched their flocks or hay-timed their acres, men and women and children knitted the fleece. They knitted while they walked to church and when they reeled home from the inn; and in order to save fuel they assembled whenever possible in one cottage; each household taking its turn on the rota. Robert Southey came over to see them from Keswick, and was deeply impressed by their industriousness. Indeed, the womenfolk were so busy that they lacked leisure in which to teach their little ones to knit; so a venerable dame held a knitting school in her parlour. I have sat in that parlour, and seen some of the old knitting needles.

Like the knitters, the Dentdale stonemasons have declined and fallen, though Dent marble was famous in the youth of men who are old. Some of the quarry out-buildings can be seen from the lane through the dale. St Pancras Station contains Dent marble; so also do several public buildings in Pennine cities, and many railway stations on the former Midland line to Scotland. One of my Dentdale friends—the son of a stonemason—has some splendid early twentieth-century marble tables.

But the most dramatic example of man's handiwork is the railway—The Long Drag, as they call it—whose summit, Dent Station, the highest in England, gets such a buffeting from the wind that the stationmaster's house was fitted with double panes

of glass. In 1968 the last steam train on British railways made a
ceremonial tour up this steep way. Now the station is a half-
ruinous serve-yourself halt; but in years past I have sat beside a
cavernous fire in the station office, hearing tales of snowbound
trains, of linesmen marooned in their huts, of gales so fierce that
one of them got hold of a locomotive on a turntable and spun it
round as though it were a toy.

The Long Drag is the engineering epic of the Pennine Way. It
began on a November morning in 1869, when an Irish labourer
swung the first spade that should build a line across the Pennines
from Settle in Yorkshire to Carlisle in Cumberland. It was indeed
a costly effort to keep up with the Joneses and the Smiths—that
is, with the Great Northern and the London North-Western.
Each of the seventy-two miles cost (in modern currency) about a
million sterling. Blea Moor Tunnel, five years in the making, cost
£900 per yard (the bill for candles exceeded £1,000). Shanty towns
sprang up beside the line, and then withered like mushrooms.
Now only their names are remembered, and only by the oldest
dalesfolk: Inkerman, Sebastopol. Jericho, Salt Lake City, Betty
Wife Hole. At Ingleton the policeman was re-inforced by thirteen
others, with special reference to Saturday nights. The population
multiplied as never before, nor since; in North Ribblesdale alone
a few hundreds became three thousand. The navvies themselves
earned more in one day than a shepherd earned in one week;
and their moral welfare was uplifted by the directors of the
Midland Railway, who contributed towards the cost of sending
two missionaries into the Catholic field. One of them, William
Fletcher, was stationed at Kirkby Stephen; the other, James
Tiplady, ministered at Betty Wife Hole, a shanty town of five
hundred labourers and their camp-followers. From Lord Kenlie
the church of St Leonard at Chapel-le-Dale received a plot of land
as a burial ground for labourers who had died either from drink
or from the hazards of their occupation.

Through the courtesy of British Rail I was able to travel The
Long Drag on the footplate of a steam locomotive, and I still
cannot decide which was the more impressive—the wild landscape
or the skill with which a railway was heaved and hewn across it.

Some of the pillars for Arten Gill viaduct were sunk fifty-five feet before they reached their rocky foundation. A man whose grandfather had helped to build the line told me that some of the viaducts rested on a layer of fleece which helped to absorb the dampness.

But not even the country of The Long Drag is quite so lonely as High Cup Nick. Many a wayfarer, arriving here for the first time, gives up all hope of ever arriving anywhere else; yet he does arrive—rather by necessity than from conviction—along a Way that at last descends from the mountainous Beacon to Peeping Hill (1650 feet) then to Horthwaite (1242) feet) and so to the white cottages and green grass of Dufton's all-weather welcome to wind-whipped winter and thirsty summer.

The sun was shining when I first saw Dufton, on a March afternoon. It was shining when I last saw Dufton, on a May morning. And with every intermediate visit—at all seasons over many years—still the sun shone. Truly this was a dovelike place, *Dove tun*, the farmstead with doves. Dufton for me is a perennial sun-spot, all the more remarkable because it lies on the wettest and wildest sector of the Way. As though to emphasize this role as a fortress built against inclemency, Dufton is set around a square, having in its centre a green with many trees and one decrepit fountain inscribed with a watery pun in poor Latin. The houses are sheer Westmorland—squat, sandstone, stolid— and their occupants seem pretty well supplied by the inn and a shop. Bedouins, no doubt, would describe Dufton as an oasis among callous heights. Certainly I cannot recall a more vivid contrast of Pennine landscape within so small a space. In Dufton and for a few hundred yards north of it there is pastoral serenity, dappled with cattle and geese and orchards, recalling Westmorland's earlier name of Applebyshire, part of the kingdom of Northumbria. But beyond Dufton are heights so scoured and bleak that the eye looks in vain for a path up them or along.

Dufton used to be a centre of the lead-mining industry; and in my childhood the barytes mines were still working. Now only their ruins remain, like cairns at the foot of the fells. The church stands outside the village, on a knoll overlooking a farm, and was horribly rebuilt during the 1880s. I believe that the parish registers have been kept since 1570. In Dufton you will discover that Westmorland maintains an old-world courtesy. For example, although most Britons nowadays address their beloved as though she were a public meeting, the men of these parts still observe 'thee' and 'thou', even as the French and the Germans have kept their *tu* and *du*, which are bestowed on those who deserve them. If a man at Dufton assumes a familiarity where none exists, he will be told: 'Don't thee thou me. Thee thou them as thou's thee.'

It is likely that Dufton never was so hard-pressed as Dentdale and its do-without small-holders; and even when poverty did exist, it stood a fair chance of enjoying good health, as De Quincey noticed when he wrote of Westmorland nearly two centuries ago: 'Poverty—how different the face it wears looking with meagre staring eyes from a city dwelling . . . and when it peeps out, with rosy cheeks, from amongst clustering roses and woodbines, at a little lattice, from a little one-storey cottage!' De Quincey was keen-eyed. He knew the London slums as closely as he knew the Westmorland fells. He did not write of 'rosy cheeks' where none was to be seen.

De Quincey noticed, too, a feature of Westmorland domestic architecture: 'The porch, for instance . . . pierced with holes for air . . . has evidently been dictated by the sudden rushes of wind through the mountain ghylls . . . by the hospitable wish to provide a sheltered seat for the wayfarer.' He remarked on the skill with which these cottages and farms were sited: 'The native Dalesman, well aware of the fury with which the wind often gathers and eddies about any eminence, never thinks of planting his house there; whereas the stranger, singly solicitous about the prospect or the range of lake which his gilt saloons are to command, chooses his site too often upon points better fitted for a temple of Eolus than a human dwelling-place; and he belts his house with balconies and verandas that a mountain gale often tears away in mockery.' Wordsworth himself described the indigenous charm of Westmorland farmhouses and cottages. Such places, he observed, '. . . may rather be said to have grown than to have been erected—to have risen, by an instinct of their own—out of the native rock—so little is there in them of formality, such is their wildness and beauty.'

I have acquired a knowledge of the fells above Dufton of a kind which few men possess unless they are shepherds, and it happened like this: against our better judgement, without troubling to plot a course with map and compass, my companion and I followed a villager's misdirections, and began to make for Cross Fell by walking away from it. When the wrong track petered out, having lured us nearly two thousand feet up, we looked back and saw the error of the villager's ways. But the sun shone, the larks sang, we had breakfasted well, and would dine likewise. So, instead of going down, in search of the right path, we went up, seeking a wrong one. No such path existed. We were charting a sea on which, like Wordsworth,

> . . . we find
> No appanage of human kind;
> Nor hint of man . . .

We found only boulders and becks and strips of sour grass among green turf. Again Wordsworth spoke for us, this time in prose: 'The stillness was not of this world.' Silent as the explorer on his peak in Darien, we looked down and all around. Far to the north the Solway Firth winked a slit of its blue eye. Everywhere the textbook of geology lay open; and that, too, Wordsworth had read:

> . . . record of commotion
> Which a thousand ridges yield;
> Ridge, and gulf and distant ocean
> Gleaming like a silver shield!

Chiefly we looked down at our own feet and then up at the crags and morasses that awaited them. Cross Fell itself stood clear and challenging, but of the Way thither—even of a faint track—we saw no sign because there was none. Up the sides of ravines we clambered, sometimes on all fours, and then down the sides of ravines, sometimes on no feet; and then again up and down the dizzy gorges until we reached the dizziest of all, known as Knock

Hush, 'hushing' being the old miners' trick of building a dam and breaching it so that the beck would scour the surface soil. At last, on the port bow, we sighted the Way; and after much stumbling and scrambling we rejoined it, and went on, even higher, to the top of Great Dun Fell, nearly three thousand feet above Solway Firth. Far to the west we saw Lakeland's peak-poised skyline. At our feet, and reaching to the middle distance, the Eden valley unfolded a carpet green as Wordsworth's:

> Lo! the dwindled woods and meadows!
> What a vast abyss is there!
> Lo! the clouds, the solemn shadows,
> And the glistenings—heavenly fair!

Away to the south, staunch as a sleepless sentry, Barbon Fell kept watch above the little town of Kirkby Lonsdale, to which John Ruskin came, and stood near the church, gazing across the River Lune. On the hill there—or brow, as they call it—a plaque records Ruskin's opinion of the view: '. . . one of the loveliest in England . . .'

Turning about, I imagined Sedbergh—so nearly in sight, below the skyline—that outpost of Yorkshire, half-islanded in Westmorland. The parish of Sedbergh once covered 52,665 acres, and from it were carved the parishes of Dent, Howgill, Cautley, Garsdale. Like Dent Town, Sedbergh lived by wool. A century ago Benjamin Newton wrote: 'In this town all the boys and girls are employed in knitting . . . blue woolen caps of yarn which make all the children look as if they came out of a dyeing factory . . . A good knitter knits 12 caps per diem which on examining must be worn by convicts and prisoners . . .' Not every Sedbergh lad was so employed. A fortunate few attended Sedbergh School, the only public school within a few miles of the Way. Nowadays, of course, a large number of schools style themselves public; but the name was first used a century ago, by the Board of Education, to describe some dozen schools or so, of which the most eminent and ancient were Eton, Harrow, Winchester, Westminster, Shrewsbury and Merchant Taylors'. These great schools followed a more or less common pattern, for most of them were founded wholly or chiefly for poor boys; all suffered their lean seasons; many shifted their sites; and each became the object of ill-informed envy.

The story of Sedbergh School begins in 1525 when a local man, Roger Lupton, Canon of Windsor and Provost of Eton, founds a chantry school in the town. Lupton himself chooses the masters, and stipulates that after his death their successors shall be chosen by twelve governors drawn from 'the more discreet and better inhabitants of the town and parish'. A master, says Lupton, may be dismissed after three warnings against unbecoming conduct.

Lupton's Free School of Sedbergh died young, for under Edward VI much of its property was forfeit, and the school faced suppression. However, Lupton had provided eight scholarships from Sedbergh to St John's College, Cambridge; and in 1551 that College used its influence to re-found the school. Five years later the governors exercised their right to dismiss wayward masters: '. . . the said Richard Jackson hath been a common frequenter of Ale Houses and hath beene for 3 or 4 days together distempered with drinke and hath been drunke upon several Lordes Days.' Jackson's successor was no saint, either. In 1677 the judges at Appleby Quarter Sessions ordered him to keep the peace by not renewing his quarrels with Mrs Sibella Lowther.

In 1716 a new school was built; today it is a museum and library; the present school buildings are scattered over a large area. Sedbergh's prestige was founded by Henry Hart, who had been at Rugby under William Temple, sometime Archbishop of Canterbury. In 1879 Hart encouraged the Sedbergh boys to explore the Pennine dales and to shoot the rapids of the Lune.

During the seventeenth and eighteenth centuries many of the pupils were Quakers, which is not surprising, because their school stands scarcely a mile from Briggflatts, one of the oldest Meeting-Houses in Britain, founded shortly after George Fox's second visit to Westmorland. This beautifully simple haven stands at the end of a track from the Kirkby Lonsdale road. The oak-panelled interior has a gallery on three sides, and a stone floor indented by centuries of meditation. Even when no one

else is present at Briggflatts, you perceive the sincerity of Charles
Lamb's invitation: 'Would'st thou know what true peace and
quiet mean; would'st thou enjoy at once solitude and society . . .
come with me to a Quaker's Meeting.'

Great Dun Fell, by contrast, lost its own peacefulness when
progress transformed it into a type of television centre, mocked
by four enormous masts and a tin-shack slum. Such is the fate of
the second highest point along the Way. Sir William Watson
diagnosed the disease before it had galloped to the summit:

> I think the immortal servants of mankind,
> If still they are watching by how slow degrees
> The World-Soul greatens with the centuries,
> Mourn most Man's barren levity of mind . . .

Watson did not wag a vaguely puritanical finger at life's good-
humoured 'cakes and ale'. He pointed precisely at

> The ear to no large harmony inclined,
> The witless thirst for false wit's witless lees,
> The laugh mistimed in tragic presences,
> The eye to all majestic meanings blind.

The majesty of Westmorland so appalled Defoe that he dismissed the entire county as: '. . . the wildest, most barren and
frightful of any I have passed over in England . . .' And he under-
lined his horror with a postscript: '. . . or even in Wales . . .' But
Defoe suffered the blind eye of a journalist who seeks chiefly
to observe the balance of trade. Even at Durham he apologized
for mentioning the cathedral: 'But what do I dip into antiquity
for . . . which I have avoided as much as possible everywhere
else?' Posterity cares little for the fat stock prices in 1726, but it
still wanders admiringly among Durham's uncommercial cloisters.
In any event, Westmorland is not and never was barren. The foot-
hills of Great Dun Fell are lapped by one of the most fertile regions
in Britain. Is not Appleby—that town of apple orchards—the capital
of Westmorland? And does it not lie within sight of the Way?

Appleby is probably the smallest and certainly the most consistently beautiful of all the English county towns. Yet many
travellers never see Appleby; they race along a main road on the

edge of Appleby. The true town is guarded by the River Eden, which, having been crossed, reveals a steep street, tree-lined and graced by handsome houses. At the bottom of the hill stand the church and its cloisters; razed by the Scots, rebuilt, restored. At the top of the hill stands the castle, much renovated since the reign of Henry VI. Midway between castle and church, the red brick of Lady Anne Clifford's almshouse casts a warm sunset upon twelve superannuated souls. And both the top and the bottom of the street are marked by tall crosses. The lower cross lacks an inscription, but the upper issues an exhortation: 'Retain your loyalty; preserve your rights.' This the townsfolk used to do in council at their ancient Moot Hall, a timbered building near the church, which convenience has been partly converted into a public lavatory. Appleby's legal status remains as it was when Celia Fiennes visited 'the shire town where the session and assizes are held'.

A sixteenth-century Grammar School, on the edge of the town, is now housed in decent Victorian sandstone. On its books are three famous names: Addison, father of the essayist; Washington, elder brother of Colonel George Washington, sometime President of the United States of America; and Robinson, a schoolfellow of the Washingtons, who became Member of Parliament for these parts. Tradition says that Robinson was attacked anonymously by Sheridan during a debate. When challenged to name the culprit, Sheridan retorted, 'I could name him as easily as I could say Jack Robinson.'

But all these are overshadowed by the great lady of Westmorland, Lady Anne Clifford, only surviving child of the third Earl of Cumberland. Her education was entrusted to a poet, Samuel Daniel, whose plays were acted at Court to settings by Inigo Jones. Daniel had written:

> I know I shall be read among the rest
> So long as men speak English . . .

But he lived to qualify his praise:

> Years hath done this wrong,
> To make me write too much and live too long.

The pupil, at all events, proved as apt as her master. She could, said Donne, 'discourse of all things from predestination to slea-silk.' Daniel, in short, had implanted a love of art and scholarship which, when she grew old, enabled her to share the companionship of 'good books and virtuous thoughts'.

At the age of nineteen Lady Anne married the third Earl of Dorset, to whom she bore five children. At the age of forty, after six years' widowhood, she married Sir Philip Sidney's nephew, the fourth Earl of Pembroke (Daniel himself had served as tutor to the third Earl). Neither of the marriages bestowed much joy, but each bequeathed large estates which she ruled as one who had been born to that manner. Thus, when an Appleby man refused to pay his feudal due of a yearly hen, the Countess sued him, and, having won the hen, invited the defaulter to share it with her at dinner. In no sense was the Countess a Quaker Lass. Her motto became 'Retain your loyalty; preserve your rights.' This no-non-sense *noblesse* was extended to matters of higher estate. For example, her second husband had fought for King Charles against the rebels; and when Cromwell became military dictator he warned the widow not to restore her castles at Appleby, Skipton, Brough, Brougham, Pendragon. The Countess ignored the warning. Her castles were duly and handsomely restored. Two of them—Brougham and Brough—stand at the foot of the Westmorland Way.

Brough Castle was built by the Normans on the site of a Roman camp. The Countess restored the ruins in 1659. Two years later, as her diary tells, she 'came to lie in it herself for a little while in September, 1661, after it had lain ruinous, without timber or any covering, ever since the year 1521, when it was burnt by a casual fire'. Now it is once again in ruins. However, Brough village maintains its annual fair, a famous *rendezvous* for farmers, gipsies and fell ponies. This fair takes place in October, and local people still use the phrase 'Brough weather' to describe the autumnal or back-end climate along the Westmorland Way . . . snow, sleet, frost, thunder, flood, mist, and sometimes a St Martin's summer.

Brougham Castle—another ruin on a Roman site—was rebuilt in 1657. The parish contains also Brougham Hall, seat of Lord

Brougham and Vaux whose barony is Victorian, though the family held lands here seven centuries ago, in what was then Whinfell Forest, thick with deer, whereof one led a famous chase, beginning when a stag named Heart o' Grease, was hunted by a hound called Hercules. Into Dumfriesshire they went and then back to Brougham, where the stag leaped the park paling, and fell down dead. The hound failed to leap it, and also died. In ‚the Countess's day the stag's antlers were nailed to the tree where it had expired.

Two poets received their due from Lady Anne. The first was her tutor, Daniel, who died at Beckington in Somerset, where the grateful pupil erected a statue on his grave; the second was Edmund Spenser, to whom she gave the memorial in Westminster Abbey, for he had been her mother's favourite poet. In memory of her mother the Countess built a plinth, half a mile to the east of Brougham Castle, at the spot where mother and daughter had taken what became their last farewell on earth. Even Defoe's keen business sense was moved by the relic of antiquity: '. . . a famous column,' he remarked, 'called the Countess Pillar. It is a fine column of freestone finely wrought, enchas'd, and in some places painted. There is an obelisk on the top, several coats of arms, and other ornaments in proper places all over it, with dials also on every side, and a brass-plate.' When Wordsworth passed by he copied the inscription on that plate: 'This pillar was erected, in the year 1656, by Anne Countess Dowager of Pembroke, etc. for a memorial of her last parting with her good and pious mother, Margaret Countess Dowager of Cumberland, on the 2d of April, 1616; whereof she hath left an annuity of £4 to be distributed to the poor of this parish of Brougham every 2d day of April for ever, upon the stone table placed hard by. Laus Deo.' Wordsworth added his own tribute:

> Many a Stranger passing by
> Has with that Parting mixed a filial sigh . . .

The Countess of Pembroke lived to be eighty-seven, having throughout her life eschewed both wine and medicine. She died at Brougham Castle, in 1676, a splendid relic of the Middle

Ages, and was buried beneath a comparable tomb at Appleby church.

But now, step by step. Westmorland approaches Cumberland, and neither yields precedence to the other. A Cumbrian will tell you: 'There's nobbut two counties in England. And the second is Westmorland.' Westmorland will reply with an even more exclusive arithmetic: 'There's nobbut one county in England. And the folk frae Cumberland live next door.' It is all good fun and therefore not ill-humoured. As Kipling said, each man loves his home above the rest. The men for whom this Way is home, have good cause to love it. Eastward a moorland rises and falls away invisible. Westward shines the Eden Valley, its orchards and cornfields and pastures; and beyond them the lakes and the mountains. Ahead, Cross Fell sits upon its throne, the peak of the Pennines. Here indeed is de Lisle's active repose: *Tout se tait*. But the supreme spokesman is Wordsworth, who spent most of his life in Westmorland, and explored much of its Way. His prose *Guide to the Lake District* is still the best introduction. His poems are an illuminating map. Not to know them is to remain partly unacquainted with Westmorland. No other Englishman—no other man in any land—owed so much to his home, and paid the debt so greatly. From him these mountains received a son's blessing:

> Dear native regions, whereso'er shall close
> My mortal course, there shall I think on you.

10 Cumberland

HAVING climbed Little Dun Fell (which is only nineteen feet littler than Great Dun) the Way descends slightly until, at Tees Head, it enters Cumberland, near a famous watershed, for the Tees rises on the east, the Eden is fed by tributaries from the west, and the South Tyne by tributaries from the north. Here, too, the Way recovers from its westerly detour, and now marches north-east through grassland, swamps, and saxifrage. About twenty miles of Westmorland followed the Way, but in Cumberland only a dozen follow it; yet those twelve are enough to suggest some of the differences between the two counties.

The word 'Cumberland' recalls the Celtic *Cumbras*—from the Welsh *Cymry* or Welshfolk—who formed part of the kingdom of Strathclyde. It was not until William II had annexed the territory that 'Cumbrian' acquired its present meaning. Cumberland itself is nearly twice the size of Westmorland, but, unlike its smaller neighbour, it contains a large and impoverished industrial area among obsolete collieries near the sea. The happier parts—the mountains and lakes—are as fine as anything in Scotland, though less extensive and therefore more crowded by tourists. A considerable part of Cumberland belongs to the National Trust, a piece of good fortune that is epitomized by an inscription on Great Gable: 'In glorious and happy memory of those whose names are inscribed below, members of this [the Rock and Fell Climbing] Club who died for their country in the European War, 1914–1918, these fells were acquired by their fellow members and by them vested in the National Trust, for the use and enjoyment of the people.' Well done and truly said; but 'the use and enjoyment of the people' will remain uselessly unenjoyable until the people's sight-seeing cars are banned from inner Lakeland, and replaced by motor-coaches that can carry the contents of fifty cars.

Now the Way climbs again, past cairns and plinths, to the summit of Cross Fell. Despite the great height, the grass track keeps remarkably dry, except after very heavy rain. The Fell itself is neither the most dramatic nor the most beautiful part of the Way, but beyond doubt it is the highest. Could it stand on tiptoe it would touch three thousand feet. The view from the summit is disappointing, for you see only a few hundred yards of turf, which appear to end at a precipice. In other words, the summit is a plateau, and you must walk to its brink in order to look down. Eastward lies an undulation of empty moorland, sullen as a Sargasso Sea; in the north the Scottish Lowlands transcend their own name; westward, a glint of Lakeland pinnacles—Skiddaw, Helvellyn, Saddleback—jagged as the ruins of a giant's castle.

In 1747 *The Gentleman's Magazine* published a description of Cross Fell, written by a geographer, George Smith: 'A mountain,' he said, 'that is generally ten months buried in snow, and eleven in clouds . . .' Smith was mistaken. Snow does sometimes sprinkle the summer summit—in 1937 it lingered until 10 June—but not even during the severest weather will it lie for ten months. As for clouds, in 1962 and 1963 I passed within sight of the Fell four times a week from April till October; and on nine days out of ten it was *not* buried in clouds. Smith emphasized the barrenness: 'This immense plateau has no verdure . . . so inconceivably barren is this distinguished eminence.' Nowadays much of the mountain is grazed by Herdwicks, a hardy Lakeland breed; but little grain is grown, even in the valley, for short summers and cold autumns make this a sheep and cattle country. Despite the bleakness Cross Fell has drawn its crowds. In the early years of Queen Victoria's reign political meetings were held on the summit, enlivened by brass bands, wrestling matches, and refreshments carried on pack-horses. Presumably the richer tub-thumper was elected. Presumably, too, some of the electors found that to go up Cross Fell was easier than to go down.

Why was the Fell named Cross? There are two answers to that question; one of them is simple, the other is subtle. The simple answer falls back on the Fell's earlier name, Fiends' Fell, which itself recorded a primitive belief that certain places are possessed or, as we now say, haunted by spirits, some malign, others benign. In an effort to exorcise the fiends, Christians built a Cross on the Fell.

The other and subtler answer falls back on the nature of the belief in spirits. William James analysed the problem in his *Varieties of Religious Experience*: 'It is,' he wrote, 'as if there were in the human consciousness a sense of reality, a feeling of objective presence, a perception of what may be called *something there*.' The average modern man refuses even to examine this hypothesis. He dismisses it unexamined as an illusion. But Tennyson would have none of such unscientific fellows:

> Dark-browed sophist, come not anear,
> All the place is holy ground.

It seems worthwhile to pause on Cross Fell, meditating modernity's ostrich-like attitude in the presence of mystery. Now the three major philosophical influences in post-medieval Europe were Galileo's announcement that the sun does not circle the earth; Darwin's announcement that men were not created late on the sixth day; and Freud's announcement that reasonableness is neither the sole nor the most powerful human motive. Each of those facts eroded man's belief that he was in every sense the centre of cosmic importance. One might therefore have expected a reaction, an attempt to justify Wordsworth's belief that we are 'greater than we know'. Instead, the tide of self-belittlement continues in spate. Blinkered by the accidents of grammar, philosophy is absolutely relative (except *vis-à-vis* relativity); physics reduces Chartres cathedral to a wave of uncoloured probability; psychology classifies mankind as a bundle of chemical reflexes; and while surgery transplants actual life into imminent death, biology boasts that it cannot tell the ultimate difference between a dead cat and a live one. Cross Fell, on the other hand, suggests that the truth is more likely to lie with those primitive people who *could* detect the presence and power of good and evil. Among some tribesmen only one question is asked when a man dies: 'Who wished him dead?' A crude version of that wishful-thinking is frequently expressed by non-tribesmen when they exclaim, 'I could have killed him.' One day, perhaps, we shall understand more about the creatures whose thoughts do indeed cause men to die, and may for all we know move mountains, and coax the rain to fall, and help the sun to shine. Until that time, the Disunited Nations will continue to pour irresolutions upon the troubled waters of man's psyche; and here and there, when two or three are gathered together, the emanation of their love will fight the good fight against evil odds.

Meanwhile, anyone who has climbed Cross Fell will understand why the ancients believed that it really was haunted by evil spirits. Even modern science allows that there is much turbulence on the Fell, though its fiendishness is nowadays called the Helm Wind, which bowls over hikers and hayricks and horses. The dynamics of the Helm can be stated as follows: when warm air crosses a cool sea it produces an inversion-layer at a height of about three thousand feet. In the presence of that layer the wind will rush down a hillside with great force, which is what happens when the wind on Cross Fell blows strongly from the north-east. The first account of the Helm was written in 1696 by Thomas Robinson, who lived at Ousby under the lee of the Fell.

The Helm can strike at any season, though most likely during winter, and may extend for several miles, both north and south. Sometimes it is accompanied by a bank of cloud—'the bar' they call it—which darkens the land for miles around. A Victorian traveller, Thomas Wilkinson, was caught by the Helm: 'If I advanced,' he wrote, 'it was with my head inclined to the ground, and at a low pace; if I retreated and leaned against it with all my weight, I could hardly keep erect; if I did not resist, I was blown over.' Yet only two miles away 'all was calm . . . while behind me the Helm continued raging in unbated fury'. I met the Helm myself once, driving from Appleby to Kirkby Lonsdale. The gusts moved the car several feet across the lane.

Even in calm weather the wind on Cross Fell is seldom still; but when it does die away, you overhear the wisdom of George

Eliot who said: 'If we had a keen vision and feeling of ordinary human life, it would be like hearing the grass grow . . .' Another eminent Victorian, Dorothy Wordsworth, painted the very likeness of these heights: 'Not Man's hills, but all for themselves, the sky and the clouds, and a few wild creatures.'

Having scaled its own summit, the Way lopes downhill into a more sheltered terrain, past the derelict lead mines that were once an important feature of the Way in general and of Cumberland in particular. It seems likely that the Celts had practised a crude form of mining. Certainly the Romans took Cumbrian lead for their own needs. However, there can have been little domestic demand for lead until the rise of the castles and great churches. Defoe said of the Cumbrian mines: 'Here are still mines of black lead found, which turn to very good account, being, for ought I have yet learned, the only place in Britain where it is to be had.' Defoe was mistaken in regarding these mines as unique. Wales, for example, had many lead mines; and in 1968 one of them—near Llanidloes in Montgomeryshire—was preserved by the Ministry of Public Building and Works (in 1945 the mine had employed three thousand workmen). The Cumbrian lead mines reached the zenith of their prosperity during the early nineteenth century, but declined rapidly when steamships carried cheap lead from overseas. One or two of the mines have been re-opened, not indeed for their lead but for a by-product, fluorspar, which is used to toughen steel.

You cannot walk far in these parts without hearing a beck. It may be a very small one, scarcely a yard wide, or it may be almost a river, of a kind which at one time enriched the county. Defoe was impressed by the northern fish trade: 'Notwithstanding the great distance, they at this time carry salmon (fresh as they take it) quite to London. This is perform'd with horses, which, changing often, go night and day without intermission, and, as they say, very much out-go the post; so that fish come very good and sweet to London.' The Industrial Revolution killed that trade by fouling the water and by outstripping the pack-horses. Within a century the number of salmon taken from the River Ribble fell from fifteen thousand to thirty-four. But it was sheep, not salmon, that had built the pack-horse bridges along the Way from Derbyshire to Cumberland. Several such bridges are claimed as the smallest in England. The smallest I ever saw is near Underley Grange on the outskirts of Kirkby Lonsdale. A thin pony might pass over it, but a fat man could not. The pack-horse bridge near Otley in Yorkshire was built as late as 1738, and all such bridges were used throughout the Industrial Revolution.

It seems a long time and a hard climb since the Way last hobnobbed with humanity at Middleton-in-Teesdale. It did condescend to look down on Dufton, and then farther afield on Appleby, but it never entered those places, and, having climbed Cross Fell, it seemed unlikely ever to enter any place again. Nor does the descent from Cross Fell suggest a change of heart, for although the heights are left behind, the land itself remains as lonely as ever. Indeed, the traces of derelict lead mines tend to sharpen the solitude.

From Long Man Hill to Pikeman Hill the Way runs more or less parallel with a walled track that was built by the miners. This track may be a mile or so longer than the official Way, but it is certainly easier and usually drier. Down then it goes, like a parting in the heather, through a high ravine that becomes narrower with every footstep. The sides of the ravine seem to mount up, but there is nothing illusory about their shelter from the wind. Out of the clouds you come, down from a treeless skyscape, and presently you do sight a tree, and then another, and after that a third, and after the third a copse which confutes Yeats when he complained:

> The woods of Arcady are dead,
> And over is their antique joy . . .

After the copse comes a farmhouse, apparently as lonely as Birkdale, but the trees and the track and the valley itself suggest that the loneliness may be an illusion, as indeed it is, for the Way becomes a tree-lined lane between cottages, and so enters the village of Garrigill, whose name means 'the narrow valley where Gerard's people live'. Of Gerard we know nothing; of the descent into his narrow valley I know much, having made it several times in several weathers.

At Garrigill, my conscience pricks me for naming the place. I wish that it might stand without being stared at. As Dorothy Wordsworth remarked of Grasmere, 'It calls home the heart to quietness.' Not that the place is pretty; few northern places are; they seem too busily engaged in not being wind-swept away. Not, then, pretty; but certainly comely; a few cottages draped around a small green, and on the green one cottage whose front door stands at the top of a stone block carved with steps. From the green a lane ambles a few hundred yards to a bridge across the stripling Tyne. There is one shop here, a small hotel, and a twelfth-century church that was decently renovated two hundred years ago. The church bell is said to have served as a dinner bell at Dilston Hall, the Northumberland seat (demolished in 1768) of James Radcliffe, third and last Earl of Derwentwater, who in 1716 was executed as a Jacobite.

If only for its smallness and isolation, Garrigill church underlines Sir Maurice Powicke's remark that the medieval Church was 'Something to which all men and women could respond and at all levels'. This simple building was the hub of a small universe. Good or bad, its priest was certainly poor and probably ignorant even by the standard of his own day. Yet in the eyes of his flock he was a shepherd, able to rescue the wretched and to daunt the mighty who had caused their misery. At his best he was indeed the parson—that is, *the* person—among his flock. Chaucer described such a man:

> That Cristes gospel trewely wolde preche;
> His parisshens devoutly wolde he teche.
> Benigne he was, and wonder diligent,
> And in adversitie ful pacient . . .

Such men must be set in the balance against the decadent friars and arrogant bishops whom Chaucer and Langland condemned. Garrigill church, at all events, was once the most important feature along this part of the Way, for men believed that Heaven and Hell were more lasting than Earth. Despite their daily backslidings, not a single aspect of life was conducted without reference to religion.

Whenever I come to Garrigill, and sit upon the green among the trees, or hear rain beating against the hotel window, I ask myself why this feature of the Way has changed so drastically that the average parish church is now a week-day museum and a Sunday handful. Partly it is because we reject many orthodox dogmas (that is nothing new: Arianism rejected the fourth-century invention of the Trinity). Partly it is because we reject the belief that our knowledge of God was revealed and at the same time limited for evermore (that also is nothing new: Euclid's geometry became demonstrably *non quod erat demonstrandum*). Partly it is because our new masters, the machines, have duped us into supposing that we ourselves are God (not even that is new: the brainbox played the same trick on uncountable ancients). Here then is a new aspect of life along the Pennine Way—orthodox Christendom confronted by an agonizing reappraisal. With language of incomparable beauty, in churches built by a faith that has withered, orthodoxy continues to preach a gospel which cannot evolve because, two thousand years ago, it was delivered whole, mature, unalterable. Fond indeed are the beliefs of youth, when men have grown old; and if those beliefs are held sincerely, then the psyche itself turns at bay against change. Men die for their faith because they live by it. Faith and life are indivisible. But until Garrigill church does make that agonizing reappraisal, it must fight for its existence against the thoughtless and the hostile, and will estrange many allies who believe that what we call God is best described as a spirit which has become encrusted with presumptuous dogma. Even so, let no one suppose that Garrigill and the other Wayside churches are spent. From the best of their members you will receive a quantity and quality of loving-kindness not elsewhere to be found. A mystic is by definition solitary; he prefers to commune alone upon Cross Fell; but most people seek God in corporate worship and among the give-and-take of good neighbourliness. At present one must report that along the Pennine Way and throughout England the priest has been supplanted by the publican.

Garrigill itself is happily placed, for it enjoys Lamb's Quaker-like blend of 'society and solitude'. Though it lives alone, at the end of a lane in a remote ravine, it has a neighbour, Alston, only two or three miles distant. The Way to Alston crosses a foot-bridge, follows the stripling Tyne awhile, and then steps on to the main road. While crossing that road I was knocked down, not by a car but by a hiker, at a point where some steps lead to the highway. The hiker jostled me as he came from behind, top-heavy with a portable house which forced me to the wall, so that I stumbled and fell. Our conversation went very much as follows:

'I say, I'm terribly sorry.'

'I'm not pleased, either.'

'Are you all right?'

'I shall survive. What was the idea?'

'Actually, I'm trying to beat the clock. Thirty miles a day with all this gear.'

And then he was off, before I could say what I thought, which is this: to travel a memorable country with the sole intention of seeing as little as possible as quickly as maybe, is like entering Westminster Abbey with a view to crawling blindfold among the pews. That hasty hiker, I thought, had not paused to savour Garrigill, to gaze from Cross Fell, to read Dufton's watery pun. He may have heard of Kingsley, but he had never seen Arncliffe. Wuthering Heights as he swept by was a pile of stones, and he may not have noticed it. All the curios and vistas and characters that had enriched my own journey . . . these were not for him. He had taken his striding orders from Defoe: 'antiquity is not my search in this work.' Not even modernity was his search. He looked only at his watch and at the gradients and swamps that might defeat it. He was like the motorist who, having raced from London to Exmoor, exclaims to the barman: 'Had a marvellous trip. Averaged forty the whole way.' Am I the only man who wonders why such people ever bother to go anywhere?

Alston claims to be England's highest market town. So does Buxton in Derbyshire. I leave them to quibble their contours, for there cannot be much difference between them. But one fact is self-evident; Alston is the steeper. Indeed, it is so steep that in 1967 a lorry careered down the cobbled street, demolishing the market cross and its miniature timber roof. In 1968 the ruins were still unrestored. Like Middleton-in-Teesdale, Alston is best approached by road—the road from Appleby or Penrith. I know at least two people who, having seen Alston Fell from afar, concluded that there was no road across such skyhigh desolation; but there is, and it resembles a serpent pursuing its own tail through a land where the trees grow sparse and more stunted, and then give up altogether. Behind, the Eden Valley appears as the Garden must have appeared to Adam when he looked back from his exile. And above it are those Lakeland pinnacles. The summit of Alston Fell has a summer-time tea-shack which in winter heightens the solitude. I must have travelled this road fifty times, and with every journey the prospect seems more barren. Left and right, there is no end to the sullen moors. A stranger wonders where and why Alston exists. Presently, however, a tree appears, and a hillside farm; and soon afterwards the road dips steeply into a less barren region, and then again climbs, and there is Alston at last, strung out on the side of a hill.

The southern approach has been spoiled by the motor trade, that nationwide network of chromatic vulgarity. But the blemish is soon passed, and when the road bears right, almost every prospect pleases (even the 1857 town hall, which seems too big for what is no larger than a village). The church of St Augustine also is modern (1869), though its pennoned weathervane was made in 1770, and the porch contains fragments from a medieval church on the site. Many of the houses are set dizzily above the cobbled street and along the alleys that slope away from it. One house especially catches the eye—a whitewashed residence, three centuries old, near the church gate. To borrow of Miss Wordsworth: '. . . there is a look of ancientry in the architecture of it that pleased me'. The town centre is, appropriately, the remains of the market cross, from which several by-streets thread their own ways among venerable houses. Tucked out of sight, a derelict railway station appears to have been axed but not killed. During a blizzard the railway is Alston's only exit and entry, for the roads may be

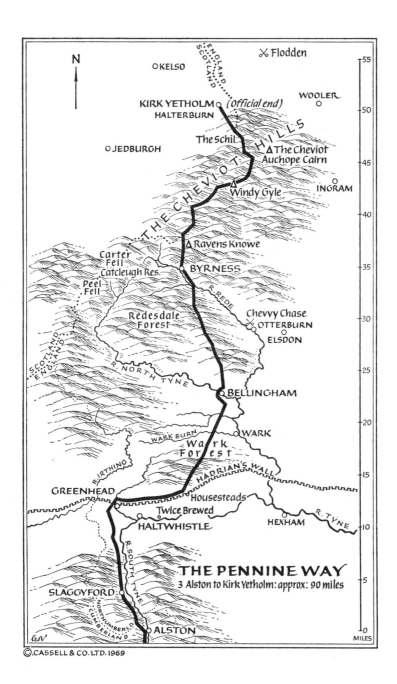

N

× Flodden

o KELSO

ENGLAND
SCOTLAND

WOOLER
o

KIRK YETHOLM o *(Official end)*
HALTERBURN

The Schil

T
H
E

C
H
E
V
I
O
T

H
I
L
L
S

o JEDBURGH

△ The Cheviot
Auchope Cairn

△ Windy Gyle

INGRAM
o

△ Ravens Knowe

Carter
Fell
Catcleugh Res.

BYRNESS

Peel
Fell

Redesdale
Forest

R. REDE

Chevvy Chase
× OTTERBURN
o
ELSDON
o

SCOTLAND
ENGLAND

R. NORTH TYNE

BELLINGHAM o

WARK BURN

o WARK

Wark
Forest

R. IRTHING

HADRIAN'S WALL

GREENHEAD

Housesteads

Twice Brewed

R. TYNE

HALTWHISTLE

HEXHAM
o

R. SOUTH TYNE

THE PENNINE WAY

3 Alston to Kirk Yetholm: approx: 90 miles

SLAGGYFORD o

NORTHUMBERLD.
CUMBERLAND

o ALSTON

MILES
55
50
45
40
35
30
25
20
15
10
5
0

© CASSELL & CO. LTD. 1969

blocked *sine die*. Although the town is in Cumberland, its church belongs to the diocese of Newcastle-upon-Tyne.

The manor of Alston was held by several families—Cliffords, Stapletons, Hiltons—before it came to the Earls of Derwentwater in the reign of James I. Less than a century later, as we remarked at Garrigill, the last Earl of Derwentwater was executed on Tower Hill, and his lands passed ultimately to Greenwich Hospital. Few towns—or few villages, for that matter—are set so superbly. From its hill among hills, Alston looks up to the moors and down at the Tyne.

Many fortunes were made, and one or two lost, in the lead mines on the fells. In 1913 a guidebook noted that mining '. . . is still the main industry apart from agriculture'. One of the Victorian lead assayers was Hugh Lee Pattison (*obiit* 1858), who patented his own recipe for extracting silver from lead ore. In 1852 he was made a Fellow of the Royal Society.

But a greater man than Pattison came to work here—John Smeaton himself, who was born at Austhorpe Lodge, not a great way from Leeds. For sixty-eight years Smeaton lived at Austhorpe; and there he died. In that Lodge he built a forge on the ground floor, a workshop on the first floor, a museum on the second, a study on the third, a store room on the fourth. The twentieth century demolished the lot. Smeaton had been apprenticed to the law, but his genius lay with civil engineering (it was he who first coined the phrase 'civil engineer'). Having studied on the Continent, he returned to lay the foundations of his fame upon a rock, the third Eddystone lighthouse, which he designed and built. While work was in progress he would remain alone on the rock at night, surveying by lamplight. For one hundred and twenty years his lighthouse stood one hundred and twenty feet above the waves. Then it was taken down and re-erected on Drake's Hoe at Plymouth.

Smeaton came to Alston in order to build an underground canal through the fells, but the project hung fire, and was soon out-dated by the railway. Some of Smeaton's work may be seen at Nent Head Force on the outskirts of Alston. Everyone seems to have liked John Smeaton. Robert Stephenson rated him the most intellectual of all engineers, past or present. James Watt declared, 'his example and precept have made us all engineers.' What a race of technical giants begat and were begotten by the Industrial Revolution, with Telford and Brindley among them. The most sophisticated of their tools was a crude steam hammer. Everything else was navvies and nous.

Beyond Alston the Way goes downhill, which is why I always linger on the summit, looking back at the most dramatic county in England. And what a host of images come to mind; some of them visible, others out of sight. Among the former is Penrith—you can see from Hartside Fell—an interesting capital despite the day-and-night traffic, the weekend Lakelanders, the motorway like a loud scar. Penrith is dominated by the ruins of its hilltop castle (once the seat of Richard Crookback) to which Bishop Strickland, of a famous Cumbrian family, added a tower. Thereafter the castle decayed. But in 1913 the townsfolk, hoping that the decay might profitably be pieced together as a tourist attraction, bought the land from the railway company, and set about tidying the ruins. Today the castle and its grassy mound extend our thanks to Penrith's altruistic self-help.

A Grammar School was founded here in 1340; the first church may have been built during the so-called Dark Ages. The present church of St Andrew (was its dedication a sop to the Scots?) was rebuilt in 1719, before architecture went out of fashion. The churchyard contains a group of stones known as the Giant's Grave, which may have been erected by the Celtic Kings of Strathclyde: certainly Penrith is a Celtic word, from the Welsh *pen rhyd* or chief ford.

Wordsworth was schooled awhile here; and here, as a child, he met his wife, Mary Hutchinson. His own mother was buried in the churchyard, having died when Wordsworth was eight years old. Yet those eight years lasted a lifetime:

> My honoured mother, she who was the heart
> And hinge of all our learnings and our loves.

Penrith was the town—or, as we now say, the nearest shopping centre—for John Peel, the most widely known of all Cumbrians.

In so far as I can discover some grains of truth among the tares of tradition, John Peel lived in a squat house near the lane beyond Caldbeck. I have been there several times; it is a land of fells, of which the natives are very proud; whence the old saying, 'Caldbeck and Caldbeck fells are worth the rest of England.' John Peel, at all events, wished to marry Mary White, daughter of a farmer at Uldale, a hamlet down the lane; but both families disapproved. Peel therefore eloped to Gretna Green, having caught the lady while she jumped from her bedroom window (the window was formally shown to me). This elopement took place on Mr Peel Senior's best horse, which the son had borrowed without permission. It is said that the father himself had eloped to Gretna. However, all ended well, for the families accepted the *fait accompli*, and the couple were remarried, this time by the parson at Troutbeck.

Peel, by the way, hunted on foot, for in the trackless mountains a horse can become a hindrance rather than a help. He died in 1854, and was buried near the church door at Caldbeck. Would the world have heard of him, I wonder, were it not for a man of whom the world has not heard—John Woodcock Graves, author of the words of the famous song? I have sat in the room where (says a plaque) that song was written, in a house facing the Caldbeck Inn. Graves himself described how the song came to be written. 'We sat by the fireside hunting over again many a good run, and recalling the feats of each particular hound, or narrow breakneck scapes, when a flaxen-haired daughter of mine came in, saying, Father, what do they say to what Granny sings? Granny was singing my eldest son with a very old rant called "Bonnie Annie". The pen and ink for hunting appointments being on the table, the idea of writing a song to this old air forced itself upon me, and thus was produced, impromptu, "D'ye ken John Peel with his coat so gray?" Immediately after, I sung it to poor Peel, who smiled through a stream of tears which fell down his manly cheeks; and I well remember saying to him in a joking style, By Jove, Peel, you'll be sung when we're both run to earth.'

Would that song still be sung were it not for another unknown man, the composer of its tune, William Metcalfe? For nearly half a century Metcalfe sang in the choir of Carlisle cathedral. In 1868 he happened to hear the song sung to the 'very old rant called "Bonnie Annie"', which so pleased him that he polished it and produced the present melody, the march of the Border Regiment.

Near Penrith, in what used to be the Forest of Inglewood, stands Hutton-in-Forest. In 1212 the village was called Hoton, that being the name of the bow-bearers and forest rangers who held their lands in return for keeping the forest of Plumpton Hay, and for holding the King's stirrup when he mounted his horse at Carlisle Castle. In 1605 the manor was bought from the Hotons by the Fletchers, a Cockermouth family (Christian of the *Bounty* was one of them). The Fletchers then married with the Vanes; and in 1969 one of their descendants, William Morgan Fletcher-Vane, first Baron Inglewood, lived at the great house here.

Nearer yet is Kirkoswald, one of the most endearing villages along the Way, a haven of red sandstone and green trees, with a ruined castle and a College (seat of the Fetherstonhaughs since 1613), previously occupied by twelve priests serving the collegiate church. The College contains a portrait of Charles I which was presented by Charles II in recognition of Sir Timothy Fetherstonhaugh's devotion to the royal cause. The Norman church of St Oswald stands some two hundred yards from its nineteenth-century tower. But Kirkoswald is only one village in a litany of loveliness—Melermby, Glassonby, Langwathy, Lazonby—showing what Cumberland can offer, even in regions farthest from its lakes and mountains.

There is one Wayside place which deserves a fame greater than it has received, for in it was fought the last battle on English soil. The story begins near the start of the Way, where Bonnie Prince Charlie and his army have reached Derby, and hope to capture London. But their own jealousies, and the King's men, send them northward in confusion. Near the West Riding Way, facing Cautley Gap above Sedbergh, a felltop track is still called the Old Scots Raik or road. Even in summertime the going can be damp; yet over that track, in December, the rebels somehow haul their artillery. Having reached the inhospitality of Shap, they divide; one party going east, the other continuing north along what is now the main road to Penrith. These latter are intercepted by the King's brother, the Duke of Cumberland, on the outskirts of Clifton. And there is fought the last battle on English soil. The Jacobite cavalry gives way in a *sauve qui peut*; their Foot stands fast and fights. But there can be no victory for a defeated rabble. In the darkness they retreat to Penrith, having lost half a dozen men.

The church register at Clifton recorded the battle: 'The 19th of December, 1745, ten Dragoons, to wit, six of Bland's, three of Cobham's and one of Mark Kerr's Regiment, buried, who was killed ye evening before by ye Rebells in ye skirmish between ye Duke of Cumberland's army and them at ye end of Clifton Moor next ye town.' Tommy Atkins, the typical English infantryman, had his counterpart at Clifton, and died of his wounds there, three weeks after the battle: 'Robert Atkins, a private Dragoon of General Bland's Regiment, buried ye 8th day of Janry, 1745[6].'

Clifton lies on a mad main road, yet its best parts are worth seeing, even although you cannot hear them. The church of St Cuthbert has withstood much persecution. Shortly before the 1914 war a corner of its burial ground became part of a new road; during the 1960s one of its outbuildings became part of a newer road. Clifton Hall, facing the church, is now a farm, though for centuries it was the seat of the Wyberghs. Defoe may have had the place in mind when he remarked of Cumberland 'almost every gentleman's house is a castle'. Clifton Hall has a peel tower, thirty-seven feet high, whose disintegration I have watched for more than thirty years.

Clifton village is sheer Cumberland—red sandstone and green fells—but Alston town is not sheer Cumberland; the gruffer accent and a wider skyline tell of Northumberland. Almost everywhere else in Cumberland and Westmorland a brook is called a beck; hereabouts it becomes a burn. Burn or beck, the young South Tyne—growing plumper now—follows the Way. A railway follows, too, and the road for Brampton, climbing north. Seeing the roofs of Alston astern, you wonder whether you really had been looking down on the world *from* Alston.

After a mile or so the Way sheers westward from the road, and once again plunges into moorland solitude. At Gilderdale, having crossed a burn, it enters Northumberland.

11 Northumberland: South of the Wall

'NORTHUMBERLAND is the land of far horizons.' So said George Macaulay Trevelyan, a Northumbrian who had walked the by-ways and the highways. 'I have,' he declared, 'two doctors, my left leg and my right. When body and mind are out of gear . . . I know that I have only to call in my doctors and I shall be well again.' But Trevelyan marched in search of something rarer than wellbeing. He sought the summit of experience: 'The fight against fierce wind and snowstorm is among the higher joys of Walking, and produces in shortest time the state of ecstasy.' This he found in his native county, 'where the piled or drifted shapes of gathered vapour are forever moving along the furthest ridge of hills, like the procession of long primeval ages that is visible in tribal mounds and Roman camps and Border towers. . . .'

Northumberland is spacious, ranking next in size after Yorkshire, Lincolnshire, Devon and Norfolk. Its farthest point, some forty miles north of southernmost Scotland, seems almost apart from the rest of England, even as Caithness seems apart from the rest of Scotland. No other English county contains such a vast area of uninterrupted beauty. Trevelyan told the truth poetically when he said: 'In Northumberland alone, both heaven and earth are seen. . . .'

Most of the county's industry is concentrated at or near to Newcastle-upon-Tyne; the rest of Northumberland is rural. In the south-west the twin Tynes wander through moorland and pasture; north-west the Tweed and the Cheviots preside over the widest vistas in England; eastward a coastline stretches seventy miles from Tynemouth to the Border, guarded by castles, decorated with islands; a corridor of sand dunes and seabirds and silence. Swinburne knew this coast:

> Waste waves thereunder
> Are blown in sunder,
> And winds make thunder
> With cloudwide wings . . . .

The great names of Northumberland span the centuries; their achievements bestride the arts, the crafts, the professions. The first of all was St Cuthbert, Bishop of Holy Island, who, though his home was an islet, would sometimes retreat to an even smaller islet—a mere rock—where the site of his cell is marked by a cross. There was George Stephenson, designer of 'The Rocket', born at Wylam . . . Grace Darling and her father from Bamburgh . . . Earl Grey of Reform fame . . . Viscount Grey, who in 1914 watched the lights of Europe go out one by one . . . Sir Daniel Gooch (Great Western was his monument) . . . Birket Foster, a North Shields man, among the finest of our water-colourists . . . Thomas Bewick (we shall have a long talk with him) . . . Wilfrid Gibson, the Hexham poet, who longed

> Just to see the rain
> Sweeping over Yeavering Bell
> Once again!

The Way follows the best of all those worlds, avoiding the industrial zone, wandering instead through forests, beside rivers, over mountains, in a solitude deeper than any since Edale. But the passage from Alston into Northumberland is something more than a crossing-over from one county to another; it is an exchange of hills and ought therefore to become an exchange of names in so far as the Pennines give place to the Cheviots. North of Alston there is no Pennine Way because there are no Pennine Hills. The Way, in short, becomes the Cheviot Way, and would probably bear that name were it not more convenient to travel with a Pennine passport. Certainly it seems inconsistent to speak of the Pennine Way when you are in the heart of the Cheviots and out of sight of the Pennines; and having crossed the border into Scotland, the inconsistency becomes inconceivability.

The matter is made even more confusing because, having entered Northumberland, the Pennine or Cheviot Way follows the Maiden or Roman Way, which has itself been shadowing the Pennine Way since Appleby. The Maiden Way, twenty-six miles long, led from Kirkby Thore in Westmorland to Carvoran in Northumberland. The parts of it which I happen to know best are near Kirkland, under the lee of Alston Fell. I remember sitting there, so steeped in summer and sandwiches that I did not even glance at what I had come to study. The Maiden Way, after all, is a hardy perennial, in flower throughout the year, but a Pennine summer may winter abroad for weeks on end. So there I lay, listening to the birds, even as the Legions must have listened while they marvelled at a colony that shivered their bones for ten months of the year, and then suddenly produced a day out of the bag. Perhaps some ghostly Roman turned in his grave, shocked by my insouciance; perhaps I merely came to the end of my sandwiches, and decided that it was time to be up and Romanizing. The point is, I did get up, and looked northward, and saw there the Roman track, faint as an indelible shadow through the turf, striding a bare and bitter country, over the parapets of Alston, and then entering Northumberland a little to the east of Nog, which is a mountain.

Before joining this ancient road the Way wanders beside a South Tyne so tree-lined and shallow-banked that you can sit with bare feet on the pebbles, fancying yourself back at Middleton-in-Teesdale. There was a Roman camp hereabouts, built on a knoll —they call it Whiteley Castle—which covered nine acres and was probably set to guard the neighbouring mines against Scots or any other picker-up of considerable trifles. It is all grass now, but archaeologists have detected traces of the baths.

Soon the Way passes Kirkhaugh, the church in a 'haff' or enclosure. If Kirkhaugh were a shade smaller it would become invisible. So far as I remember, it contains a farmhouse, a miniature school, another house or so, and a Victorian church with a medieval font and a very thin spire. A man at Lintley Farm told me that the

Alston, Cumberland: the market-place

The Pennine Way near Bellingham,
Northumberland

The Cheviots, near Wooler,
Northumberland

Northumberland National Park mobile
H.Q., near Rothbury, Northumberland

church had been designed by its vicar, and was a copy of one in the Black Forest. In the earlier church they had baptized John Wallis, who was born in 1714 at a farm near by. Many years later Wallis wrote an account of Northumbrian antiquities, with a stirring preface: 'Northumberland being Roman ground, and receiving my first breath in Whiteley Castle, one of their *castra*, I was led by a sort of enthusiasm to an inquiry and search after their towns, their cities, their temples, their baths, their altars, their tumuli, their military ways, and other remains of splendour and magnificence.'

But the Way would be magnificent even if the Romans had never guarded it, for it continues to wander beside flowing water among many trees. There is a bridge over the Tyne—ugly, modern, concrete—though in old days men walked across, and floundered so deeply that they named the place Slaggyford, from the Middle Ages *slag* or slithery. Slaggyford slithers no longer. It is a trim village, built to outlive the climate, and it illustrates how misleading the Way can be, for although the Way approaches from apparent remoteness, the road and the railway are still near by, and in summer Slaggyford becomes quite busy.

I was only once in Slaggyford, yet the visit was rewarding because it introduced me to a literary clergyman who in turn introduced me to the writing of John Story, a Northumbrian poet, whom Carlyle praised for his 'breazy freshness, as of the Cheviots'. Story was among the peasant-poets whose songs are worth reading for their own sake, not simply as curios of unkindly circumstance. The man himself knew this Way as surely as he loved it, but his life was a battle against poverty. In the end he went to London, failed to find his fortune, and died there in 1860, worn down by grubbing crumbs from the gold-paved streets. In those streets he one day closed his eyes, and saw these hills, and anticipated Rupert Brooke by asking

> Rests the light and downy cloud
> Upon Hoseden still?
> Is the sky-lark's carol loud
> Upon Hoseden still?

Is the cuckoo seldom dumb?
And the wild bees, do they come,
As of old, to sip and hum
Upon Hoseden still?

Beyond Slaggyford, near a derelict quarry north of Burnstones, the Way becomes the Maiden Way, and for two miles or more follows the footsteps of the men who made it, through heather and bilberries. Burnstones is a handsome house near a viaduct over Thinhope Burn. According to the old guidebooks it was once an inn. The present house has a walled drive, several byres, and a cluster of trees for wind-break. On this sector the going is grassy and straight, flanked by wire posts and several stiles which climb the wire for no apparent reason.

At Lambley, the ley or pasture for lambs, a disused colliery and its rusty railway write a silent chapter of economic history. Here lived John Charlton, fourteen hundred feet in the clouds, keeping his record of the annual rainfall. Here, too, is a church whose turret contains a bell from a neighbouring nunnery which was raided by the Scots and then swept away by floods. The raid was described by a chronicler at Lanercost Priory along the Cumbrian Way: 'In this assault,' he wrote, 'the Scots surpassed the cruel fury of the heathens . . . they speared little children and left them to expire on pikes and so fly away to Heaven. They burnt consecrated churches . . . they herded together a crowd of little children in the school at Hexham, and having blocked the doors they set fire to the place. They destroyed Lanercost of the Canons Regular, Hexham of the same order, and that of the nuns of Lambley.' Lanercost itself was not wholly destroyed. Part of the walls and roof, well tended by the Ministry of Public Building and Works, now make a church where winter Evensong is said by lamplight and candleshine.

Left and right meanwhile the Way overlooks much loveliness. I remember especially a foot-bridge across Hartley Burn, and another across Kellah Burn, leading to Greenriggs Farm and four wind-bent trees. Under the third tree I mislaid a tin of tobacco, and came back a year later, and found it fresh as the day I had bought it in Alston. But houses larger than Greenriggs are to be seen along the Way, and two of them invite inspection: Bellister Castle and Featherstone Castle.

Fetherstone Castle stands beside the Tyne, and is circled with hills and woods. There was a castle here eight centuries ago, and in all that time only five families have held it. The first, the Fetherstonaughs, occupied the castle from the thirteenth century until the Civil Wars, when the rebels stole it and then sold it to the Earl of Carlisle. In 1711 a member of the Fetherstonaugh family (he was Mayor of Newcastle-upon-Tyne) bought back his own heritage, but the son disposed of it to James Wallace, co-founder of the Hope-Wallace family. During the 1940s the castle was again sold, this time as a school. In 1968 it belonged to Colonel John Clark, a Northumbrian.

When R. S. Surtees was staying at Featherstone he presented Sir Walter Scott with part of what he called an old Border ballad which described the murder of Sir Albany Fetherstonaugh, High Sheriff of Northumberland, in 1530. Quite apart from its value as history, the ballad is useful because it intones the very voice of the Border country:

> Hoot awa' lads, hoot awa'
> Hae ye heard how the Ridleys and Thirwalls and a'
> Ha' set upon Albany Fetherstonaugh,
> And taken his life at Deadmanshaw?
> There was Williemoteswick,
> And Hardriding Dick,
> And Hughie o' Hawden and Will o' the Wa'
> I canna' tell a', I canna' tell a',
> And mony a mair that the Deil may knaw.

Those lines so impressed Scott that he used them in *Marmion*, not knowing that Surtees had composed them himself. However, Surtees certainly caught the local timbre. You will have noticed the Scottish 'hae' and 'mony' and 'mair'. They are, of course, not Scottish; they are relics of an English dialect that was spoken both north and south of the Border.

The second castle, Bellister, is the home of a Northumbrian who graciously invited me to occupy a room there while I explored the countryside. Bellister always was small, and has become smaller through decay; but the present owner has restored much of the medieval remains, and blended them with a less warlike residence. The castle stands at the end of a long avenue that is said to be haunted by the Grey Man or wandering poet who, arriving here one night, was given what poets cannot now earn, which is board and lodging. Unfortunately, the poet arrived at a time when the lord was more than usually preoccupied by the business of killing his enemies before they could forestall the compliment. Noticing a stranger at his table, the lord stared so suspiciously that the guest, being a travelled man and worldly-wise, escaped while he could. Alas, his sudden departure sealed his fate, for the lord, convinced that the stranger was indeed a spy, unleashed a pack of bloodhounds in pursuit. They made the kill near some willows beside the Tyne. Thereafter, says legend, the ghost haunted the castle.

Now suddenly the Way finds itself surrounded not only by castles but also by villages and small towns. Three miles eastward, for instance, is Haltwhistle, whose name means 'the meeting of two rivers near a hill'. Parts of the town, troubled by industry and tourism, tally with Dorothy Wordsworth's description of another eyesore: '. . . frightful, dirty, brickhousey, tradesmanlike, rich, vulgar. . . .' But the best parts of Haltwhistle are good; notably a Norman church and some agreeable old shops set back from the street. Yet neither the shops nor the church is so evocative as the name of Ridley, an ancient Northumbrian family, one of whom, Sir Nicholas Ridley, was High Sheriff of the county. The most famous Ridley, also Nicholas, became Bishop of London in 1550.

No one knows when nor where the future bishop was born. Some say that it was at Unthank Hall, a gabled mansion in a valley near the town, with traces of a medieval tower. Others say that Ridley was born at Willimotswick, once the chief seat of the Ridleys, which also stands on the edge of the town. Most local people accept the story that young Ridley was once reprimanded for pilfering a neighbour's apple orchard. Ridley's first recorded date is 1518, when he went up to Pembroke Hall, Cambridge, whose Master he became. But he had studied, too, at Paris and

Louvain; and preferment came swiftly. He was made chaplain to Henry VIII, a Canon of Canterbury, Canon of Westminster; but he had the misfortune to hold high office at a time when the official religion varied with the Sovereigns. His own star, having waxed and waned with Edward VI, was dimmed when Mary Tudor sent him to the Tower. Yet even there he defied Rome. How, he asked, can the common people understand a Latin liturgy? 'What showing can there be whereas no man heareth, that is to say, understandeth what is said? No man, I mean, of the common people, for whose profit the prayer of the Church ought specially to serve.'

Ridley saw the writing on the wall of his cell. He continued to see it when, with Cranmer and Latimer, he was transferred to Oxford, under orders to debate transubstantiation with Roman theologians from the two universities. In the Tower he had been treated with courtesy, but at Oxford he was cast among thieves and prostitutes in the Bocardo. Cranmer, as all the world used to know, lost his courage, and several times recanted, and at last made brave amends. But Ridley and Latimer never did waver. Accepting death, and rejecting bribes, they were burned alive because they would not disown their Protestant creed. Although one may reject any kind of dogma about Mystery, one cannot discount the heroism of men who supposed that their own orthodoxy was Heaven's *ipse dixit*. Of all the words of dying men, few are so gallant as those that were spoken by Bishop Latimer to Bishop Ridley when the flames began to rise: 'Be of good comfort, Master Ridley, and play the man; we shall this day by God's grace light such a candle in England, as I trust shall never be put out.' Master Ridley took that good advice, for, although Latimer died soon (his brother had set a bag of gunpowder around his neck), the faggots nearest Ridley were damp, and he suffered unspeakably for a long while. His last words were, 'Lord have mercy upon me.' So ended a hideous caricature of Christianity.

From Greenhead, which the Way touches, comes a sweeter air, able to dispel the stench of damp wood and scorched flesh. The church here was designed by that John Dobson who, with Grainger and Clayton, built the Regency glory that is rapidly ceasing to be Newcastle-upon-Tyne. Here stood the Roman fort of

Carvoran, until Progress pulled it down. Now only a few stones are to be seen. In 1915 the village postman noticed an old bucket, as he thought, lying on the ground. He picked it up and showed it to someone who showed it to someone else who passed it to a third party, which is why the exhibit now adorns Chesters Museum, a rare bronze measure into which the native British poured their tribute of corn. An inscription on the measure states that it holds seventeen and a half sextarii (about sixteen pints). In fact, it holds nearly twenty pints: so someone did well, from the quartermaster downward.

The river here is the Irthing; and beside it, hidden among trees, stands Wardraw House, where Sir Walter Scott first met his wife, Charlotte Carpenter. Many years later, when he was fifty-four, Scott began to write a *Journal*, which he kept secretly under lock and key. One of the early entries refers to his love for Williamina Stuart, whom he had met in Edinburgh more than thirty years before: '. . . the crack will remain to my dying day.' Two years later he revised that version: '. . . these things are now matters of calm and solemn recollection, never to be forgotten, yet scarce to be remembered with pain.' How deeply this great Scotsman loved England. Four of the six Epistles in *Marmion* are addressed to Englishmen: its hero, Lord Marmion, is himself an Englishman; the whole of the second canto is set in England; and the battle of Flodden is seen through the eyes of an English squire:

> St George might waken from the dead,
> To see fair England's standards fly.

Both sides of the Border have much to learn from the courteous patriotism of Sir Walter Scott.

Scott, Surtees, Ridley, and a brace of medieval castles: Defoe would hardly have approved, for his own Northumbrian notebook was concerned rather to record the balance of trade: 'Here is the present state of the country describ'd, the improvements . . . in commerce, the encrease of people, and employment for them. . . .' Times had changed since the priest at Garrigill warned his flock that businessmen were heathens: *Nullus christianus debet esse mercator.* However, the priest may have added that the word 'pecuniary' came from the Latin *pecus* or flock of sheep. Judged by that ancient yardstick, the men of Northumberland are moneyed indeed, for most of them still live by sheep, either as farmers or as suppliers of goods and services to those farmers. The principal breeds of sheep are the Black Face and the Cheviot (pronounced Cheeviot). Black Face mountain sheep do best on coarse and mossy soil. They are short-tailed, wide-nosed, with black or mottled faces and legs. Fifty years ago they were the most numerous breed in Britain, though seldom seen south of Lancashire. The Cheviots, on the other hand, are natives and perhaps the most beautiful of all sheep, having white faces, sharp withers, black nostrils, long tails fringed with wool. But they seem less hardy than mountain sheep, and do best on grassy uplands. As long ago as 1900 they and the Suffolks were winning more Smithfield competitions than all the other breeds combined. From Cheviot fleece came Scottish tweed.

These pecuniary matters are discussed in the taproom, or leaning over a gate, or casting beside a burn. There will be moments when a stranger supposes that no other topics ever are broached in these parts, unless someone mentions the hunt, or a football team, or the price of beer. Yet the stranger himself will find more than enough money to occupy his thoughts, for at Thirwall Castle, a fourteenth-century ruin, he approaches the remains of something greater than a castle, and older than the Middle Ages. He has reached the Wall.

12 Northumberland: The Wall

CAESAR invaded Britain, and then came back and did it again, to the dismay of uncountable schoolboys who construe his campaign while they curse his memory.

Caesar, of course, did not come to Britain simply because the wind happened to be blowing in that direction. He came because he wished to increase his own prestige. Having increased it, by punishing a people who showed little respect for Rome, he left his victims more or less to their own devices. Roman merchants succeeded Roman mercenaries; and, as ever, it became fashionable to ape the foreigner. This colonization by imitation continued in peace until the year A.D. 43 when another Caesar felt the need of another triumph. Again Britain became the victim.

The invasion by Claudius was both politic and profitable. The British leader, King Cunobeln of the Catuvellauni, had died; the British themselves continued disrespectful towards Rome and therefore hostile to the Province of Gaul; and their corn and their tin invited attention. So, four legions and their auxiliaries landed in Kent. Within a few weeks they had established themselves along the lower Thames, and were securing their lines of communication with Gaul.

The south and east of Britain offered little resistance to the invasion. They may even have welcomed it. But the men of the hills did resist. Indeed, it took the Romans thirty years to entrench themselves at Eboracum (York), and several more years to contain Wales. Much of this subjugation was the work of Agricola, father-in-law of Tacitus. In A.D. 79, from a base at Deva (Chester), Agricola turned to the north and north-west of Britain, whence he advanced into Scotland, which the Romans called Caledonia. The Scots themselves were Irish. Their wholesale emigration into Caledonia did not take place until the fifth century A.D. Agricola, at all events, built a chain of forts across the Forth – Clyde isthmus. Then came Hadrian, imperial and imperious.

The Emperor Hadrian was an Italian, born in Spain. The Legions loved him because he marched with them, fully armed, and visited their sick-bay. His private life was interesting but not here relevant; though I cannot omit to mention that he ordered his brother-in-law, Servianus, to commit suicide lest he outlive and succeed the Emperor. Servianus obeyed, being then ninety years old. In Britain meanwhile the Emperor faced a problem, which Defoe—with one of his rare sallies into antiquity—summarized neatly: 'The Romans, finding it not only difficult, but useless to them, to conquer the northern Highlands, and impossible to keep them, if conquer'd; contented themselves to draw a line, so we now call it, cross this narrow part of the country, and fortify it with redoubts, and stations of soldiers to confine the Picts and Irish . . . and defend the country from their incursions.' So it was that Hadrian ordered a Wall to be built, such as Europe had never seen before, and is unlikely to see again. From the Tyne to the Solway it stretched, seventy miles uphill and down, curbing the wildest country and the fiercest tribesmen in Britain. Like the Latin poet, Hadrian created something that would outlive him: *Exegi monumentum aere perennius.*

The construction of the Wall was supervised by the imperial Legate, Aulus Platorius Nepos. Within ten years his work was complete; later generations merely added or modified. The Wall is eighty Roman miles long, or about seventy-three English miles. It began at Wallsend-on-Tyne and ended at Bowness-on-Solway. Time has whittled the height of the Wall from twenty to a maximum of six feet, and many sections of it have disappeared, partly through neglect, partly from pilfering. The Wall was built of rubble and mortar, with facing stones quarried along the Way. Archaeologists say that two million cubic yards of rubble and stone went into its making.

Seventeen forts were built on the Wall, from three to seven miles apart. The largest were manned either by a thousand infantrymen or by five hundred cavalrymen; the small forts, by five hundred infantrymen. Each fort contained a year's store of grain, supplied by the natives as tribute (hence the fraudulent bronze measure at Greenhead). Every fort had its baths, shrines, and housing estates for families and civilian auxiliaries. Beside these forts, the Wall was defended by mile-castles holding fifty men each; and between the mile-castles were two turrets, manned by four guards apiece.

On its northern side the Wall was protected by a ditch twenty-seven feet wide and nine feet deep. On its south side ran a vallum or more complicated ditch, set between two mounds of earth. Near by, a military road linked the forts, mile-castles and turrets. Here was a classic feat of engineering, worthy of Vauban himself. Sixteen centuries after the Romans had left Britain, it took an English army three days to travel from Newcastle to Hexham; but a Roman army would have made the journey in five hours. In 1751, having at last learned from the lessons of the '45 rebellion, the English government ordered a turnpike road to be built between Chollerford and Hexham, within sight of the Wall. If a farmer was lucky enough to have a section of the Wall on his land, he sold it as rubble to the contractors.

The dozen miles beyond Greenhead are a hop-skip-and-jump on-and-off the Wall. My own favourite viewpoint is Cuddy's Crags, about half a mile from Housesteads mile-castle, where the hilltops march eastward over a bare moorland tufted with two copses. Beyond and all around, other hills arise, so that the earth resembles a green sea caught and miraculously held in the act of surging. 'Verily,' cried old William Camden, 'I have seen the tract of it over the high pitches and steep descent of the hills, wonderfully rising and falling. . . .' Wonderfully indeed, like an indomitable serpent; and if you would set the march to music, you have no choice but Schubert's striding Ninth, booting its way against climate and crags.

It is irrational to speak of this scene except with awe, not simply at the Wall itself, though that is wonderful enough (the vallum alone consumed twenty-four million man-hours), but also at the men who made it . . . the Roman soldiers chivvying and chasing, the natives hewing and carrying, children gaping and larking, young girls old as Eve, ancient men disapproving every-

thing that was younger than themselves, itchy-palmed go-be-
tweens, short-measure contractors, clerks filling in forms for other
clerks to file; and rain falling, and mist rising, and then again in
spring the corn; and all the while, like shadows on a skyline, the
Caledonians come to spy what it was they must destroy. There,
perhaps, lay the deepest drama; the eternal battle between the
civilized and the savage, the law and the disorder, Ego and Id.
Matthew Arnold passed the final verdict:

> . . . imperial City! that hast stood
> In greatness once, in sackcloth now and tears,
> A mighty name, for evil or for good,
> Even in the loneness of the widow'd years.

The way follows the Wall to a point just west of Housesteads,
where it veers north. So much is to be seen—past and present,
Roman and English, natural and manufactured—that only impressionism can proceed coherently. First comes the fort of Great
Chesters or Aisica, now partly hidden beneath a farm. An aqueduct
carried water to the fort from Caw Burn, two miles away. At
Cawfields the Wall is well preserved, but soon declines near a
turret. Then again it reappears, and at Winshields reaches its
summit, nearly thirteen hundred feet above the Solway Firth,
which can be seen in clear weather. And Cross Fell can be seen,
too; the crux of Christianity saluting the height of paganism.

From Peel Crag a lane leads southward a few hundred yards
to the Twice Brewed Inn on the Carlisle road. The original inn,
a port-of-call for carters and pack-horsemen, became Twice
Brewed Farm, so a new inn was built farther to the west, near what
is now a Youth Hostel called the Once Brewed.

It seems strange that England was so tardy in conserving its
largest monument. Nowadays, of course, one expects that any
ancient monument will be razed by a new power house or another
motorway; but one does not expect that sort of vandalism from
men for whom education meant Latin and Greek. Even Celia
Fiennes mentioned the Wall by dismissing it. The road, she remarked 'was exceeding steep, full of great rocks and stones,
some of it along on a row the remainder of the Picts walls or

Fortification. . . .' Miss Fiennes was concerned rather with the weather: '. . . its a black moorish sort of ground and so wet I observ'd as my man rode up that sort of precipice or steep his horses heeles cast up water every step . . .'

Defoe offered his customary apology for mentioning the past: 'Here I must take notice, though, as I have often said, antiquity is not my business, that we saw the remains, and that very plain, of the antient work which they call Severus's Wall, or Hadrian's Wall, or Graham's Dyke, for it is known by all these.' Of the state of the Wall he said nothing. The name Graham's Dyke, by the way, is not Caledonia's attempt to co-opt Hadrian as an Irishman. Graham was old Scots *Graem*, meaning the Devil; and if it existed when the Picts did, it probably expressed their opinion of the Romans.

Not until the nineteenth century did the Wall become a fashionable curio. The fort of Chesters, for example, owes much to John Clayton, on whose estate it stood: and not only Chesters, for he bought whatever parts of the Wall were for sale, and acquired five forts. His museum at Chesters is an abiding monument. But Clayton's interest had been preceded by William Hutton, a Birmingham businessman with a flair for history and hiking.

When Hutton was nearly eighty years old he walked from Warwickshire to Northumberland, averaging twenty miles each day, and thence along the Wall and back again. For his journey he chose a sober uniform of black—a 'kind of religious travelling warrant' he called it—and a satchel for maps. Like Miss Fiennes, he walked with a weather-eye: 'To this little packet I fastened with a strap, an umbrella in a green case, for I was not likely to have a six weeks' tour without wet. . . .' Hutton did not travel the whole way alone. He was accompanied into Cumberland by his daughter, she riding behind a servant; her task being to prepare lodgings for her father, who started at four o'clock each morning and breakfasted at seven, having travelled nearly eight miles by way of aperitif. At Penrith he parted from his daughter who went south to Lancaster, until he should join her there. The Wall he walked alone, from west to east and back again; but men before and after have confounded his modest pride in the achievement:

'Perhaps I am the first man that ever travelled the whole length of the Wall, and probably the last. . . . Who then will say he has, like me, travelled it twice?' One feels that many a Roman soldier travelled it twice, and thrice, and for a fourth time maybe, until the mist and snow so mocked his memories of Naples or Provence that he cursed the evening when that recruiting sergeant fuddled him with wine at the tavern. And while he marched he may have chanted the couplet in which Florus thanked the gods that he was not with Hadrian, trudging the contours of a cold colony:

> Ego nolo Caesar esse,
> ambulare per Britannos.

Neither before nor after, one feels, did the Way so resoundingly echo the lilt which Rupert Brooke imagined:

> From the hills and valleys earth
> Shouts back the sound of mirth,
> Tramp of feet and lilt of song
> Ringing all the road along.

Even so, Hutton rushed in where many younger men would faint to tread. Having walked the Wall and back in a week, he became a seven days' wonder: 'It has excited the curiosity of the towns and causes me frequently to be stopped in the street to ascertain the fact.' Hutton's return journey of six hundred miles lasted thirty-five days. The cost of board and lodging for himself, his daughter, the servant, and a horse averaged six shillings each per day. He lost a stone in weight, but found that his shoes were still good for another six hundred miles . . . our own cattle seem to have become thin-skinned. William Hutton would not recognize the road whose high-summer whine now disturbs even the meditations of Peel Crag; but if he could return at twilight in December, he might yet relive his wonder on first seeing the Wall: 'I forgot I was upon a wild common, a stranger, and the evening approaching . . . lost in astonishment, I was not able to move.'

A village has been named after the Wall, as though to maintain a tradition from Walltown, a village that has disappeared except for one farmhouse (when Hutton passed by he found two Roman altars there, used as a water trough). In 1555 Bishop Nicholas Ridley's family lived at Walltown, and it was to them that he wrote his last letter to 'Dear Cousin, John Ridley of the Walltown'—asking John to remind his wife, the bishop's sister, that the Haltwhistle folk used to say she loved Nicholas more than any other of her brothers. A postscript praised the gentle manners of the bishop's niece, John's daughter, Elizabeth Ridley, whose descendants were living near the Wall during the twentieth century.

In 1962, while making a television programme about the Wall, I called at Sewingshields Farm, near the site of Sewingshields Castle, sometimes known as Arthur's Castle because that King and his Court lay there under an evil spell. Sir Walter Scott mentioned the castle in *Harold the Dauntless*: Seven Shields Castle he called it, yet even in those dim days

> No towers are seen
> On the wild heath, but those that Fancy builds.

An inscription in one of the farm buildings recalls that this sector of the Wall, which no longer stands above ground, was made at the time of Gellius Philippus; and in so far as it was built of stones taken from the Wall, the farm itself is Roman. When I congratulated a farmhand on working at such a classic place, he looked blank.

'Built on't auld stones? Nay, there's summat ah never knawed.'

Soon after that brief encounter, having wandered off the Way and wishing to find someone who could put me on to it again, I saw an old shepherd training his dog in a field at the foot of the hill on which I stood. I hailed him, and he replied, but I could not understand what he was saying, which piqued me because I had assumed that I knew the North. My companion, a Westmorland farrier, undertook to translate; but not even he could do so, for the shepherd's words were of another land and of an older generation.

Although the Wall dominates this part of the Way, it is not the only ancient monument. A little to the south are Hexham, a former city, and Blanchland, a perennial village. Modern Hexham is prosperously 'brickhousey', cluttered with more garages and serve-yourselves than is good for anyone's landscape. They manufacture something here, but I have forgotten what it is. Old-fashioned Hexham looks different, and has another kind of history. In or about the year 674 Queen Etheldreda gave this place to Wilfred, a monk from Holy Island, who built an abbey in the heart of a diocese so famous that it became known as Hexhamshire. In 821 the diocese was merged with that of Holy Island; and fifty years later the Danes destroyed the church. During the twelfth century the Archbishop of York founded Hexham Priory for Black Friars or Austin Canons. In 1296 the Scots came down and destroyed the nave of the priory. Seven centuries later the nave was rebuilt, so that Hexham is again the largest church in Northumberland, and for splendour among the first half-dozen in the North.

Near the Georgian shamble or market shelter the townsfolk placed a sandstone plinth, crowned with a lamp and a Cross 'for the common good placed here near the site of the old market'. And on the plinth they inscribed some lines by their own poet, Wilfrid Wilson Gibson.

Blanchland seems best described conventionally, as one of the loveliest villages in the north country. It is set—you may say it is hidden—among heathery moors, beside the River Derwent, under the lee of high woods. Its name refers to the Abbey for White Canons, founded during the twelfth century by Walter de Bolbec. One of the Blanchland abbots was summoned to Parliament by Edward I. But the Scots soon got wind of the abbey, and now only their destruction remains. The parish church, however, they spared. During the sixteenth century it began to collapse; during the eighteenth century it was restored by the Lord Crewe estates.

John Wesley came to Blanchland, having set out from Newcastle in a blizzard. He preached in the churchyard, standing beside the Cross. On the church wall, despite bitter weather, the village children (said Wesley), sat like mice, making no sound while he spoke. There is a tradition that Wesley preached a second sermon here, in the Crewe Arms, which was then an inn (though formerly the Abbot's house), named after an eighteenth-century Prince

Bishop of Durham. The bishop's wife, Dorothy, was the daughter of General Forster, who lost his lands—and nearly forfeited his life—by supporting the Old Pretender in 1715. The present dining-room of the inn used to be a ballroom. Another room, called the Dorothy Forster Room, contains that lady's portrait.

But all this beauty lies along the southern border. The Way itself is northward bound; and at Hotbank Crags it takes leave of the Romans, even as the Romans took leave of Britain, having long since ceased to be an army of Romans. The *gravitas* of Rome —its austerely patrician ideals—were superseded by a cosmopolite plutocracy and a mob demanding its dole of bread-and-circuses. Private soldiers became generals; generals became emperors; and while barbarians advanced against Rome, other barbarians pierced even the Roman Wall. But it was not only the Wall which fell, for when the last legion did leave Britain, the deserted islanders faced another invasion. Edward Gibbon etched their plight with twelve words: '. . . the seacoast of Britain . . . was exposed to the depradations of the Saxons.' Bede recorded the new invasion, and with it the traumatic birth of the English people.

Yet seedtime and harvest come and go and return, enriching a countryside which Wilfrid Gibson painted in the poem that was inscribed on the Hexham plinth:

> O, you who drink my cooling waters clear,
> Forget not the far hills from whence they flow,
> Where over fell and moor and year by year
> Spring summer autumn winter come and go
> With showering sun and rain and storm and snow;
> Where over the green bents forever blow
> The four free winds of heaven; where time falls
> In solitary places calm and slow,
> Where cries the curlew and the plover calls. . . .

Neither plover nor curlew calls upon the next sector, for the Way bears north-east, into a great Forest.

A Cheviot farm

Burnhead Farm, Kirk Yetholm,
Roxburghshire

Crossing the border: near Kirk Yetholm,
Roxburghshire

Flodden Field, Northumberland

13 Northumberland: North of the Wall

D O not be dismayed by the conifers which the Forestry Commission has foisted on these Northumbrian skylines. Above all, do not be drawn into an argument, either with the foresters who admire them or with the farmers who abominate them. Both sides feel little concern for anything except money; and each will assure you that its own kind of moneymaking is the more likely to prosper the nation. For better or for worse, the Forestry Commission has enclosed hundreds of miles of moorland where once the moss troopers lay swaddled in their plaid. From the Wall to the Cheviots, too many skylines are smudged with monotonous spruce. Granted, these alien invaders employ more men than could ever live by sheep. Granted also that this kingdom contains at least forty million more people than it can comfortably hold. Therefore it may be argued that—until the surplus can fly to the Moon, or otherwise be picked off by Progress—it is better to see foresters at work, even although their trees are alien, than to watch estate agents at work, scheduling land which by some oversight the Almighty omitted to 'develop'.

Under the shadow of these trees the Way becomes first a footpath and then a drovers' track, making for Wark Forest, only to shy away from it, as though fearing to fathom such artificial darkness. While the Way makes up its mind as to whether it really will enter Wark Forest, the Wayfarer himself has a small duty to perform, for here he takes leave of a spritely fellow-traveller, Celia Fiennes, whose own ways went eastward to Edinburgh, and our paths will not cross again.

Now when Miss Fiennes reached Westmorland, she 'tooke a

Guide . . . and so went for Scotland'. Having explored such a large area, without a guide, why did she lose her bump of location at the River Eden? The answer is, she neither lost it nor hired a guide to impersonate it. Her guide was what we would now call a guard, and his duties emphasize that this was once the wildest and most blood-stained part of Britain. Here, when the Assize Judge came, he was given an armed escort by the tenants of every manor through which he passed; and the escort was made stronger the nearer he approached to Scotland, for, as Macaulay observed: 'No traveller ventured into that country without making his will.' Whether Miss Fiennes made a will before entering Scotland, no one knows. If she did, she must have cancelled it, because her last will was dated 6 November 1738, forty years after her final visit to the Northumbrian Way. As though expressly in order that we might bid adieu to two birds with one codicil, her will was witnessed by another of our fellow-travellers, Daniel Defoe. What good talk they must have shared, those intrepid explorers of a widely unknown island: he, the butcher's son, the voice of *homines novi*; she, the patrician, keen-eyed as he, and to the very end as up-to-date, but less deafened by what Adam Smith was about to say. What a tribute to the individual and civic sanity of their time and place, that two such odd assortments could meet upon such easy terms, and so freely share the goodwill which disagrees without becoming disagreeable.

It is pleasant to report that Celia Fiennes made her will when she was seventy-seven and enjoying 'perfect health, praise be to my good God, but increasing in infirmitys of body. . . .' She begins very sensibly by requiring a simple funeral 'without ostentation . . . I forbid all escutcheons or bearers'. The cortège itself must be 'as private as can be a hearse and one coach'. Like many other old ladies, she leaves a titbit to her doctor; but William Butcher, loyal servant for fifteen years, receives (in modern terms) several hundred guineas, as does her personal maid. Even the 'cookemaide' and washerwoman are remembered. Of the manuscripts of her remarkable travels she makes no mention at all, yet in them she wrote her own epitaph, being herself foremost among those who 'spend some of their tyme in Journeys to visit their native Land,

and be curious to inform themselves of the pleasant prospects, good buildings, different produces and manufactures of each place'.

As for her fellow-traveller, Defoe, the Northumbrian Way so impressed him that he changed his tune, or at any rate repented of ever having whistled it: 'I cannot but say,' he confessed, 'that since I have entered upon the view of these northern counties, I have many times repented that I so early resolved to decline the delightful view of antiquity, here being so great and so surprising a variety. . . .' Surprisingly great indeed: and most surprising when the Way at last enters Wark Forest, for the going is like nothing on earth because your feet are not on the ground. Densed-in by soundless spruce, you tread a nether soil of fibrous droppings, in a close-canopy plantation that destroys all flora by shading them from the sun and then by stifling them with needle-leaves. In summer the forest resembles an ill-lit Turkish bath; in winter, a cistern with a tendency to leak.

These coniferous woods are not a novelty to Britain. Much of the ancient Caledonian Forest was pine. In 1705 Lord Hamilton planted eight hundred acres of Scotch pine on his estates; twenty years later a larch wood was planted at Dawyck; and in 1919 the Forestry Commission began to repair the wartime havoc among woodlands. Crippled by taxation, many noblemen and lairds sold land to the Commission at rock-bottom prices. Soon the grouse moors and deer forests bristled with pine from Corsica, spruce from Norway, hybrid larch from Japan. This see-saw of deforestation followed by afforestation was not new. As long ago as 1685, when Englishmen were shocked to discover that the King's ships were being made from foreign oak, an Admiralty spokesman (his name was Samuel Pepys) pointed out that the King had no other choice, for in all Britain there was not enough oak to defend Britain. Industry had felled it as firewood. The problem in 1969 is different, and may be stated thus: Progress having brought us to a point where every kind of beauty—and health itself—must be sacrificed to the business of filling our bellies, it is better that Northumberland should be sprinkled with foreign trees rather than spattered with native factories.

Within Wark Forest a stranger may be misled by tracks in various stages of obsolescence, suggesting Kipling's dilemma:

> They shut the road through the woods
> Seventy years ago.
> Weather and rain have undone it again,
> And now you would never know
> There was once a path through the woods . . .

Near Hawkside the Way emerges and becomes a grassy drive, but at Kimmins Cross it re-enters the woods, as though to emphasize that this is the Border Forest Park, the largest of its kind in Britain, established in 1955 on a tract of reclaimed heath stretching from the Wall to the Scottish Lowlands. Six forests comprise this new landscape—Kershope, Newcastleton, Wauchope, Redesdale, Kielder, Wark—and Wark itself is divided into south, central and north sections.

Now for a second time the Way comes into the open and then returns to the shade, and once more emerges, again as a grass track. Soon it crosses Warks Burn, a tributary of the North Tyne. I was last here in April, when the leaves come out to play, and a wren flits from sprig to sprig, spilling his song like the best of good news. Warks Burn flows through a deep ravine dappled with hawthorn; though why they call it Warks is something I never did understand, because the burn is obviously named after Wark village. If you do come here, be sure to visit Low Steads, one of the snuggest little farms along the Way, tacked on to a byre that is reached via a block of stone steps.

Wark village lies off the Way. There are two Northumbrian Warks; one on Tweed, the other on Tyne. Wark-on-Tyne was the capital of Tynedale when these parts were Scottish. Here the Scottish Kings held court, in a Norman castle long since razed. The present castle, called Chipchase, recalls Wark's medieval importance, *chip* meaning a market. The fourteenth-century tower blends well with the Jacobean additions. As Celia Fiennes remarked of another place: 'It looks finely.'

At Houxty Burn the Way crosses a wooden bridge, in a setting so sylvan that you might fancy yourself on a backwater of the Thames which Robert Bridges loved:

> Straight trees in every place
> Their thick tops interlace,
> And pendant branches trail their foliage fine
> Upon his watery face.

Houxty Farm stands on a hill beyond Wark. In 1898 it was a down-at-heel place, but so haunted by blackcock that Abel Chapman bought it as a bird sanctuary, and then rebuilt it, and laid out fine gardens, and made his home there. Like Thomas Bewick and the Kearton Brothers, Chapman was a dedicated naturalist. His first book, *Bird Life of the Borders*, appeared in 1889. He travelled widely and wrote many other nature books. 'The Borders,' he declared, 'were my first love and today, sixty years later, remain my last. Never during the long period has the charm of the Cheviots and of Ettrick Forest, with all the far-flung mountain-land that lies between, abated or suffered eclipse.'

Wark was a local capital; the next village, Bellingham, still is. The Way thither crosses some streams, follows a track, and so enters the village via the Hexham road.

Bellingham—they call it Bellinjam—is not the *belle* but the *bel*, meaning a hilltop. Shall we say that its appearance is more than skin-deep? I like especially the Regency bridge and a small church massively roofed against Scottish firebrands. But the chief showpiece is a wooded walk, across six foot-bridges to a waterfall, Hareshaw Linn, which I first saw on a morning so bitterly cold that the spray had formed stalactites and stalagmites. On my next visit the afternoon was so intensely hot that one of the townsmen collapsed and was carried home by three Boy Scouts from Battersea. On my third visit the evening was so misty that I turned back at the second bridge lest all six of them vanish from sight. Small wonder that Dr Johnson remarked: 'When two Englishmen meet, their first talk is of the weather.'

There is a derelict colliery to the north of Bellingham. When I passed it in 1950 the place was very active, but they closed it soon afterwards, and in 1968 I found that even the colliers' cottages had disappeared. The great house here, Hesleyside Hall, contains a spur that was used by the Charlton family more than three centuries ago, not on horses but against horsemen, for, when food ran low, the lady of the house served her lord with the spur on a dish, to remind him that his next meal must be stolen from somebody else's larder. Charltons still reside at the Hall.

Over the hills, not much above an hour's walk, lies Kirkharle, which is linked with Hesleyside because the Hall contains a second heirloom, the plans for its gardens, drawn in 1776 by Capability Brown, a Kirkharle man. There are no shops at Kirkharle; neither pub nor garage nor bus stop; only a stately farmhouse, a church that was rebuilt in 1336, a comely vicarage, and a row of cottages whose gardens would please Brown himself. In 1728 the lord of the manor, Sir William Loraine, erected a stone in a field near the church to commemorate his ancestor, Robert Loraine, who, says an inscription, '. . . was barbarously murdered in this place by the Scots in 1483 for his good services to his country against their thefts and robbery, as he was returning from the church alone, where he had been at his private devotions'. They are proud of Capability Brown at Kirkharle. Indeed, one of those trim-garden cottagers gave me tea while he recounted facts and legends about a local lad who made so good that his fame spread throughout England and across the Channel.

Lancelot Brown was born in 1716. As a boy he went to work in the gardens of that Sir William whose ancestor the Scots had murdered. So great was the youngster's skill, his temperament so sunny, that he was soon invited to work with William Kent, the architect and pioneer landscape gardener. While still a young man Brown was designing gardens for some of the greatest houses in the land. The Dukes of Northumberland and of Marlborough were only two of his patrons. All over England, Brown's capability made its mark, and not only on the landscape, for he became High Sheriff of Huntingdon and Cambridge and father-in-law to Lord Holland.

I visit Kirkharle once or twice each year, and, having arrived, I stroll across to Capheaton, the home of the Swinburnes, by way of Stamfordham, which lies hidden in trees among fields beside a steep green. During the eighteenth century Stamfordham held an important cattle fair; now it is unknown, except among those who happen to know it, or to know that it bred a man not less influential than Brown of Kirkharle. The story began in 1849 when the wife of the vicar of Stamfordham gave birth to a son, Arthur John Bigge, who became a Gunner and had Napoleon III's son in his battery. When that Prince was killed during the Zulu War, it fell to Lieutenant Bigge to break the news to the French Empress. This he did so tenderly that the bereaved mother invited him to remain awhile as her guest. In that entourage the subaltern was introduced to Queen Victoria; and she also admired his forthright yet tactful manner. Within a few months he was appointed groom-in-waiting. Thereafter, as we say, he never looked back: assistant private secretary to the Queen; secretary in succession to Lord Ponsonby; then secretary to King George V, who rewarded his lifelong service with the Barony of Stamfordham. When this great courtier died, in 1931, the King wrote in his diary: 'Dear Bigge passed away peacefully at 4.30 today. I shall miss him terribly. His loss is irreparable.' Historians have shown that the vicar's son played more than a walking-on part in the drama of the twentieth century.

The lane from Stamfordham to Capheaton is as beautiful as any in Northumberland, not least because so few people ever use it. For all I know, I am the only person who does use it. Six times I have come here—four by car, two on foot—without seeing or hearing anyone at all. Perhaps that is why the trees here seem nobler, the grass greener, the surge of the hills more stately than anywhere else along the Northumbrian Way. This is among those places of which G. M. Trevelyan said: 'The silence is broken only by water's ancient song, as the burn makes its way down rocky hollows towards the haymakers at work under a sycamore beside the grey stone farm below.'

Capheaton must have been born tidy. In such a well-bred hamlet even a stray bus ticket would glare like a placard. A row of sleek cottages points the way to the seat of the Swinburnes, Capheaton Hall, which, like their baronetcy, dates from the Restoration. The

Hall once contained a cat and a punch bowl, where from hangs a remarkable story: the father of the first baronet was murdered by a rebel during the Civil Wars, and for safety's sake his small son was sent to a monastery in France where he lived more or less forgotten until, quite by chance, the monastery was visited by some of his cousins, the Radcliffes. Impressed by the boy's family likeness, they took him back to England, and there he was able to prove his identity by describing the markings on a cat and a punch bowl which he remembered from his early childhood. The Swinburnes had owned Border castles since the Middle Ages. One of the Swinburnes, Sir William, was cousin to that Earl Derwentwater whose dinner bell summons the faithful at Garrigill. A later squire, Sir John Swinburne, married a niece of the Duke of Northumberland, and so begat Admiral Charles Swinburne, who married Lady Jane Henrietta, fourth daughter of the Earl of Ashburnham. Their son was the poet Algernon Charles Swinburne, a misfit if ever there was one. 'Generally and admirably ignorant,' was Swinburne's description of himself at Eton. Up at Balliol he read discursively in four or five languages, which is one reason why he came down without a degree. Thereafter he lived chiefly in London, among other Bohemian psychopaths. In so far as free association is a condition of psycho-analysis, no man can deeply analyse the dead; but even a layman perceives that Swinburne's tragedy was contained in the family motto, *Semel et Semper*, which may be translated as 'Always the same'. In other words, a part of his emotional life never grew up. Because the family had for centuries been Christian monarchists, he chose to become a republican atheist; and although the gods had granted him brilliance and birth, he turned sour and remained so until he died. Watts-Dunton, who nursed Swinburne's old age at Putney, wrote to the dead poet's sister: 'his antagonism against Christianity . . . increased with the years . . . and at the last (if I must say what I am sorry to say) it was bitterer than ever.'

Despite his eminent unsuitability, one wishes that Swinburne could be ranked among the sons of Northumberland, but the truth is, he was never more than an ungrateful orphan. Only his earliest childhood and some of the Eton holidays were spent at

Capheaton. For the rest, he chose to live hundreds of miles south of the Border, which diminished somewhat his praise of it:

> In fierce March weather
> White waves break tether,
> And whirled together
> At either hand,
> Like weeds uplifted
> The tree-trunks rifted
> In spars are drifted
> Like foam or sand . . .

Many people can write that sort of thing once or twice; but to maintain and to improvise upon it through hundreds of pages of varying metres—that belongs only to genius. One may say that it belongs only to Swinburne. His style, of course, has fallen from fashion; his predilections are now widely accepted; his republicanism is derided because it was aristocratic; his atheism is a mere *fait accompli*. Yet it seems early days to write him off, for, if the ancient norms of human life are indeed destined to be supplanted, then posterity may find in Swinburne both a precedent and a panache.

Appearances are famous for their powers of deception, and genius continues to confound the geneticists; even so, the more one thinks about Swinburne, the more one marvels that such a family and such a landscape should have begotten such a freak. Sipping absinthe in a Bloomsbury bedsitter . . . swooning over Baudelaire amid the dog-ridden fastness of Wimbledon Common . . . what have such things to do with the Way at Gib Shiel Farm, which is a house and a byre and one tree, set near the summit of Padon Hill, ringed with an interminable dry-stone wall, reached by a track so lonely that, if it were signposted, the words would surely say To Heaven? In order to get here the Way has crossed the Bellingham–Otterburn road, and then plodded through heather and marsh, against a wind whose winter will burn your cheeks, on to summits in sight of the Cheviot Hills. This is Redesdale, the wildest and fiercest of all Border battlegrounds; both sides so given over to brigandage that they joined forces in a war against mankind. In 1555 the King's Commissioners rated the Redesdale men as savage as the Scots; and the old ballads added their own assent:

> I lighted down, my sword did draw,
> I hack'd him into pieces sma',
> I hack'd him into pieces sma'.

The Border battles needed no declaration. They were waged even when the two kingdoms had signed a truce. History proves that the Scots were the more brutal, the more transgressive, yet there cannot have been much to choose between the worst of both sides. Sometimes a tribe of horsemen rode out. At other times only a dozen came, creeping like snakes through the heather. A brand, a sword, a shriek; then silence; and after the silence a rainbow of midnight flames and the terror of bleating sheep as a strange dog harried them over the Border. Occasionally the battle was fought between armies, as at Chevvy Chase on the outskirts of Otterburn, an unpleasing village, except for one or two cottages and a vener-able tweed factory beside the Burn, where for generations the Waddell family have manufactured a famous commodity. If all rural factories were half so handsome as this, everyone would feel the better for it. Summer after summer I come to the Burn and gaze across the water at the factory's flower-bright garden.

The Battle of Chevy Chase is so well known that few English-men could say why, when or where it took place. A Cross used to mark the alleged site of the battle, but it was removed two centuries ago to make way for a wider road. The present Cross stands on a knoll, about a mile to the west of the village, and somewhere very near to it was fought the battle of which Sir Philip Sidney wrote: 'I never heard the old song of Percy and Douglas, that I found not my heart moved more than with a trumpet.'

This famous encounter began during the summer of 1388 when the Scots under the Earl of Douglas ravaged Durham and North-umberland. At Newcastle, which had shut its gates against them, they were defied by Sir Henry Percy, whose banner they cap-tured. In those years, of course, a banner signified honour, which itself symbolized life. When therefore Douglas boasted that he would fly his trophy from Dalkeith Castle, Percy vowed to avenge both the insult to himself and the injury to his fellow-countrymen. Having mustered an army, he set off in pursuit.

At Otterburn the Scots halted, lying in wait for the enemy: and there the two sides met by moonlight, on 19 August 1388. Despite their long day's march, the English attacked at once. Froissart described the battle, having heard about it from an eye-witness, but the Border ballads chant their own *ex parte* statements. Some facts, however, can be verified. We know, for example, that the Earl was killed and that Sir Henry was captured. A Scottish version, *The Battle of Otterburn*, sets the ghostly scene:

> The moon was clear, the day drew near,
> The spears in flinders flew,
> And many a gallant Englishman
> Ere day the Scotsmen slew.

The English version, *Chevy Chase*, was for centuries the favourite ballad among Northumbrians. The present Duke of Northumberland—the only English Duke who maintains his own piper—sometimes hears the ballad sung to a swirl of those pipes:

> Of fifteen hundred Englishmen
> Went home but thirty-three;
> The rest in Chevy Chase were slain,
> Under the greenwood tree.

The ballad ends with a noble stanza:

> God save our King, and bless this land
> With plenty, joy, and peace;
> And grant henceforth that foul debate
> Twixt noble men may cease.

Four centuries later another Northumbrian said the same thing: 'It is horrid to contemplate the ferocious battles of that day, between men descended from the same stock, and bearing the same names on both sides of the Border, only divided from each other by a river, a rivulet, a burn . . .' So wrote old Thomas Bewick, a

Borderer who claims our affectionate esteem, partly because he was a great artist, partly because he knew and loved the Way.

Thomas Bewick was born in 1782, in the parish of Ovingham, away to the south-east. His father—a peasant who rented a one-man coalmine—sent the boy to be schooled by a parson who grounded him in Latin and arithmetic. At the age of fourteen Bewick went as apprentice to a Newcastle engraver, but without receiving any tuition in the art that he was soon to master. His *Memoir* declares: 'I was never a pupil to any drawing master. . . .' Despite an arduous apprenticeship, Bewick found time to read good books and to walk prodigious distances: 'In my solitary walks . . . the first resolution made was that of living within my own income.' There spoke the voice of northern self-help; there it still does speak, preserved in the pages of his *Memoirs*.

Like many a country lad, Bewick tried his fortune in London, but soon wearied of the soot. Home haunted him: 'The scenery of the Tyne seemed altogether to form a Paradise, and I longed to see it again.' So, he decided to go home. A friend asked whether he would return to London: '"Never" was my reply, at which he seemed both surprised and displeased.'

At home the prodigal prospered. He married the daughter of his former employer—'I had formed a strong attachment for her' —and received a business partnership from his father-in-law. He also resumed the walks that were his university: 'I often stopped with delight by the sides of woods, to admire the dangling woodbines and roses, and the grasses powdered or spangled with drops of dew.' Like Tennyson, he knelt before the flowers: 'The primrose, the wild hyacinth, the harebell, the daisy, the cowslip . . . these altogether, I thought, no painter ever could imitate.' That, of course, was written in years before people had accustomed themselves to a framed portrait of the artist's Unconscious.

In 1791 Bewick began work on the illustrations for the first volume of his classic *History of Birds and their Figures*, which owed much to his own observations in these hills. The task demanded wide research and frequent correspondence: 'Many a letter I have written after being so wearied out with the labours of the day, that I often forgot how to spell the commonest words.' Bewick's labours included the engraving of plates for banknotes and cheques, and his modesty was such that the *Memoirs* say less about his books than about the difficulty of detecting forged banknotes. Once or twice, however, he does discuss the technique of his art, and then a grateful pride appears: 'At that time this department of the arts was at the very lowest ebb in this country. . . . It may perhaps be of some use to know the part I took in recovering or bringing into use, this to me new art, as far as I was able, with the slender means at my disposal. . . .' But chiefly he wrote of Northumberland and the ancient norms: 'I have often thought, that not one-half of mankind knew anything of the beauty, the serenity, and the stillness of summer mornings in the country, nor have ever witnessed the rising sun shining forth upon the new day.' Bewick's *Memoir* reveals him as a man brusque as Cobbett, tender as St Francis, wise as a shepherd. Like Brown of Kirkharle, he looked back in gratitude on a memorable life: 'To be placed in the midst of a wood in the night, in whirlwinds of snow, while the tempest howled above my head, was sublimity itself.'

Bewick would certainly have met a wind on Padon Hill, for it is 1,230 feet up, the highest on the Way since Cross Fell. He would have exulted also in the skyline above Elsdon, a short walk from Otterburn. Certainly he would have discovered that a nation's memory may, like the mind of a child, relive traumatic terror. For example, a friend of mine, who farms at High Shaw, told me that 'raiking' is still observed as a legacy of the Border wars. In other words, some farmers drive their flocks on to the hills at twilight. Why? Because the grass there is greener? Or the air more bracing? By no means; the farmers are repeating the nightly drill of medieval forebears who chose a hilltop as their watch-tower against the Scots. On those heights, when the warning beacons blazed, sheep were less vulnerable than they would have been in a valley fold. But if you ask a farmer why he indulges this nightly charade he will either decline to answer or proceed to offer a rationalization which he *may* believe but probably does not. The custom of raiking is dying, and seems likely to disappear within a generation or two. Until that time, a handful of Northumbrians observe it religiously:

> Therefore from such danger lock
> Every one his loved flock;
> And let your dog lie loose without,
> Lest the wolf come, as a scout
> From the mountain, and ere day
> Bear a kid or lamb away.

When John Fletcher, a Sussex man, uttered that warning three centuries ago, he spoke for some of the Borderers today. So much for the spirit of the Border battles; their substance may be seen in the peel tower at Elsdon.

The entry into Elsdon from Otterburn is marred by a breaker's yard and other mechanized symptoms, but the sore eye is soothed by a village green whose cottages confront one another across the sward, overlooking an ancient pound. The shop here is so leisurely that, were you to ask for last month's newspaper, you would still sound ahead of the times.

Set on a knoll, Elsdon church is dedicated to St Cuthbert, whose body, they say, rested here during its devious journey along and around the Way, until at last the bearers eluded the heathen invaders, and set their burden in its final resting-place at Durham.

A grassy cul-de-sac beside the church contains an Anglican school. What pleasant days I have enjoyed there, with the master and his sixfold family. On one of my visits the children were rehearsing a song of greeting to the Bishop of Newcastle, who arrived that afternoon to bless their three R's.

Beyond the school, on rising ground, stands the Elsdon peel tower, in which the rector and his people sheltered from the Scots. This peel was also the rectory, and remained so until recent times. Its former role is remembered by some of the elderly villagers, who still call it the Castle. Both the Castle and the climate were so cold that one eighteenth-century parson slept between two feather mattresses, wearing three nightcaps on his head, and a muffler round his neck 'to keep me from being frozen to death'. This bachelor parson slept in the parlour while the curate with his wife and maid snored in a kitchen on the first floor, and their cows grazed on the ground floor. In 1820 Archdeacon Singleton enlarged and rearranged the rooms; in 1969 the rector's peel was a very gentlemanly residence.

When a traveller looks south from the Elsdon hills, he remembers things past and, like Robert Bridges, is seized

> With like suspense of joy as any man may know
> Who rambling wide hath turn'd, resting on some hill-top
> To view the plain he has left, and seeth it now out-spread
> mapp'd at his feet, a landscape so by beauty estranged
> he scarce will ken familiar haunts, nor even his own home,
> maybe, where far it lieth, small as a faded thought.

Over these hills, though far away, a traveller sees Brougham Castle and the Lady Anne's *memento amare* for her mother. He sees High Nick Cup and the Narrowgate Beacon whereon, like Elsdon shepherds, the Westmorlanders peered north for news of the Scots, or south in search of Philip's Great Armada. He sees Sedbergh and the schoolmaster who was '. . . drunke upon several Lordes days'. He sees those Irish navvies hauling a railway over the Pennines . . . and Tan Hill Inn, the tallest of them all . . . and Dickens and Smirke at Dotheboys Hall . . . and that happier school to which Richard Kearton limped while curlews answered his call . . . and the ruins that became imperishably *Wuthering Heights* . . . Bill Buckley, Admiral Sir Clowdisley Shovell, Izaak Walton, Robin Hood, and Charlotte Brontë's Hathersage. In one mood the visionary grieves for Branwell Brontë's pilfered cash-box at Luddenden Halt; in another, he rejoices at the best legacies of an industrial revolution. And having seen those visions, he continues his journey, along the loneliest twenty miles throughout the Way, which here plunges into Redesdale Forest, darker even than Wark. The Way, in fact, becomes a road, on which flocks and herds were driven to Bellingham market, in the years before the alien trees arrived. There is a farm on the eastern fringe of Redesdale Forest, but nothing else except silence until a wind gets up, and then you overhear what Thomas Hardy reported in his Wessex novel, *The Woodlanders*: 'Gusts in innumerable series followed each other from the north-west, and when each one of them raced past the sound of its progress resolved into three. Treble, tenor and bass notes were found there.'

After several miles the River Rede chimes in, at a point near the long-sounding Blakehopeburnhaugh; hope meaning a valley, burn meaning a stream, haugh meaning a riverside enclosure. The Rede is joined by the wild road to Jedburgh, and presently Byrness appears, the last English village on the Way.

The only relics of the real Byrness are some old houses and a bell-coted, tile-roofed church with a window dedicated to the memory of sixty-four people who perished during the building of Catcleugh Reservoir, which occupied a thousand workmen for fifteen years. The rest of Byrness is a new village, created by the Forestry Commission for its employees. Some of the immigrants remain and settle down; others, from cities, cannot endure a natural existence. This clash between buildings ancient and modern is not peculiar to the twentieth century. Dorothy Wordsworth noticed it at Dover: 'There was also a very old Building on the other side of the road, which had a strange effect among the many new ones that are springing up everywhere.' What is peculiar to this century—and to much of the nineteenth also—is the dissonance of the clash. A Tudor manor house looks well beside a Regency cottage, and each blends with every type of English landscape; but three-ply palaces and twenty-storey blocks of flats do not blend with any type of English landscape.

The hotel at Byrness was the home of Jacob Robson, Master and then Joint Master of the Border Hunt for more than half a century. Through one hundred and fifty years the Masters of this pack were either Robsons or Dodds. Their territory includes both sides of the Border. In 1969 Northumberland had eleven packs of fox-hounds and one of beagles, but none of them would find much sport at Byrness, in a claustrophobia of conifers that climb almost to the tops of the hills. Scotland lies very near, just beyond Carter Bar, the eighteenth-century toll-house that stood beside a desolate road, nearly 1,400 feet high, now studded with snowposts. The road at Carter Bar confirms the accuracy of another of Thomas Hardy's observations: 'A deserted highway expresses solitude to a degree that is not reached by mere dales and downs, and bespeaks a tomblike stillness more emphatic than that of glades and pools.'

In 1575, Carter Bar witnessed a famous Border skirmish, of a kind that must have been familiar to these parts in those years. Sir John Forster, Warden of the Northumbrian Middle Marches, has come with his men to talk with Sir John Carmichael, Scots Keeper of Liddisdale, concerning the Scots' treatment of an English robber. The two sides talk indeed, but their words soon become wounds. The Scots cry 'Jedworth' while the English shout 'Tynedale'. This time the Scots win, having chased the enemy across the Border, and taken several prisoners. The affair at Carter Bar is sometimes called the last Border battle, but fighting continued for many years, even when James VI of Scotland had been crowned James I of England.

Now begins a climb gruelling as any since Edale, if only because the wind on this heath is seldom still. After a few hundred yards of forest track the Way regains the open air, heading due north towards Windy Crag, which lives up to its name. Mountains rise up from hills, guarding a land where the River Coquet is born, in a *cocwudu* or forest of wild birds; and here rise the burns that breed Kale Water and the Tweed. This region never has known peace. First came cavemen, practising mankind's immemorial unneighbourliness; then came the Romans, to build outposts—the Chew Green Camps, as they are now called—near the Roman Dere Street to York; when the Romans left, the Nordic pirates arrived; next, the Border battles; now, an artillery range.

The Roman camps near Byrness make the Wall seem an easy posting. The largest of them, Great South Camp, was built on twenty-two acres of the least sodden ground. The Great North Camp, of fifteen acres, must have seeped and leaked when the wind came out of the west. The South-East Camp, some two acres, shows traces of ramparts and a vallum. In the West Camp a medieval chapel was found, and near by the bones of Roman soldiers who had been buried according to their rites. Though I have passed by several times in a car, I only once walked into the heart of these hills. When I did, and looked around at the burial site, I remembered the words of Sir Thomas Browne: 'Man is a noble animal, splendid in ashes, and pompous in the grave, solemnizing nativities and deaths with equal lustre, nor omitting ceremonies of bravery. . . .'

Having returned to the highway, I met a party of youths and maidens, each sex striving to out-walk the other. They were half out of sight before it occurred to me to make their journey more comfortable by reminding them that its speed was in vain, because women never will out-race men, because men's metabolism exceeds theirs in the ratio of 141 to 100. Moreover, in proportion to the size of their bodies, women have smaller lungs than men, and a smaller heart. Nature is not a suffragette.

North of Byrness the Way enters Scotland, returns into England, again enters Scotland, and continues to and fro for several miles. It seems therefore convenient to regard the rest of the Way as English until, near Burnhead Farm, it enters Scotland and remains there.

Near Ravens Knowe an Army signboard urges the traveller to watch his step while walking into Redesdale. Some people argue that Redesdale ought to be Risdale, which was the ancient spelling. But they spelt it as Redesdale in the year 1212, and that is old enough for me. Anyway, after the warning you reach Ogre Hill (and two more warnings) overlooking the Border Fence between England and Scotland. But a great deal of Englishry still remains to be seen because it is relevant and exciting. A good vantage point is Brownhart Law, 1,664 feet above the North Sea, where mounds of peat and stone point the Way. From Brownhart you see the Cheviot clearly, an English mountain 2,676 feet high, liable to be snow-streaked at any time between November and April. Defoe wished to climb the Cheviot on foot, but a native '. . . laugh'd at us, and told us, we should make a long journey of it that way.' So they went up on horseback, Defoe and a party of friends. Even that was bad enough: 'As we mounted we found the hill steeper than at first, also our horses began to complain, and draw their haunches up heavily. . . .' Defoe was honest with himself and his readers also: 'I must own, I wish'd myself down again. . . .' As the party approached the summit, they wondered whether it would be big enough for them to sit down upon it: 'We all had a notion, that when we came to the top, we should be just as upon a pinnacle.' Their guide reassured them. Like Ingleborough, the Cheviot is big enough to hold its own horse race, though some people prefer a different sport: 'One of our company, a good botanist, fell to searching for simples, and, as he said, found some nice plants, which he seem'd mightily pleased with.' At that point the commercial traveller remembered his brief: 'But as botany is out of my way, so it is not of the present design.' One of my own botanical friends assured me that the Cheviots sustain *S. andersoniana* and *S. phylicfolia*, from the summits down to a height of about three hundred feet. No one at all needed to assure me that the roe deer flourish here. The forests above Rothbury are dappled as in Debussy's prelude; their fawns haunt the glades like shadows in April. Grouse abound, too, and complain when you stumble on them.

Ingram lies at the foot of the Cheviot, only a short walk from the Way. There may be greener valleys in Britain, but there cannot be many of them. Here a stream illustrates the meaning of the word meander, and beside it graze the Cheviot sheep (not to be mistaken for the North Country Cheviots, which one of the Robsons imported from the Scottish Highlands). The head of this valley is blocked by the Cheviot itself.

Ingram hamlet contains a medieval church, a former rectory, one or two farmhouses, and the home of John Hope, Warden of the Northumberland National Park. Born and bred on Holy Island, Mr Hope lives as good a life as any in Northumberland. With him for guide I have watched the birds, stalked the deer, studied the rocks, and roamed among places known only to the initiate and only by consent of the Forestry Commission. The Warden and his family have created their own museum, which is open to the public. Among its exhibits is a sledge, standing by against the moment when misfortune, or more likely folly, sends a distress signal from the Cheviot. In dry and calm weather these hills sight the sea, usually grey, sometimes silver, in sunlight blue; and by the edge of it is Bamburgh Castle, that red sandstone fortress, poised on a cliff so dramatic that the ramparts and towers

seem no more than an ornament, as it were a carving on a carving.
Sir Walter Scott passed by and was amazed:

> Thy tower, proud Bamburgh, mark'd they there,
> King Ida's Castle, huge and square
> From its tall rock looks grimly down,
> And on the swelling ocean frown.

Here were crowned the Northumbrian Kings; one of whom,
Edwin, gave his name to Edinburgh or Edwin's Burgh. Here
Queen Philippa defied the Scots. Here another Queen, Margaret
of Anjou, held court during the Wars of the Roses. Here Lord
Crewe of Blanchland founded a Trust, having bought the castle.
Thirty-four girls, he said, were to be trained there as servants. A
free surgery was opened, a mill to grind poor men's corn, a light
and a warning bell for sailors, room if they were swept ashore
alive, a grave if they landed dead. Horsemen patrolled the coast
in bad weather, ready to sound the alarm when they sighted a ship
in trouble. Parts of Bamburgh Castle have been made into resi-
dences, but restoration and rebuilding scarcely ruffle the warlike
surface.

Who has not heard of Grace Darling? Who can say precisely
why Swinburne wrote one memorable line for her and for her
father? 'Thee and him shall all men see for ever.' This famous tale
deserves to be re-told, even to a generation whose heroes are
unheroic. On the night of 6 September 1838, a coastal steamer,
Forfarshire, was blown off course by a gale so violent that it carried
her towards the dreaded Farne Islands, and at length hurled her
against a mass of basalt, known as Big Harcar or Harker's Rock.
Forty-three people perished before the hulk was sighted by Grace,
daughter of William Darling, keeper at the Longstone Light near
Bamburgh. The Darlings had one small boat, a cockle-shell. But
the brotherhood of the sea is an everlasting Yea. So, the mother
helped to launch that cockle-shell, and then watched while her
husband and daughter rowed—the word may be repeated—rowed
into a gale. The rest belongs to them, as it was reported in a letter
by Darling to Trinity House: 'I have to state that on the morning
of 7 September, it blowing a gale with rain from the north, my

daughter and me being both on the alert . . . one quarter before five my daughter observed a vessel on the Harker's Rock; but owing to the darkness and spray going over her, could not observe any persons on the wreck . . . until near seven o'clock, when the tide being fallen, we observed three or four men upon the rock; we agreed that if we could get to them some of them would be able to assist us back, without which we could not return . . . we immediately launched our boat, and was enabled to gain the rock, where we found eight men and one woman, which I judged too many to take at once in the state of the weather, therefore took one woman and four men to the Longstone. . . .' Then the coble returned to rescue the others. What were their feelings when, having said their prayers, or cursed their fate, those nine sighted a row-boat come to restore them to life? In my time I have gone down a little into the sea in ships, and have seen some of the wonders in the deep, but whenever I am at Bamburgh during a gale, I still cannot understand by what miracle of psychic energy and daring seamanship that girl and her father got there, and went alongside, and then came back.

These Northumbrian shores are not conventionally beautiful. Parts are flatly monotonous. But is there in all Britain a coast crowned with such castles, or flanked by such a stately hinterland? One place especially catches the eye, and fires the imagination, on these Wayside summits. The place is Lindisfarne, or Holy Island, which appears as a speck of land about a mile and a half long, steeped in many kinds of drama.

St Aidan and St Cuthbert came to Holy Island, and there lit one of those beacons which shone above the darkness of their age. The island, in fact, became a diocese, and its fame spread beyond the seas. The illuminated Lindisfarne Gospels are beyond price because they are not for sale. A ruined sandstone Priory recalls some words of Bede: '. . . heathens miserably destroyed God's church in Lindisfarne with savagery and slaughter.' Happily, the medieval parish church is intact.

On the pinnacle of a natural mound, dizzier than a giant's castle, a real castle was built against the Scots. After many vicissitudes it was restored and skilfully modernized by Sir Edwin

Lutyens. Now it is supervised by the National Trust, and never so memorably as at nightfall when the candles are lit.

Although the island's lifeboat was superannuated during the 1960s, the few acres of farmland flourish, and a depleted fishing fleet ekes its pittance for a dwindling band. This tiny community—my friends through many years—have so far withstood the wiles of tourism. Their little ones attend a school beside the sea (in 1969 half of the eight pupils were children either of the vicar or of the schoolmistress). In winter on Holy Island you receive that peace and quiet which the world never gave, because it never possessed. Even the summer visitors seem to be old acquaintances and therefore orderly. And at any hour of any day the vicarage may welcome one of thousands of pilgrims who have come across the seas to worship at a shrine famous throughout medieval Christendom. *Floreat insula sacris.*

No matter where you look from the Cheviot, you see either the past or the present prestige of the greatest layman in the north of England, Hugh Algernon Percy, His Grace the tenth Duke of Northumberland, Lord Lieutenant of this County, Knight of the Most Noble Order of the Garter, Earl of Northumberland, Baron Warkworth, Earl Percy, Earl of Beverley, Lord Lovaine, Baron of Alnwick; the heir of men who once ruled like kings and dared to overrule their Sovereign.

The Percy family were Normans. Throughout the Middle Ages they held vast estates, and their hereditary foe was Douglas across the Border. The last of the male Percys, the Earl of Northumberland, died at Turin in 1670. His daughter married a Duke of Somerset; her grand-daughter, Elizabeth, having inherited the Percy estates, married a Yorkshire baronet whose family bore the respected, though scarcely exclusive, name of Smith alias Smithson. Having changed that name to Percy, the baronet was created Earl of Northumberland in 1750, and first Duke of Northumberland in 1766.

The Duke's seat, Alnwick Castle, is girt with a wall ten miles long, enclosing three thousand acres of farms, woods, moors, and a park that is graciously opened to the public. The two great Cheviot regiments are linked with Alnwick, for the present Duke served with the Northumberland Hussars during the war and became honorary Colonel of the Royal Northumberland Fusiliers. The Percy motto is *Esperance en Dieu* or Trust God. There have been moments when God must have ceased to trust the Percys; but Whiggery and its spiteful child, Socialism, have long since witnessed a rapprochement between the Kings of the North and their celestial overlord. The ducal estates are now so adroitly managed, and the castle itself contains so many precious heirlooms, that not even a vicious tax on success seems able to reduce them to failure. Alnwick Castle may be likened to a secular Holy Island, for it preaches and practises certain high ideals in time of darkness. Not yet need the north country fear the loss of a family that is *de jure* and *de facto* its social leader.

And now, from that summit of Englishry, the Way takes its last few steps towards Scotland. Having climbed Ogre Hill, it descends a little, and halts at the Border Fence by Coquet Head on the slope of a moor as wild and lonely as any in England. No trees are here; neither shrub nor scrub nor reed; only the music which we call silence, and a peace so profound that, when you lie on the grass, its vibration soothes your civilized fever. But in the old times—to make the point once again—there was so little peace here that the hills were less a No-Man's-Land than a Dead-Man's-Land. Southward for many miles the cottagers and their masterful castles dwelt under the shadow of a Bomb that really did fall. They worked and played and married and died, never knowing when the Scots would creep down by the dark of a moonless night; never knowing, until the crops were ablaze, the sheep driven off, the first firebrand thudding on a thatched roof. The Scots, of course, carried their raids far south of the Border, deep into Yorkshire and Lancashire; and one might therefore have expected a legacy of wary aloofness in these far-northfolk. Instead, they are famed for their hospitality; perhaps too famed. After all, if you ask for a glass of water, or some shelter from the rain, you are as likely to receive them in Norfolk as in Northumberland. But there is one form of welcome at which the northerners do appear to excel—tea, of Cowper's 'cups, that cheer but not inebriate'. Perhaps the climate has something to do with it, for while Sussex basks in April sunshine, these farms and cottages all along the Way are likely to have a fire and a simmering kettle. I have entered several hundred such houses between Haworth and Wooler, yet I cannot remember one of them that did not say, 'Wilt have coop?' Across the Border, of course, the cup is more likely to be a wee dram . . . and no' always sae wee. Old William Cobbett might have swallowed the dram, if only for Timothy's sake, but never the tea: 'A destroyer of health,' he called it, 'and enfeebler of the frame . . . a debaucher of youth, and a maker of misery for old age.' Strange, that a man so wise could sound so foolish.

Here meanwhile, at the frontier, you need no passport. It is three hundred years since an armed thug last shot down a man trying to cross this Border. Here solitude and silence reign over a realm of bare skyline broken only by clouds and one kestrel, poised like a full-stop. As you climb the Fence, and set foot in another land, you know that the Border feuds are merely the ghosts of

> . . . old, unhappy, far-off things,
> And battles long ago.

14 Scotland

SOME of the British Borders really do cause an Englishman to feel that he has entered a foreign land. There are parts of North Wales, for instance, which speak Welsh within a few yards of England; and even in Monmouthshire, which is an English county, the accent and the signposts seem as novel as the distant mountains. On the Roxburghshire Way it is otherwise, for there are neither signposts to be seen nor accents to be heard; and the mountains look precisely as they do in England, two yards away. Even that kestrel is the same, poised above the wire-thin frontier. For him there is neither England nor Scotland, but only moorland. Yet men can observe things hidden even from a hawk's eye; and at the Border Fence—as on Cross Fell—the sensitive traveller is aware of a spirit or influence . . . one moreover which in many ways differs from the spirit of England.

What *is* Scotland, the country which everyone knows so well? It is one of the smallest in the world, though twice as large as Denmark, and thrice the size of Belgium. A train journey from the Border to Caithness takes twice as long as from London to Glasgow. From the most northerly to the southernmost isles is about as far as from Edinburgh to Paris. The present population of Scotland is roughly one-half that of Greater London.

Who *are* the Scots, the people whom everyone knows so well? They are, like the English, partly Celtic, partly Scandinavian. The ancient kingdom of Dalriada, for example, was dominated by Gaelic-speaking Irishmen; in Strathclyde were many Welshfolk; Orkney and Caithness remained Norwegian until historically recent times. Nevertheless, the Scots maintained several sorts of contact with England. Many of their overlords were Anglo-Normans, and, as we have noticed, the English speech was crossing the Border from Northumberland. Charles Lamb could not like the Scots: 'I have been trying all my life,' he confessed, 'to like Scotchmen, and am obliged to desist from the experiment in despair.' One or two Scots may have found it equally difficult to like the English. Ultimately it is a matter of taste, as formed by knowledge and toleration or by arrogant ignorance. Far to the north-west, in places hidden from hasty tourists, the Scots bear themselves like kings who have married queens and begotten princes. No Englishman can understand such people until he has attended one of those gatherings at which the kilt is worn. There he will see a costume, and hear a skirl, to which his own nation has no reply. Though his calves are covered, he feels more out-landish than the dancers whose knees are bare; and neither Elgar nor *Greensleeves* seems an equivalent anthem. You may, of course, protest that the tartan and the pibroch have become vulgarized, and always were rather of the Highlands than of the Lowlands. That is true. But it is also true that whatever pertains to a part, belongs to the whole.

In 1296, when the King of England was compelled for safety's sake to tame Caledonia, the Scots sent a letter to the Pope: 'For so long,' they declared, 'as one hundred men of us remain, we shall never submit under any condition to the domination of the English.' That was more than the English had said to the Normans. The Scots, as we know, fought and lost, and would in any event have been invaded by Time. When James VI of Scotland became James I of England, the English themselves were invaded; and when that King asked Guy Fawkes why he had tried to explode Parliament, the reply was: 'To blow the beggarly Scots back to Scotland.' But the Scots were not content to invade England. They aspired to rule the waves also. If in the recesses of the Malacca Straits you ring down for Full Ahead Both, a voice will reply: 'Hoots, mon, this is no' a jet plane.'

The Scottish clans began to gather during the twelfth century, under the leadership of the heirs to the Norman–English knights. Their chiefs acquired an influence greater than any they might have wielded by virtue of civic office. For centuries the Gaels had been wearing a tartan or chequered cloth, which was outlawed by the Disarming Act of 1745, but became lawful again in 1782. Thereafter it so lapsed into popularity that, when George IV visited Edinburgh in 1822—the first English King to be received there since Charles II—the Lowland lairds hastened to buy tartans, though their forebears would have been appalled at such Gaelic uncouthness. Most of the present setts are relatively modern. The English use them as seat-covers, dog-rugs, neck-ties. But no self-respecting person of any nation will assume a privilege to which he is not entitled.

The latest census states that only 0·19 per cent of people in Roxburghshire have the Gaelic, but the language is 'no' deed yet'. In Ross and Cromarty more than one-third of the people speak their native tongue, and some among the old ones speak no other. But Gaelic is falling more rapidly than Welsh, and never was such a national rallying point. Scottish religion, on the other hand, remains lively—if that is what you care to call Calvinism—and also schizophrenic because many Highlanders adhered to Rome while most Lowlanders turned to Geneva. When Charles I, their own Scottish Sovereign, sought refuge with them from his English rebels, the Calvinists sold him into captivity and thence to death for several pieces of silver. It was this national division which foredoomed both the Young and the Old Pretender, each of whom may have secured a heavenly crown by deciding that not even London was worth a Mass.

The excesses of Home Rule hardly touch this Borderland. Extensive travel and persistent inquiry have persuaded me that not even a Scottish Parliament excites enthusiasm; though some of the older people do tend to shake their heads when an Englishman expresses a hope that England will one day achieve an English Parliament. Most of these Roxburghshire people—which is to say, most of the farmfolk—believe that there are more than enough tub-thumpers at large. Personal identity, they say, has no necessary connection with politics, and is nowadays in danger of being eroded by politics. Yet it is their personal identity that the Scots must preserve against international chain stores, super cinemas, and all other things which precisely resemble all other similar things. Mammon and Mars have stripped away the mere ornaments of nationalism. It is by their arts and crafts and creeds that a people maintain their identity . . . and, of course, by their language.

This Scottish landscape is as high as the English, and although the Way has crossed the Border, it re-enters England briefly, always climbing. Cairn Hill, for instance, is 2,419 feet high, the Schill is only fifteen feet short of mountainous, Auchope Cairn is 2,382 feet (in clear weather a pair of glasses will sight Balmoral more than a hundred miles away). Even the hilltops are eminent: Butts Road, 1,718 feet; King's Seat, 1,743 feet; Score Head, 1,910 feet. The most spectacular solitude lies at Hen Hole, a craggy precipice near Auchope Cairn, where even an eremite would crave companionship, unless he shared Dickens's belief that cities and streets are also lonely: 'A solemn consideration, when I enter a great city by night, that every one of those darkly clustered houses encloses its own secret; that every beating heart . . . is a secret to the heart nearest it.' However, there is some kind of company here, and Defoe's botanical friend would have found it in a star saxifrage, a dwarf conel, a black willow.

I never reached the summit of Auchope Cairn, but I did once go high enough to look down on the hills above Wooler, a little English town, which, like Holy Island, has offered me much good companionship. I remember meeting a Wooler shepherd who was so nearly one hundred years old that he recalled the coming of the railway, the relief of Mafeking, and the Wooler Hiring Fair, at which the shepherd stood with his crook, the milkmaid with her pail, ready to do business with any farmer who would engage them for the next twelvemonth. He told me that at Wooler they hold an annual Burns night, as though to celebrate the generations of marriage across the Border. The town's oldest house, he said, was the headquarters of the Earl of Surrey before he led his army against the Scots at Flodden. And having told me of such things, the near-centenarian went for a walk through the fields. Is he the freak, or are we?

A little to the north of Wooler, within view of the road to Coldstream, was fought the bloodiest of all Wayside battles, at a place called Flodden Hill, which is just in England. The Scottish King, James IV, had decided to stab England in the back while

she was fighting France. An army of thirty thousand Scotsmen
streamed south across the Border, hoping for a quick kill. They
received a swift death. Forewarned and forearmed, the English
under Surrey routed the invaders. Ten thousand Scotsmen died
that day, and with them the flower of their nobility. It was a
national disaster which Scotland has never forgotten. At Coldstream, the first town north of the Border, I once asked a shop-
keeper what he thought of Flodden. He replied: 'I think what we
all think.' And then he smiled: 'But dinna' forget, we gave you a
braw wallop at Killiecrankie.' Yet the Scots may grieve without
shame, for they fought gallantly. Their own King died fighting,
and so did every man in his bodyguard.

The Battle of Flodden has its own memorial, a simple Cross on
a bare hill, dedicated 'To the brave of both nations.' The Scots
erected it; the English have neglected it. Four times I have visited
Flodden Field; four times the steep path to the Cross was a muddy
river, and the gate resembled something from an Edwardian scrap-
heap. Twice I found the Cross islanded among nettles. On one
occasion the footpath was hidden by a crop of oats.

As at Otterburn, so at Flodden Field; sheep graze safely, while
the two enemies meet for a friendly darts match. But in 1513 tens
of thousands of corpses littered these hills; and on both sides of
the Border many a woman, gentle and simple alike, uttered the
lament of the old ballad:

> I took his body on my back,
> And whiles I gaed, and whiles I sat,
> I digg'd a grave, and laid him in,
> And happ'd him with the sod sae green.
> Nae living man I'll love again,
> Since that my lovely knight is slain;
> Wi' ae lock of his yellow hair
> I'll chain my heart for evermair.

Even the cattle were warlike. A report to the Board of Agriculture, submitted in 1818, stated: 'At the first appearance of any
person they (the oxen) set off at full speed, and gallop to a considerable distance; when they make a wheel round, and come boldly
up again, tossing their heads in a menacing manner: on a sudden

they make a full stop, at the distance of forty or fifty yards, looking wildly at the object of their surprise; but upon the least motion being made, they again turn round, and gallop off with equal speed; but forming a shorter circle, and returning with a bolder and more threatening aspect, they approach much nearer, when they make another stand; and again gallop off. This they do several times, shortening their distance, and advancing nearer, till they come within a few yards, when most people think it prudent to leave them.'

In these parts a man is usually master in his own house, and so enables the woman to become truly its mistress. The unfashionable voice of John Knox still reverberates among the cottages and farms: 'God hath revealed to some in this our age that it is more than a monster in nature that a woman should reign and bear empire above man.' And there is another, more literal, sense in which Knox's voice is heard. For example, on the lane from Wooler to Kirk Yetholm I met with some roadmen speaking the deep voice of Northumberland; but after a few hundred yards, having crossed the Border into Scotland, I was greeted by Donald: 'Away wi' it, you've no been walking all the day, surely?' Anyone coming here for the first time would need to guess whether he stood in Scotland or in England—unless the tone of talk could guide him. The difference between these two tones can be gauged by considering a passage from St Matthew: 'Behold the fowls of the air: for they sow not, neither do they reap, nor gather into barns; yet your heavenly Father feedeth them. Are ye not much better than they?' A twentieth-century version of those words was rendered into Lowland Scots: 'Look ye to the wee birdies i' the lift; for they naither saw nor shear, nor lead intil the barn; and yet yeere Heevenlie Faither gies them meat. Are-ye-na a hantle better nor they?'

Just north of the Schill, where the Border Fence becomes a Border Wall, the Way passes through a gate, out of England into Scotland, and there it remains for the last few miles of the journey. While counting-down those miles, one hopes that the next hilltop will reveal Kirk Yetholm, but it never does. Unlike Tan Hill Inn, the village remains hidden. Hopes rise again when you see the roof of Burnhead Farm, the first house on the Way since Byrness, but then again they fade because no other house is visible. Behind, you take a farewell glance at the Cheviot; ahead, other hills arise; and somewhere between them is the end of the Way.

The last three or four miles are bonnie indeed, and the man who has walked every mile of the Way feels justly complacent when he travels them. The man who has not walked every mile, but has chosen to linger and wander, enjoys a different satisfaction, for he has sampled the wide as well as the narrow Way. To do both is best; to do the latter is next best.

> Does the road wind up-hill all the way?
> Yes, to the very end.
> Will the day's journey take the whole long day?
> From morn to night, my friend.

There have been many times since Edale when Christina Rossetti's prognosis came true, but now at last the facts confound it. Downalong is the motto, smoothly from Burnhead Farm to Halterburn Valley, between arcs of green and their blossom of sheep; beneath plovers and curlews and lyrical larks that sing even through a November twilight. Down, down, down: here in spring a primrose; there in winter a Way deep and crisp as the Feast of Stephen; at all seasons a breeze, a curlew, and bleating sheep. The green path becomes a farm track; the track becomes a lane; then a byre appears, and a cottage and a little bridge across a burn, and after that the hamlet of Halterburn, whose hotel whenever I have passed was either shut or about to open but not today. And still there is no sign of Kirk Yetholm, though the maps assure you that it is only a few hundred yards away. You begin to doubt those maps because the Way suddenly presents you with a steep hill. But it is the last hill and not long, and when you have climbed it, you do at last see the roofs of the village that h₹s occupied your thoughts since first at Edale you crossed a river and climbed a ravine. The return to civilization is confirmed by two plain-faced signs, warning you not to walk faster than thirty miles an hour.

Kirk Yetholm lies in a Cheviot valley—deep, peaceful, wooded, sheep-grazed. Its Lowland cottages squat like gnomes around a village green. The inn—neither ancient nor modern—sits decently by, facing a Youth Hostel that is both alpha and omega. Kirk Yetholm resembles Edale in that nothing ever happened here, except the most important of all happenings. Its history was written long ago: 'One generation cometh, and another generation passeth away, but the earth abideth forever.'

A row of cottages, called Gipsy Row, testifies to Kirk Yetholm's ancient role as a Romany stronghold. The last Romany Queen, Esther Faa Blyth, died and was buried here in 1835. When gipsies first reached Scotland, at the end of the fifteenth century, their reception was not cordial. In 1563 Queen Elizabeth ordered them to leave the kingdom, but not even the threat of death persuaded them to comply. The latest census suggests that there are about 45,000 gipsies in Britain. Some of them are layabouts, some are fairground attendants, some possess considerable house property and use their motor-caravans as fair weather profit-makers. Very few travel by horse-drawn caravan. Gipsies used to call themselves by a generic name, Faa, but to the Scots they were Tinkers or Tinklers, an onomatopoeic word, echoing the sound of hammer and anvil. Some of the gipsies still deal in horses, or do seasonal farmwork; the women tell fortunes, sell mops or brushes, and help their menfolk at knife-grinding. The guidebooks make much ado about the gipsies in these parts, but the guidebooks are mistaken. During the past eight years—wandering widely on foot and by car—I have yet to meet a gipsy between Wooler and Coldstream or along the cross-country lanes. But along the Westmorland Way they arrive in their hundreds, bound for Brough Fair and Appleby Show.

Kirk Yetholm church is dour and almost black. Even from its porch you fancy that you overhear the voice of John Knox again, warning a Queen—and a Scottish Queen at that—to expect no condescension from him until '. . . it shall please God to deliver you from that bondage of darkness and error in which ye have been nourished, for the lack of true doctrine. . . . .' Despite its many faults these past four centuries, Garrigill church never echoed such an unlovely *ethos* as Knox and his kind imposed and still do impose upon their ain folk. But you have not travelled nearly three hundred miles in order to insult Scottish hospitality. At Kirk Yetholm, therefore, remembering what you may of Scottish history, you walk respectfully, with admiration and affection for your clever, industrious and redoubtable neighbours. Said old Fynes Moryson, that much-travelled Scot: 'Such is the delight of visiting foreign countries, charming all our senses with most sweet variety.' No matter what his nationality, a guest will find that this country is foreign in the friendliest manner.

In so far as travelling and reading are impressionism, each requires to be recollected in tranquillity. When we close the book, or unsling the haversack, we need neither a guide nor a glossary to sift our impressions and to pronounce our verdicts. Such things are matters of taste. We have followed the spine and indeed the roof of a large part of the centre of this united kingdom. All of those parts are at all times changing, and have been since they were created. Some parts have changed beyond the recognition of our youth. It is man's duty to hope that change itself will lighten the burden of living, and improve the quality of its delight. Certainly it is his privilege to believe that his children's children will see Cross Fell as he saw it, and find little difference when they too walk light-hearted into Halterburn. So shall Wordsworth's prophecy be fulfilled: 'What we have loved, others will love.'

Index